NO PUNCHES PULLED:
THE PREMIERS PECKFORD, WELLS, AND TOBIN

[A] political page-turner." — THE TELEGRAM

THE TRUE CONFESSIONS OF
A BADLY MISUNDERSTOOD DOG

"It has been a really, really long time since I read a book that caused me to both laugh out loud and get a little weepy, and Bill Rowe has done that with this book." — THE NORTHEAST AVALON TIMES

"This is an easy-to-read book that anybody who has ever had a dog can easily relate to. It's a story with warmth and humour."

— EDWARDS BOOK CLUB

"Durf's voice is full of affection and is, by his own lights, honest. And the tone is plausible and authentic. The writing is at its strongest when Durf is in some kind of exchange with That Man: '*No man is indispensable,' I heard That Man say one time about himself, and he got that right. But I never heard him say that no dog is indispensable.*"

— THE TELEGRAM

"Dog persons, likely even cat persons, will love this book. They will haul *Marley and Me* from their bookshelves and replace it with [*The True Confessions of a Badly*] *Misunderstood Dog*." — THE ADVERTISER

"[Durf's] misadventures are funny and sad, and always well-written. Definitely a book to read." — THE PEI GUARDIAN

THE MONSTER OF TWENTY MILE POND

"A fantastical novel with a mysterious creature and added thrill of a murder, Rowe creates a connection with the reader through sympathy, mystery and an overall amazing story." — TINT OF INK

"Rowe is an excellent writer and you can't really go wrong reading anything by him. This is one of his best." — THE PEI GUARDIAN

"Rowe's writing shines particularly brightly when his lawyer is chastising the (female) premier or other political discussions are underway, but the entire book is a rollicking ride with likable characters (except the skeets) in familiar settings." — THE NORTHEAST AVALON TIMES

"A well-constructed novel, weaving murder and monsters into a single speculative tale." — THE PACKET

THE PREMIERS JOEY AND FRANK

"A voyeuristic and tantalizing trip through the workings of the government by a man who was there." — THE PILOT

"Rowe's stories paint not only an interesting picture of Rowe's own life, but the lives of the two men in which the book is named, and in the process, their greed, power and lust." — THE MUSE

"*The Premiers Joey and Frank* is crack for political junkies and will be a welcome gift for even the marginally interested observer of the political scene." — THE TELEGRAM

ROSIE O'DELL

"*Rosie O'Dell* is one of those books with such brilliant writing as to lull you into forgetting you're actually reading." — THE PILOT

"Yes, it's Bill Rowe—back this time with his third novel, which I think is by far his best. Probably one of the better novels to come out in the past few years—depending on your own tastes, of course."

— THE NORTHEAST AVALON TIMES

"[A] deeply emotional page-turner by one of the country's finest writers." — MEGAN MURPHY, INDIGO

"This is a terrific story that hinges on a woman who is like quicksilver, running through all the cracks." — THE GLOBE AND MAIL

"It's well-written (Rowe is an experienced and accomplished writer), the characters are excellently drawn and much of the writing is just plain funny." — THE PEI GUARDIAN

"There is not a false note in this book. All the characters are drawn with skillful insight, the descriptions are so vibrant you can almost hear the water and feel the mist of St. John's, Newfoundland. Although it has elements of a thriller, this is no gothic soap opera, but rather a brilliantly crafted look into the hearts and souls of ordinary people who are thrown into extraordinary circumstances."

— ATLANTIC BOOKS TODAY

"This novel is a real page-turner, with lots of tension and mystery."

— THE TELEGRAM

DANNY WILLIAMS, PLEASE COME BACK

"I started to really appreciate Rowe's ability to narrow down a topic and come up with something pithy and witty to say about it, week after week." — THE TELEGRAM

"Like any columnist worth his salt Rowe is provocative and a number of the columns deal with topics whose lessons are still relevant."
— THE NEWFOUNDLAND QUARTERLY

"Rowe's columns on Williams's persona, bellicose manner and political antics truly shine. What Danny Should Do in the Crab War? (May 7, 2005) puts a delightful Shakespearian twist on Williams's strategic positioning; Is Danny a Dictator? (June 25, 2005) will stand as a classic." — THE CHRONICLE HERALD

"A brisk read and a fine book to have in your personal library."
— THE COMPASS

"[Rowe] does it all, of course, with his usual blend of droll good humour and common sense." — THE GLOBE AND MAIL

"With a mind—and a pen—as sharp as a paper cut, the elegant, affable Rowe remains Newfoundland's literary agent provocateur, provoking, teasing, sometimes coddling his subjects, but all the time digging towards truths that cause discomfort for the province's Who's Who and everyman alike." — THE BUSINESS POST

DANNY WILLIAMS: THE WAR WITH OTTAWA

"Interesting book about a successful Canadian politician . . ."
— THE GLOBE AND MAIL

"[Danny Williams] is captivating. [Bill Rowe] spares no punches."
— THE COMPASS

"The most interesting political book to be released in Canada in some time . . ." — THE BUSINESS POST

"Rowe's Ottawa chronicle [is] absorbing, humorous."
— THE TELEGRAM

"I quickly realized that this was not going to be a dry political memoir. To the contrary, not only is the book interesting and revealing of this contentious time, it is very funny in places."
— THE CHRONICLE HERALD

"An exciting read." — THE NEWFOUNDLAND QUARTERLY

"[One of] three of this year's most controversial and talked about political books." — THE HOUSE, CBC RADIO

"Rowe has a more humanistic side to politics. It is as if a citizen managed to be a fly on the wall while Danny Williams fought."
— CURRENT MAGAZINE

"An eye-opening, often hilariously funny, account of life among Ottawa power brokers and civil servants."

— CANADIAN LAWYER MAGAZINE

"Bill Rowe has a lot to say. There are dozens of interesting stories told, and comments passed on . . ." — THE NORTHEAST AVALON TIMES

"A fascinating and frequently funny read." — DOWNHOME

"Written with the knowledge and insight that only an insider could possess, this book (sub-titled 'The Inside Story of a Hired Gun') is a timely reminder of the duplicity of far too many of our elected leaders—no matter what their political stripe." — ATLANTIC BOOKS TODAY

"The writer's good English style—rare today—his knowledge of all kinds of personalities in the political world and his misadventures in getting a basic office set up (which took six of the eight months he was there) all make for amusing and exciting reading."

— THE PEI GUARDIAN

THE WORST AND BEST

of the

PREMIERS

and Some We Never Had

BY BILL ROWE

THE WORST AND BEST OF THE PREMIERS AND SOME WE NEVER HAD

NO PUNCHES PULLED

THE TRUE CONFESSIONS OF A BADLY MISUNDERSTOOD DOG

THE MONSTER OF TWENTY MILE POND

THE PREMIERS JOEY AND FRANK

ROSIE O'DELL

DANNY WILLIAMS, PLEASE COME BACK

DANNY WILLIAMS: THE WAR WITH OTTAWA

IS THAT YOU, BILL?

THE TEMPTATION OF VICTOR GALANTI

CLAPP'S ROCK

BILL ROWE

A POLITICAL REPORT CARD

THE WORST AND BEST of the PREMIERS

and Some We Never Had

FLANKER PRESS LIMITED
ST. JOHN'S

Library and Archives Canada Cataloguing in Publication

Rowe, William N. (William Neil), 1942-, author
The Worst and Best of the Premiers and Some We Never Had : a political report card / Bill Rowe.

Includes index.
Issued in print and electronic formats.
ISBN 978-1-77117-640-8 (paperback).--ISBN 978-1-77117-641-5 (epub).--ISBN 978-1-77117-642-2 (kindle).--ISBN 978-1-77117-643-9 (pdf)

A CIP catalogue record for this book is available from Library and Archives Canada.

PRINTED IN CANADA

MIX
Paper from responsible sources
FSC www.fsc.org FSC® C016245

This paper has been certified to meet the environmental and social standards of the Forest Stewardship Council® (FSC®) and comes from responsibly managed forests, and verified recycled sources.

Cover Design by Graham Blair

FLANKER PRESS LTD.
PO BOX 2522, STATION C
ST. JOHN'S, NL
CANADA

TELEPHONE: (709) 739-4477 FAX: (709) 739-4420 TOLL-FREE: 1-866-739-4420
WWW.FLANKERPRESS.COM

9 8 7 6 5 4 3 2 1

Canada — Canada Council for the Arts — Conseil des Arts du Canada — Newfoundland Labrador

We acknowledge the financial support of the Government of Canada through the Canada Book Fund (CBF) and the Government of Newfoundland and Labrador, Department of Tourism, Culture, Industry and Innovation for our publishing activities. We acknowledge the support of the Canada Council for the Arts, which last year invested $157 million to bring the arts to Canadians throughout the country. *Nous remercions le Conseil des arts du Canada de son soutien. L'an dernier, le Conseil a investi 157 millions de dollars pour mettre de l'art dans la vie des Canadiennes et des Canadiens de tout le pays.*

To my brothers, Fred, Bud, and George (1944–2008),
in appreciation of their lifelong interest in politics and history

Contents

A Note to the Reader

Many readers of my earlier political books have been kind enough to tell me they appreciated my brutal frankness in evaluating the premiers there, and they have urged me to write about other leaders in the same vein. That's the main reason for the existence of this book, and I have continued here a similar "warts and all" approach.

I've tried my hand in this volume at grading our political leaders during the nearly seventy years since we joined Canada. To make the task manageable, I had to impose a cut-off somewhere. So, I've restricted those chosen, with just two exceptions, to the men and women who actually led the Progressive Conservative Party, or the Liberal Party, or the New Democratic Party (including its early forerunners), or the short-lived United Newfoundland Party, and the Labrador Parties, into a provincial general election. Even within that limit, the number of leaders comes to a total of some forty-two since 1949.

The two exceptions happen to belong to the same family, the father, Ches Crosbie, and the son, John Crosbie. Why I included them will, I hope, be obvious when you read my commentaries on them, but I'll say briefly now that their contributions to politics and policy were so significant and interesting, and even visionary and far-reaching in impact, that it would have been plainly senseless to leave them out.

In grading the men and women in this book, I've used a scale of 0% to 100%. But I hasten to add that none of the leaders either sank to that lowliest possible percentage or attained the most exalted one. I considered no leader, to the best of my knowledge and experience, to be that bad or that good. So, I have given each of them a grade somewhere between those two extremes.

In earlier books, I dealt with six of our premiers: Joey Smallwood, Frank Moores, Brian Peckford, Clyde Wells, Brian Tobin, and Danny Williams. In this book, I have avoided repeating my remarks regarding them except merely to highlight actions or events upon which I have formed my conclusions here. Anyone wishing to have a fuller, more detailed description of the actions and personalities of those premiers is invited to consult the earlier volumes.

By far, most of the contents of this book cover fresh facts and opinions, even concerning the leaders I have already written about. Also, some of the judgments I made in the earlier books I've altered in the light of broadened realities and further reflection.

In *The Premiers Joey and Frank*, for example, I ranked Smallwood lower as premier than for his achievement in "dragging Newfoundland, kicking and screaming," into Confederation. And I made Moores one of our top premiers simply for terminating Joey's seemingly endless twenty-three-year rule. Some readers agreed with those evaluations, but others told me I was nuts. With the passage of time, and taking readers' reactions into consideration, I have revised some of my assessments.

Similarly, I've had to consider whether the high evaluation I gave the premier in *Danny Williams: The War with Ottawa* may have been eroded since then by the escalating doubts over his Muskrat Falls project.

In *No Punches Pulled: The Premiers Peckford, Wells, and Tobin*, I surprised some readers by the high or low appraisal I dealt each of them in turn. Here, I look at all three with fresh eyes, and state the reasoning for my current judgments, clearly and bluntly, but, I hope, not too cruelly.

Two premiers, Kathy Dunderdale and Dwight Ball, received fairly recent mandates from the people. They enjoyed enough popular standing with the provincial electorate to get their teams into the House of Assembly with substantial majorities of seats. Evidently, they were highly regarded then. But where do they stand now? It may be too early, in the light of history, to pass lasting judgments on them. But their actions generally, and how they dealt with the events they faced, or which overtook them, do allow for tentative evaluations.

Then there were the leaders—Tom Rideout, Roger Grimes, and Paul Davis—who became premiers solely as a result of winning their party leadership conventions, but who failed to convince enough of their fellow citizens in an election to keep them in the job. Having held the advantage of premiership, but then failing to convert it into an actual mandate from the people, how do they rank as political leaders?

Next come Noel Murphy, Ed Roberts, Don Jamieson, Leo Barry, Lynn Verge, Ed Byrne, and others before and after them, who became Leaders of the Opposition by winning their party leadership. But when they placed their fate in the hands of the people in an election, not one of them was able to get voted in as premier. They are graded here as the best and worst premiers we never had.

Finally, among the heads of the NDP, the perennial third party in the province, were found some noteworthy leaders, including Peter Fenwick, Jack Harris, and Lorraine Michael. I grade them by the way they tackled the challenges and conducted their uphill battles. Plus, like the others who never reached the Premier's Office, they are rated by how they might have made out, based on their political and other deeds, if they had ever managed in reality to achieve the top executive, decision-making status.

Without exception, I regard all the leaders in this book as spirited and courageous characters, simply because of the way they took on their always difficult, sometimes impossible political tasks. In most cases they did not achieve the ultimate political success, the premiership, which they sought. Their failure to do so was not a determining factor in my grading, but it was an important one.

Politics is a merciless, ruthless business. And leaders who encountered bad luck in timing, or faced overriding issues against them, or chanced upon a formidable opponent, have no right to complain. That's the nature of the racket they opted into. Thus, I have not unduly taken into account those elements when measuring the gap between what each leader aspired to and what he or she actually achieved. But I have looked at what they did with what they had. And I've allowed for the breadth and depth of their vision, their positions on crucial public issues, and their genuine achievements in all aspects of their public life, inside and outside of actual leadership, as indications of what they might have been like as premier.

I have tried to be as objective as possible in my judgments, but self-evidently, in the end, these gradings are my own subjective opinions. Some readers of my earlier books have forthrightly told me where they agreed or disagreed with my appraisals of the personalities therein, and I'm encouraging the same reaction to this book.

Bill Rowe
St. John's
Newfoundland and Labrador
August 2017

Ches Crosbie

WHAT MIGHT HAVE happened to Newfoundland after 1949 if its citizens had voted for the independence of Responsible Government rather than union with Canada?

I discussed that question with one of our esteemed historians some time ago, and we both surmised with some amusement that, if Ches Crosbie had gotten his own way back in the 1940s, all of us here today might well be Yanks.

It was an intriguing, if fanciful and far-fetched conjecture: we only had to make the right moves as a people, after we'd taken our independence back and pursued Ches Crosbie's idea of Economic Union with the United States. Instead of being a mere province in the relatively minor country of Canada, we could have become an important state in the most powerful nation on earth.

Mind you, this conversation took place before the advent of President Trump.

CHESLEY A. CROSBIE, known to his familiars as simply Ches, and to his mostly admiring employees as *Skipper* Ches, was born in Newfoundland in 1905. He was the eldest of a dozen children of the commercially aggressive and politically ambitious John Chalker Crosbie, later Sir John, whose family would comprise some of the most prominent business and public persons in the land.

Sir John had started Crosbie and Company at the turn of the century and used it to develop interests in hotel, insurance, shipping, and manufacturing businesses. And he became one of the Dominion of Newfoundland's top fish exporters. He also entered the Newfoundland political forum, which was primarily a raucous milieu of partisan buccaneers, but he easily held his own there. During one election, friends and foes alike were delighted to report, albeit for opposite reasons, that he refuted an adversary's argument by bellowing publicly, "The Pope and the Archbishop can kiss my arse."

He had no trouble getting elected to the House of Assembly, where he became minister of Shipping, and later minister of Finance and Customs. He even served as interim prime minister for a few days during the First World War. Knighted for his good works, Sir John Crosbie died at only fifty-six in 1932, leaving son Ches, in his twenties, to head up the family business.

Ches was equal to the task. He expanded and diversified further throughout the Island, assuming challenges of great risk, some of which thrived, some of which nosedived. His more novel investments included whaling and the herring fishery, plus Joe Smallwood's *Books of Newfoundland* and his pig farm in Gander.

Ches seemed to be fond of Smallwood in a head-shaking way and always had time for him. Some observers thought the relationship indicated Ches's breadth of vision and his appreciation of off-the-wall ideas. Others held that, in those days, Ches liked to have him around now and then as kind of a court clown. Whatever the case, Smallwood was also fond of Ches, in common with many Newfoundlanders, some who esteemed Ches generally for his audacity and industry, and some for his partiality to more than the odd nip with the b'ys.

* * * * *

OVER IN THE mother country, in the general election of 1945, Labour Leader Clement Attlee defeated great wartime prime minister Winston Churchill and became prime minister of Great Britain himself. Within months, he announced that Newfoundland had to elect a National Convention to decide its own future. That future was cloudy to many. But its past was clear enough: this fully-fledged dominion had voted its own democratic, responsible government out of existence and asked to be governed thereafter by a local dictatorship overseen, basically, by a bureaucracy on the other side of the ocean.

Back in 1934, London had appointed a Commission of Government here. This was a panel of men, three locals and three Brits, chaired by a governor from the United Kingdom, whose jobs were to sit in St. John's and run Newfoundland as they saw fit, answerable only to Westminster.

By the end of the Second World War, though, laden with back-breaking debt, the UK government desired only to off-load somehow, somewhere, this perennial nuisance.

Pretending to re-establish a semblance of democracy, London set up a process here to elect delegates to debate the options that would be put to the Newfoundland people for decision in a referendum. Candidates for election had to be residents of the district they were running in. Whether because of apathy or broken spirit, only about half the voters bothered to cast ballots to choose delegates for this National Convention. Or perhaps they surmised that the whole kit and caboodle was window dressing.

Ches Crosbie ran in St. John's West and got elected with the largest percentage of the votes of all the candidates. As he was campaigning, and when he entered the National Convention, he professed not to be dead set against the notion of Confederation with Canada. But he did deem it essential that, before anything else, we had to dump Commission of Government and recover our autonomy under our old responsible government system.

Joe Smallwood, luckily for his own future prospects, had moved from St. John's and was living in Gander at the time. He was there mucking around with the pig farm which, ironically enough, Ches Crosbie had helped stake him to. His residing there was amazing good luck, because Smallwood always claimed that, as an advocate of Confederation with Canada, he would never have been elected in merchant-dominated St. John's. But he had no trouble getting elected by a huge majority from Bonavista Centre district, which contained Gander.

Smallwood's standpoint was that we had to bypass Responsible Government and go directly to confederation with Canada. He argued then and later, inside the Convention and out, that there was not a chance in hell of confederation ever coming about if Newfoundland returned to Responsible Government: the power and control would fall into the hands of the same old gang as before our collapse, or their descendants, with a return to the same old misgovernment and corruption. And he made his case vociferously on the floor of the Convention, and everywhere else, that the confederation option must be placed right on the referendum ballot.

When the delegates at the National Convention voted by 29 to 16 to place only the two options, Commission of Government and Responsible Government, on the referendum ballot, and to keep Confederation with Canada off, it proved, in a lot of minds, Smallwood's fears about the future behaviour of his opponents.

He publicly denounced these "twenty-nine dictators" and assembled supportive petitions containing tens of thousands of names, some alleged to have been taken off headstones. Within a month or so, the UK government vetoed the elected delegates' resolution, which had been freely arrived at, and unilaterally placed Confederation with Canada on the ballot as the third option. Naturally, the Responsible Government brigade squawked in shock and dismay: So much for the promised exercise of democracy by Newfoundland's elected delegates!

Ches Crosbie and his supporters, including Don Jamieson and Geoff Stirling, now calculated that Smallwood, with his energy, his mesmerizing oratory, and his fanatical devotion to his Confederation cause, was going to beat the disordered Responsible Government League. Unless they did something drastic, Confederation with Canada was going to win the referendum.

A big problem with the Responsible Government notion was that it was cast in language very unattractive, not to say disgusting, to a lot of Newfoundlanders: a return to Responsible Government "as it existed prior to 1934." It was Responsible Government as it existed prior to 1934 that had brought about its own pitiful downfall and the imposition of Commission of Government in the first place. Clearly, something more appealing, or at least palatable, had to be hooked to Responsible Government if it was going to win the day.

Then, in 1948, someone came up with a notion so alluring that it had the makings of a brilliant political coup. A few observers have credited a young St. John's lawyer and fervent anti-confederate, Jim Halley, with the concept. Twenty years later, I would practise law with Halley under the firm name Halley, Hickman, Hunt, Steele, and Rowe, and, although Jim Halley himself was reticent on the subject, his partner Alex Hickman always maintained to me that the idea was Jim's creation. Others denied that and attributed the whole thing to Ches Crosbie.

Whatever its source, it was sort of an embellished version of Sir Robert Bond's unsuccessful attempts, as Newfoundland colonial secretary, and later premier, to implement a free trade agreement between Newfoundland and the United States. Ches's inspired notion was that once Newfoundland regained its independence under Responsible Government, it should form an economic *union* with the United States by way of a free trade agreement. Thus the newly self-governing country would survive and succeed by freely exporting its fish and other resources to the Americans.

Economic union with our good friends in the greatest nation on earth! The concept was immediately popular and took off like wildfire. The confederates, for good reason, got a big fright. Years later, Smallwood's henchman Al Vardy told me that Joey's anxiety was such at the time that he was "shitting shrapnel."

Newfoundlanders in those days experienced largely neutral, or even negative, feelings toward Canadians. But, by and large, they loved Americans. Through earlier migrations of people from here to the "Boston States," many local families already had strong, long-term ties to relatives and friends there. As exemplified by one family, they covered the gamut from Billy Bulger, former president of the Massachusetts Senate, university president, and director of library, orchestra, and hospital boards, to his own brother, Whitey Bulger, gangster boss and the FBI's most wanted murderer, and the subject of blockbuster mobster movies. Their father was from Newfoundland.

Added to such connections, Britain had granted the US government authorization during the Second World War to establish military bases here in exchange for some decrepit American naval ships. It didn't seem to matter to us that no permission was asked, locally, or that the vessels in exchange were obsolete, which gave a pretty good indication of British estimates of our worth.

More important, after a gruelling depression and the Commission of Government's tight-fisted stinginess, was the fact that tens of millions of American dollars were spent on construction jobs here. And from a personal relationship standpoint, as a result of the "Bases for Destroyers Deal," many Newfoundlanders would closely encounter at work and play thousands of Americans stationed in Newfoundland and Labrador. Hordes of Newfoundland women married American servicemen and moved to every part of the States. The ties of blood, love, friendship, sex, and money were strong.

Enthusiastically, Ches Crosbie and others defected from the Responsible Government League and formed the Economic Union Party. Ches was named leader. He was an absolute dud at speechmaking, but his empire-building reputation ignited tremendous respect and interest in the movement.

Don Jamieson became a highly effective mouthpiece for the cause. Also, Geoff Stirling's knowledge of the States and his connections there allowed him to craft persuasive articles for his popular weekly journal, the *Sunday Herald*, and to insert therein some encouraging interviews with well-placed American senators and officials.

The confederates counterattacked with the opinion of a highly regarded American lawyer that the economic union proposal was not viable. The close three-way relations between the US and Canada and the

UK, he said, would make it unacceptable to the latter two countries, and Washington would go along with their wishes. But Stirling was able to publish in the *Sunday Herald* the names of fifty-one US senators who said they would in fact confer with Newfoundland, as an independent country, to talk over free trade. This dazzling coup by Stirling was proclaimed as proof, of course, that economic union, as part of Responsible Government, was unquestionably possible and feasible.

As a result, the two referendums were close-run contests. The first referendum was held on June 3, 1948. Responsible Government led with 69,400 votes. Confederation with Canada came second with 64,066 votes. Commission of Government came in a relatively distant third with 23,311 votes. Still, it's astonishing that over 14% of the voting population were both so disillusioned by memories of the old Responsible Government days that bankrupted the country, and yet so disenchanted with the prospect of union with Canada, that they would vote to retain a paternalistic, bureaucratic, colonial dictatorship.

First-place Responsible Government had garnered 44.5% of the vote. Democratic governments, with powers of life and death, have been elected with less than that. But this was a referendum requiring a majority decision, not merely a first-past-the-post plurality. The least-favoured option, Commission of Government, was dropped from the ballot, and the choice became a simple two-way battle between Responsible Government and Confederation with Canada. A second referendum was set for July 22.

As fierce as the campaigning had been for the first referendum, it now became vicious. Smallwood's Confederate Association was buoyed by the fact that, adding together the Confederate vote and the Commission vote, most people had disapproved of a return to Responsible Government. The Economic Union Party, led by Ches Crosbie, and the Responsible Government League, led by Peter Cashin, also saw the freed-up Commission of Government vote as a leaning toward Confederation, and they tried to counter that trend by working in concert. But it was an uncomfortable alliance and their efforts were clumsy and uncoordinated.

The battle between independence and union with Canada became more and more divided along religious lines. The Confederates blasted Roman Catholic Archbishop E. P. Roche's hostility to Confederation and induced the protestant Loyal Orange Association to come out strongly against what they perceived as Catholic bias.

Ethnic prejudices were also dragged in. While the Confederates argued that joining Canada was "British Union," the Responsible Government champions retorted that "Confederation Means British Union with *French* Canada." The Confederate Association came back with the view that the anti-confederates, in cozying up to the Yanks, were really anti-British and against the king. They were anti-monarchists and pro-republican!

In the second referendum on July 22, Confederation with Canada got 52% of the vote, beating the Cashin-Crosbie forces by just 7,000 votes. Grown men among the Responsible Government forces bawled their eyes out, hung black crepe over their doors, and wore black bands of mourning around their arms.

Still, Ches Crosbie was prevailed upon to join the delegation dispatched to Ottawa to conclude the Terms of Union with Canada. But ultimately he refused to sign them on grounds of their financial inadequacy. He didn't believe that the new province, based on the financial terms offered by Canada, would be able to balance its books. As subsequent financial fed-bashing from St. John's would show, how right he was!

Ches may have bolted for home from Ottawa, but he rejected attempts to entice him into leading a nationalist party in the upcoming election. In the partisan cleavage that now occurred between Smallwood's new Liberal Party and the Progressive Conservative Party rump that formed around the old Responsible Government League, he is said to have supported Smallwood. Thereafter he retired altogether from active politics and concentrated his efforts on his businesses and trying to have a life.

Regrettably, his relations with his wife grew worse and worse, exacerbated by his heroic binge drinking and the burdens added by problems in his sister's family. He separated from her in order to marry Alice Squires, the widowed daughter-in-law of former prime minister Sir Richard Squires.

Ches got a divorce in Reno, Nevada, and married Alice. On Boxing Day, 1962, while they were on their honeymoon in Hawaii, Ches died of a heart attack. He was fifty-seven, just a year older than his father, Sir John, when he died, and the same age as his son Andrew, also a prodigious businessman, at his death in 1991.

I met Alice once at her house on Old Topsail Road. I'd been brought there by her son Richard, the namesake of his famous grandfather, Sir Richard Squires. Young Richard and I were casual friends, much the same age, and I wanted to listen to the vinyl record he had of one of Sir Richard's campaign speeches about the Corner Brook paper mill—putting "The Hum on the Humber." Alice was a lovely, friendly woman, and I could readily understand why Ches had fallen in love with her. I could also see, listening to Sir Richard's oration on the recording, why he was able to get elected handily, and re-elected much of the time, even after being politically down and out from accusations of skulduggery.

The last words from Ches Crosbie to his son John were uttered just before he left for his Reno divorce. Ches and Joe Smallwood had enjoyed, or endured, an eccentric friendship for decades, and Ches knew him all too well. He came to see John with a warning, eerie in its timing. Perhaps he had a premonition of his premature death, and it needed to be said now. The warning was basically: Never get tangled up politically with Smallwood; never run alongside Joe Smallwood in an election.

Four years later, John would be in Smallwood's cabinet and elected to the House as a Member of Smallwood's caucus. And a couple of years after that the pair of them began, Joe Smallwood and John Crosbie, one of the biggest political wars in the province since Confederation. But that's a yarn for later. Right now let's look at a vast, if fanciful and far-fetched, might-have-been:

IT IS TANTALIZING to speculate about what could have happened to Newfoundland if Confederation had been rejected in the second referendum and Responsible Government had won, especially by a narrow margin. Would Confederation, in that scenario, have indeed been dead? After all, a win by Responsible Government forces would not, in theory, have precluded the possibility of Confederation later. Could Smallwood's forces have been able to keep the confederation idea alive and feasible by leading a Canadian-union party into the following general election? Perhaps even to victory?

Smallwood himself has said—certainly he told me many times—that he thought a return of Responsible Government, with the momentum of victory gained by its supporters, would have killed the notion of Confederation for years to come. And he believed that, centred in St. John's, the Responsible Government crowd would have seized control of the levers of power and the political drive, and that he himself would have been turned into a political eunuch by defeat in the referendum.

If Smallwood was right, we next need to bear in mind that a supposed victory by Responsible Government would have been, in large measure, attributable to Ches Crosbie's attractive cause, Economic Union with the United States. That powerful faction did possess political organizing ability, plus speaking and media talent, and substantial support in its own right.

Is it likely, or even possible, then, that an Economic Union party, with their attractive idea, could have grown to dominate the political landscape, after the return of independence? Could they have won a general election by continuing to espouse such a policy? It is mesmerizing to contemplate. And although the notion of a post-1949 government of a sovereign Newfoundland actually deciding to foster closer and ever closer political relations with the US may seem improbable, let's speculate anyway. After all, ultimately, it would have, or should have, depended on the freely exercised wishes of the people here, despite attempted roadblocks by outsiders.

In such a scenario, I could see Newfoundland involved over time in a political chain of events: first a free trade agreement with the States, next some form of economic union, then the gradual process of developing into a territory, and ultimately converting into a state in the American union.

The question then becomes, if such process had actually occurred, how would our imaginary statehood status in America have compared with the reality of our becoming a province in Canada?

Strangely, little Newfoundland and Labrador would have enjoyed as a state just as much political clout, or more, in the United States nation, a country with ten times the population of Canada, and even more than ten times the economic influence, as we actually now possess as a province. We would enjoy that status because, as a state, we would be part of a truly federal country, rather than what we in fact are—a weak and powerless province in the hybrid amalgam of a pretend-federal country like Canada.

As a state in the US we'd have 2 elected senators out of 102, or nearly 2% of the Senate. At present, with Newfoundland's 7 seats in Canada's House of Commons, we have about 2% of the current 338 MPs. In other words, we'd have about the same percentage of the USA's most powerful political institution as we now have in Canada's.

Moreover, as time rolls on, the way it is now in Canada, our destiny as a province will be to see our percentage of MPs decrease far below the 2%. That will happen because the total number of seats in the House will increase with the rising population of the rest of Canada, but the number of our Newfoundland and Labrador MPs will stay the same.

In this fantasy, I'm emphasizing the Senate, because it's the Senate's power to advise and consent on presidential appointments and treaties, in addition to its regular legislative powers, that can make or break a president. In all those processes, every single senator counts. The possibilities for Newfoundland with a president who oversees the spending of several trillion dollars a year, and who feels dependent on the support of senators, are phenomenal.

US senators are the most powerful legislators in the most powerful country in the world, and we would have two of them. It's the kind of power for Newfoundland and Labrador that Clyde Wells wanted us to have in an equal and elected Canadian Senate, in his amendments to the Meech Lake Accord, as necessary to allow our weak and powerless province to thrive in a "federation" containing relatively gargantuan provinces like Ontario and Quebec.

There are some other advantages we would have had as a state in the United States: military spending here would have been many times greater than the amount the Canadian government has spent in this province since Confederation. And from a practical political point of view, it would have been hard, if not impossible, to close all the military bases the Americans already owned and operated here.

In addition to the huge free and open market for our fish and other resources that we would have accessed, we would have enjoyed enormous economic benefits from tourism, as a state. The "last frontier" aspect alone of the Island and of Labrador would be very attractive to millions of our fellow Americans. Combine that with the secular shrines that would have developed for all Americans at L'Anse aux Meadows as the first landfall in America of Europeans—the Vikings—and at Bonavista as the site of John Cabot's discovery of America.

Christopher Columbus's landing in the Bahamas would be utterly effaced by Leif Erikson and John Cabot, these true discoverers of the United States of America. And remember that John Guy founded Cupids ten years *before* the *Mayflower* pilgrims landed at Plymouth Colony. There would be no American in the rest of the country who would not, at some point in their life, make the pilgrimage to those sacred, historic Newfoundland sites in America. One's mind is overwhelmed at the thought of the cornucopia of tourist dollars that would come our way.

Churchill Falls power? Do we imagine that, with America's weight in finance and trade, our Labrador hydro power at the Upper Churchill Falls and at our Lower Churchill sites, Gull Island and Muskrat Falls, would be sold to Quebec or Canada at anything less than full market values? Contrast that with our past and current exploitation in Canada as a powerless province, vis-à-vis Quebec.

To size up how Newfoundland and Labrador would have done generally as a state, let's measure ourselves against a roughly equivalent place, Alaska. That state has been more or less equal to us in resources, and its population, while a little larger than ours, is relatively small in America. Its economy is mainly dependent on fishing and oil industries, some nine military bases, and tourism. Ring a bell? Alaska is at least as remote from the mainstream as we are, and about as challenging in climate and terrain.

Yet it has enjoyed historically a substantially higher standard of living as a US state than Newfoundland and Labrador has had as a province of Canada. A few years ago a study showed that Alaska had one of the highest standards of living in the United States, and a Gallup poll indicated that residents of Alaska were more satisfied and optimistic regarding their standard of living than the people of any other state.

Add to all this positive speculation about Newfoundland and Labrador as a state the uncanny fact that politicians from here have often punched well above their weight as premiers and federal MPs and ministers in Ottawa. We can imagine how effective it would have been for us in Washington to elect senators of the calibre of, say, Joe Smallwood, Richard Cashin, Don Jamieson, John Crosbie, and Brian Tobin, among others.

Would there be any disadvantages of statehood for us? Yes, there would have been a few downsides. For example, I personally would probably have been brought home from Vietnam in a body bag. I was just the right age for it. But I can think of a good few Newfoundlanders who might have been prepared to see me make that sacrifice for the greater good.

More generally, the US, as the self-appointed policeman of the world in the last half of the twentieth century and onward, has gotten involved in a lot of questionable or pointless conflicts and wars with toxic consequences to present and following generations.

The ingrained conservatism which has seemed to choke off rational debate on health care and gun control might also be deemed a negative by many, compared to the atmosphere in Canada. And a presidential system that elects a President Trump might give some people here pause, if not the outright willies.

Still, weighing the pros and cons, the idea of our becoming a state in the USA remains an intriguing scenario. But, realistically speaking, even if we had gone back to Responsible Government, could union with the United States ever have actually come about?

I tried the conjecture out recently on a highly respected Canadian historian, and he replied that it certainly could have if the Newfoundland people really wanted it. But it would have taken extraordinarily strong leadership and solid will of the populace to achieve it, especially against outside naysayers. There's the rub! Those elements—the necessary leadership and the will for such a cause—would have been hard to find. But even assuming the popular desire and the inspired leadership, the barriers, most likely, would still have been impossible to overcome.

The overt and behind-the-scenes machinations of America's close allies, Canada and Great Britain, would, realistically, have made it impossible for the United States to give Newfoundland's unification overtures the time of day. There are ample precedents in our benighted history where the Canadian and UK governments have, by themselves or jointly, thwarted any independent action by Newfoundland that they didn't like the look of.

STILL, FOR HIS leadership in the referendum battles, which created a vision and a cause that nearly won Responsible Government in 1948, and which can still stimulate thought on one of the fascinating might-have-beens in our history; and for seeing at the time of our joining Canada the deficiencies being foisted on the new province by the Terms of Union; and for the amazing fact that forty years afterwards, his idea on economic union via free trade between Newfoundland and the United States would be taken over and implemented in part by the government of Canada; I would award Ches Crosbie a rating of 75% as one of Newfoundland and Labrador's historic leaders. He built better than he knew.

Joey Smallwood

JOSEPH ROBERTS SMALLWOOD was born near Gambo, at Mint Brook, Newfoundland, on December 24, 1900, and died nearly ninety-one years later on December 17, 1991. It was during his political campaigning that he imposed on himself the endearing diminutive "Joey."

His life was more than half over when he produced his epoch-making contribution to history. If Joey had abandoned politics completely on April Fool's Day, 1949, his leadership legacy, as the last Father of Confederation, would have been secure. Leading Newfoundland into joining Canada, whether one agrees with the step or not, would have placed him among the most important leaders of this land since the first arrival of Europeans 950 years before.

Add to that his dedication to writing, editing, and publishing. He assembled books about every aspect of the place, its politics, economy, geography, characters, and general history. That heritage, particularly his *Books of Newfoundland*, and his conception of and work on the five-volume *Encyclopedia of Newfoundland and Labrador*, would have increased his lustre as one of our very great public figures.

But what about his twenty-three-year stretch as premier of the province from 1949 to 1972, and then his monkeying about on the political scene, mostly as a spoiler, during the next five years? Do his activities over that period increase or decrease the sheen on his leadership? Did his long haul in elective politics make him a greater or lesser leader?

Over the years, many knowledgeable Newfoundlanders I've talked to, and not necessarily just those with a natural or partisan prejudice against him, would give him low or even negative marks as premier and in later politics. They have evidenced his "hare-brained" development schemes—factories making boots, batteries, chocolate, and so on ad nauseam—plus the ill-starred Come By Chance oil refinery, Stephenville linerboard mill, and Upper Churchill hydro deal, and his role as a spiteful vote splitter in keeping his own Liberal Party out of power in his last election.

Moreover, his strong taste for hobnobbing with offshore swashbucklers like John Shaheen, even to the point of corruption with the likes of Alfred Valdmanis and John C. Doyle, did him little credit. So, before we move on to the positive matters, if any, let's get some of the negative baggage out of the way.

I spent five years in Joey's caucus as an elected Member of the House of Assembly, including three years in his cabinet as a minister of various portfolios. One of the personal characteristics I observed about him during that time was that he was mostly a prick. And I wasn't surprised that I could discern around him, discounting the many sycophantic brown-nosers, no real friends.

It was hard for anyone to remain on a friendly basis with the old fart, because he constantly placed a dreadful strain on your loyalty and camaraderie. Just about everyone he was ever close to, ultimately and inevitably, became estranged from him, including me. He had sought, early in my career, to make me some sort of protege of his. He put me at a young age in several government portfolios; he took me on a remarkable jaunt around the world with him; he asked me to take charge of financial aspects of his 1969 leadership campaign against John Crosbie; and he took me into his confidence on political and policy matters entirely outside my departments. But then . . . ?

When Ed Roberts and I, as his cabinet colleagues, combined our efforts to stop the worst excesses of John Shaheen's Come By Chance refinery and John C. Doyle's linerboard mill, he sided with them and gradually soured on us to the point of enmity. Like a mafia godfather, he considered me dead to him at the end and refused to speak to me or write anything about me. I think he was trying to make me a non-person in his world. Mind you, I was more than okay with that.

And then, having tried and failed, in his seventies, to knock Ed Roberts out of the Liberal leadership in 1974, he engineered, in cahoots with his former worst political enemy, Frank Moores, in the 1975 general election, Moores's victory against Roberts, Joey's former closest colleague. Go figure out that psychology!

The paradox about Joey was that, simply as a person, outside of his place in politics, he was an engaging, humorous, often fascinating conversationalist and companion. Some of his erstwhile friends, but by no means all, who'd been forced into rancour and conflict against him, returned to some form of companionship later, particularly when he was old and disabled and no longer in a position to dominate or humiliate them politically.

Perhaps Les Curtis and O. L. "Al" Vardy were the closest to the status of friends to Smallwood. Curtis, a former law partner of Joey's early mentor, Sir Richard Squires, was his long-time Attorney General and minister of Justice. Joey used to joke that he only had Curtis around to keep him (Joey) out of jail. Evidently, judging by the results, Curtis was pretty good at that.

I always had the impression Smallwood kept Vardy around as a convenient henchman, perhaps sometimes for less than salutary purposes. Vardy was born in Channel–Port aux Basques and later sought his fortune in the United States, where he ended up doing a stretch in prison for armed robbery in New York State. Back in Newfoundland in 1936, he met Joey through his involvement in broadcasting and newspapers and, in the only elective politics available at the time under Commission of Government, the St. John's municipal council.

Then, having been elected under Smallwood to the House of Assembly right after Confederation, and appointed to the provincial cabinet, he was forced to resign his seat in 1951. Peter Cashin was on the verge of making public Vardy's stateside criminal record. Vardy had brought this on himself by going around insinuating that someone close to Cashin was a homosexual, which was a decidedly negative political slur in those benighted days.

But Joey was able to keep his "friend" around by appointing him as the director of tourist development and, later, as deputy minister of Economic Development, and having lunch with him nearly every day in Smallwood's private dining room.

The government of Frank Moores in 1972 would appoint a Royal Commission under former lieutenant-governor and prominent lawyer Fabian O'Dea to inquire into the alleged wrongdoings of Vardy, Smallwood, and others. O'Dea reported that Vardy was in a blatant conflict of interest for leasing several buildings that he was part owner of to the Newfoundland Liquor Commission, a government agency. And he'd been massively overcharging for rent for twenty years, to boot.

O'Dea also alleged that Joey was one-third owner of the company that leased the premises to the Liquor Commission, but Joey claimed complete ignorance of the transgressions, or even of the transactions. The commission alleged a further flagrant conflict of interest by Vardy and Joey when they had put the liquor store leases up as collateral for loans of hundreds of thousands of dollars each to buy shares in the British Newfoundland Development Company (BRINCO). That was the company Joey's government was dealing with at the time regarding the Upper Churchill hydro development.

For years to come, Smallwood always defended himself against accusations that he'd given away the billions of dollars of Upper Churchill power to Quebec, by arguing that it wasn't he but BRINCO that entered into the contract with Hydro-Québec. But, of course, it was he that had empowered BRINCO in the first place to give away virtually all the value of that great public resource.

But back to the time of O'Dea's royal commission report: Smallwood and Vardy defended themselves against his conflict of interest allegations by asking everyone in view a rhetorical question: Well, what else would you expect from a big Tory like O'Dea, they queried, who had been, after all, appointed lieutenant-governor by Joey's mortal foe, John Diefenbaker?

A year later, though, in 1973, Vardy was charged criminally with fraud, bribery, and breach of public trust in connection with the financing of John C. Doyle's Labrador Linerboard Limited mill in Stephenville. He took off for Panama. When he was nabbed there the next year, and was in the process of being flown back to St. John's to face charges, his American lawyer secured his release after the plane put down in Florida. From his Clearwater home, Vardy managed to fight off extradition to Canada until he died there in 1980.

Some St. John's lawyers who were close to all that speculated to me that the failure to bring him back to Newfoundland was a lucky stroke for Joey, since Vardy would have sung like a canary, and implicated his leader, in return for a more lenient punishment. As justice, or good luck, would have it, Smallwood was never charged with anything.

JOEY WAS BIG on loyalty, but that was entirely a one-way street leading *to* him from others, never *from* him to any other human being. Unless, that is, the other human being was an offshore buccaneer type, pitching down here to "save" the province, economically. Then Joey seemed to fall right in love with the guy, at least in the sense that he would become enamoured of the buccaneer's off-the-wall promotions and loony development notions, especially if they involved hefty government layouts of money. Take for example his "bromance" with Alfred Valdmanis, the suspected Nazi Latvian.

In 1950, on the advice of C. D. Howe, the famous federal minister of Trade and Commerce, Joey had the provincial government hire Valdmanis as his director general of Economic Development at a salary, large but not outrageous for a top civil servant in those days, of $10,000. Soon, though, Valdmanis would be demanding and receiving additional remuneration and positions. He spent his time around Joey clicking his heels, bowing obsequiously, and purring the words, "Yes, mein premier." Even some ministers and supporters of Joey, let alone opponents, used to whisper to each other that they expected to hear him any time now emitting a Freudian slip along the lines of, "*Ja wohl, mein führer.*"

Joey himself told me many years afterwards that, within a year following his hiring, a Jewish periodical in Canada alleged that, during the war, Valdmanis had been involved in murdering Latvian Jews. But Valdmanis denied all that, exhibiting, as proof of his innocence, the "torture scars" on his back received during his resistance to German and Soviet tyranny. A German professional would later assert that the scars had resulted from a medical operation when Valdmanis was a child.

Within two or three years of his hiring, Valdmanis had used his German and Latvian connections, together with extensive tours of Europe with Smallwood, and a flood of Newfoundland tax dollars, to build gypsum, hardboard, tannery, cement, rubber, and cotton plants, among others.

During this period there was speculation that Valdmanis and Smallwood were personally on the take from this great economic leap forward. Even some members of the cabinet were concerned by Valdmanis's zeal for finding jobs and projects in Newfoundland for old European buddies. But opponents of Smallwood, who hoped a scandal involving Valdmanis would bring him down, were disappointed when it turned out to be Joey himself who alerted the police.

In the spring of 1954, he came across evidence of kickbacks to Valdmanis from some European builders of the various mills. Newfoundland's economic white knight was arrested, criminally charged, convicted, and sentenced to four years.

He served twenty-seven months at the prison farm in Salmonier. Joey felt so betrayed personally by his one-time saviour that he refused to have anything else to do with him after his arrest. He also refused Valdmanis's entreaties to see him when he was out on bail, and complained about Valdmanis's cushy treatment on the prison farm, and said no to his request for support in his parole application. When he died in an accident years later on the mainland, Joey's icy reaction, entirely devoid of sympathy, was that he was a brilliant but tragic figure.

It seemed clear that Joey himself was not in on the scheme; he escaped serious criticism by painting himself as the victim betrayed by the greatest male love of his life and describing the pain of having to turn in his golden boy to the police. That heartbreak over Valdmanis, though, didn't stop Joey from falling for other lesser or greater buccaneers, John Shaheen and John C. Doyle.

Those further ill-begotten projects—the Come By Chance refinery and the Stephenville linerboard mill—would end up costing the province hundreds of millions of dollars for minimal returns. When one considers how these earlier and later ventures added to the public debt and deprived the province of further improvements to education and health care, it can be heartbreaking.

So, those are a few perceived deficits of Joey's tenure as premier. What else should go on the liability side of the ledger before we see if we can dig out some positive material?

Quite a few people today would place squarely in the negative column Joey's draconian reaction to the strike of the International Woodworkers of America that began at the end of 1958 against the paper mill in Grand Falls. But such an attitude at this distant date would not have been shared by as many Newfoundlanders at the time.

I was in first year at Memorial University when the strike started. I can recall that, although most loggers had voted to have the IWA as their union, public opinion generally in the province inexorably mounted against the union during the winter weeks that the acrimonious strike continued. Joey's stated intention to "send [the IWA] packing!" had strong support.

When he caused the House of Assembly to pass legislation decertifying the IWA and stripping it of its right to bargain in this province, Canadian and international labour organizations, and much of the mainland media, condemned him. But local support for Joey's actions continued to grow, and when a confrontation between police and loggers in Badger in March became a riot in which Newfoundland Constabulary member William Moss was fatally injured, the support in the province for Smallwood's position, including at the university, escalated prodigiously.

Memorial students were so partial to Joey's stance that student leaders wanted to organize a march supporting him and the new puppet union led by Minister Max Lane, and denouncing the IWA and its leader, Landon Ladd. A chant, which gave new meaning to the word "sophomoric," was rehearsed throughout the campus for the march: "Pick up your axe and follow Max and lop off Landon's lad." University Vice-President Mose Morgan banned the student march, not because he was against anyone's anti-IWA sentiment, but because he feared the possibility of violence in the streets.

My point is that it's easy with the benefit of hindsight to criticize Joey for his antediluvian attitude regarding the IWA. Such disapproval did happen decades later when Landon Ladd returned to give a speech at Memorial and received a deserved, tumultuous standing ovation for his outstanding oratory. But it's well to remember that when the events were actually going on, it was Joey who was receiving, at least locally, the accolades and standing ovations.

JOEY LAUNCHED A provincial election a few months later, in 1959, by attacking Progressive Conservative Prime Minister John Diefenbaker. His issue was Term 29 of Newfoundland's Terms of Union with Canada, and it involved Diefenbaker's cancellation of an annual federal grant of $8 million. Smallwood fought the Tory PM tooth and nail over that money, both in the provincial election, which he won handily, nearly annihilating the local PC Party in the process, and leading up to the federal election of 1962. He travelled the entire country speaking out against Diefenbaker. Some commentators attributed a substantial amount of the Tory decline in that election, and the party's ultimate defeat soon afterwards, to Joey's war with the federal PCs.

Other analysts are perplexed by Joey's aggressiveness in the Term 29 dispute, compared with his tame acquiescence, later, when Liberal Prime Minister Lester B. Pearson would not lift a finger to further Newfoundland's constitutional right to transmit its Upper Churchill power through Quebec. To many, it has seemed that Liberal partisanship trumped everything else in Joey's mind: he didn't hesitate to attack a

Tory PM savagely over the *relatively* minor Term 29, but he lay down and rolled over like a whipped dog before a Liberal prime minister regarding the hugely important transmission of Labrador power. But perhaps, as we shall see, there may have been a quid pro quo involved in Smallwood's dealings with Pearson.

IN THE AREA of purely partisan politics, Joey was not a healthy influence. In my experience, his reign was not, as often alleged, a dictatorship or tyranny. His party "organization" was far too loose-knit for that. But it certainly was, when he felt the urge, a one-man show. And it consisted frequently of government by whimsical enthusiasm and impulse, with little consideration given to consultation of colleagues, provincial or federal.

One interesting side of his political technique was that, although he personally selected all Liberal candidates for elections, he did not simply pick loyal yes-men known to be his devoted uncritical supporters. He went out of his way to bring into his caucus men (there were no women) of independent reputation in the province, even including some businessmen, professionals, and labour leaders with a history of ambivalence, if not outright hostility, to his policies and methods. Many whom he courted declined, but not because they weren't fervently wooed.

A glance at some of the stalwarts he did succeed in recruiting shows how much he favoured having men of some consequence around him, well regarded in their professions: Jim Chalker, Bill Adams, Rupert Bartlett, Bill Callahan, John Crosbie, Les Curtis, Eric Dawe, Val Earle, Charlie Granger, Gerry Hill, Bill Keough, Dr. Hubert Kitchen, Max Lane, Dr. Fred Rowe, John Mahoney, Dr. Cliff Joy, Nat Noel, Art Mifflin, Aidan Maloney, Beaton Abbott, Steve Neary, Dr. James McGrath, Tom Burgess, Dr. Noel Murphy, Myles Murray, John Nolan, Gus Oldford, Herbert Pottle, Ted Russell, Greg Power, Ed Roberts, Clyde Wells, Alec Hickman, Earl Winsor, Mel Woodward, and Harold Horwood.

But despite their abilities as individuals, Joey never regarded his cabinet as a team. He viewed each member as a mere extension or appendage of himself, and he never shirked from using the powers of the chief minister to "guide" weak and strong colleagues alike. "A leader's job," he would proclaim to disparagers of his capriciously bossy methods, "is to lead."

Some of his choices were not able to stomach his ways as premier and had to quit, or were forced out: Harold Horwood, Ted Russell, Herb Pottle, Greg Power, John Crosbie, Clyde Wells, Val Earle, Alec Hickman, Tom Burgess, Gerry Myrden, and Beaton Abbott.

When Ed Roberts and I were still in cabinet at the end of Smallwood's reign, we found ourselves carrying the entire burden of dealing with Shaheen and Doyle on the oil refinery and the linerboard mill. With Joey usually supporting them against us, we were often on the point of resigning ourselves. But Joey was by then in the position of not being able to survive further hemorrhaging from his cabinet and would, therefore, have to resentfully yield, while muttering curses against the two of us, the obnoxious "Bobbsey Twins."

From the start of his premiership to the end, and well beyond, Joey was wholly unable to visualize any other person ever replacing him in the leadership of the Liberal Party. I wouldn't say he was paranoid about possible conspirators toppling him in a coup. He had too little esteem for the political talents of any other person or group for that. But he was constantly Machiavellian in his alertness to nip any such ill-advised attempt in the bud.

His main technique was to "divide and rule." Every now and then, throughout his premiership, he would publicly name his new "next premier." This was intended to set all the aspirants secretly at each other's throats, especially those whom he had earlier named, but had now superseded, as his heir apparent. Mainly, though, it made the newly anointed next premiers cackle and chortle.

Richard Cashin, for example, used to laugh that he was the *original* next premier, having been so designated when he beat Billy Browne in the 1962 federal election. He was certainly one of the early ones, but I believe he was preceded in the 1950s by Harold Horwood, Greg Power, and Fred Rowe. In the late 1960s, the "next" premiers were, among others, John Nolan, John Mahoney, Bill Callahan, Ed Roberts, and myself.

In the early 1970s, around the time of his ill-starred 1971 election, his next premiers were Tom Burgess and Andrew Crosbie.

Earlier, leading into 1969, though, there was such a rift in the party, between him and John Crosbie, that he had little choice but to announce an actual leadership convention. He assured the province that he was going to retire and had no intention of being a candidate. But then it turned out that the one man who really, really wanted to be the next premier, John Crosbie, had the "wrong hands." At least that was Joey's appraisal of his anatomy. And since there was no way, for the good of the people, that Joey was going to allow the party or the province to fall into the wrong hands, he had no option but to deny himself the joys of retirement. No, he had to make the supreme sacrifice and run for leader himself. He did so, and won the battle against Crosbie. But two years later he would lose the war.

NOT BEING SATISFIED with maintaining an iron personal grip on the leadership of his own Liberal Party, he wouldn't keep his nose out of the leadership of the Tory party, either. Despite the fact that most of the PC leaders were politically weak enough to be positively helpful to him in winning elections, he could not seem to resist bullying them out of existence. He knocked out the harmless Malcolm Hollett, leader of the PC Party, by running directly against him in St. John's West in the 1959 election. The fact that he and some other Liberals called Hollett, privately, "Malc the alc" should have been enough to persuade him to leave well enough alone.

Then, in 1966, he decided to remove the equally unfeared Dr. Noel Murphy from the Tory leadership. He put Clyde Wells up against him in Humber East and ran himself in the adjacent district. Campaigning vigorously for Clyde and pouring limitless money into the task, he did the job.

Next, he allegedly connived at the forced resignation of the brand new Tory leader, the learned but namby-pamby Gerry Ottenheimer. It was whispered, with some claim to plausibility, that he set his minions the task of luring Gerry into a Montreal whorehouse, where he was "discovered" by the police and charged.

Some of us in Joey's caucus suggested that he should stop rooting out unthreatening Opposition Leaders: one of these days, we argued, a leader might percolate to the top who could be an effective challenge to him. But Joey only scoffed. "And who might that be?" he asked in derision at one of the candidates in the Tory leadership race he had caused with Ottenheimer's downfall. "Frank Moores?"

NOR COULD JOEY keep his fingers out of who could be Liberal candidates in federal elections, or appointments to the federal cabinet. In 1967, his meddling in federal politics started his own precipitous slide to political doom. That year, Jack Pickersgill, Newfoundland's minister in Ottawa, resigned from parliament and the Pearson cabinet and was appointed president of the Canadian Transport Commission.

Either Richard Cashin, first elected in 1962, or Don Jamieson, elected in a by-election in 1966, would have been an excellent replacement in cabinet. But, instead of letting the prime minister choose the new federal cabinet minister for his own cabinet from this province, Joey took over. According to him—I never heard it from anybody else—there'd be a brawl to the death between Richard and Don over who should get the appointment, so Joey had to step in and exercise "statesmanship."

I suspected that his motive was to keep both of these potential rivals for his own job from gaining the power and prestige of becoming a federal minister. So he looked around for someone mild and risk-free. And his eye settled on provincial cabinet minister Charlie Granger.

Poor Charlie must have been starting to feel like a rat in a maze. He'd been re-elected to the House of Commons in the federal election of 1965. A year later, Joey inveigled him into abandoning Ottawa and running in the provincial election of 1966, to be appointed to Joey's cabinet. Now, just a few months later, Joey cajoled him into resigning from the provincial House of Assembly to run federally again in the by-election for Pickersgill's old seat, whence he was appointed minister without portfolio in Ottawa.

That convoluted series of machinations now necessitated a provincial by-election in October 1967 in Charlie's former provincial district of Gander. In this hitherto safe Liberal seat, the PC candidate, Harold Collins, startled Smallwood and the rest of the Liberal Party by winning the by-election.

Only one year after Joey's near-sweep of 1966, he himself had caused the first cracks in his monolithic power to become obvious to the whole province. That, and the ill-fated federal election for the Trudeau Liberals in this province in 1968, scared him into putting off the next provincial election until 1971, five full years after the last one. By doing so, in retrospect, he all but guaranteed his own defeat by Frank Moores in October 1971, with his forced resignation as premier being the *coup de grâce* in January 1972.

IN 1974, AFTER failing to grab back the Liberal leadership from Ed Roberts, he performed his last pathologically resentful act toward the ruination of the provincial Liberal Party for the next decade and a half. Shortly before Premier Frank Moores called an election in 1975, Smallwood set up his very own faction, the Liberal Reform Party, to contest seats. Frank Moores's bagmen helped to fund Joey's "new" party, with the result that in the election, the Liberal vote was divided two ways in many seats.

There have been arguments, pro and con, about how much this may have benefited the PC Party in the election. My own view is that Joey's Liberal Reform Party probably kept his former protege and colleague, Ed Roberts, from winning a majority of the seats and becoming premier. Instead, Smallwood was instrumental in turning the government back to Frank Moores and John Crosbie, the despised political opponents who had unseated him from power in the first place.

DID JOEY SMALLWOOD ever do anything good as leader after bringing Newfoundland into Confederation? Some people would still answer, no, not much: He spent most of his time and energy, they believe, on blowing tax dollars on lunatic schemes. Oh sure, he oversaw roadwork, sewer construction, rural electrification, and the like, but where was the glory in that? A committee of bureaucrats could have overseen those mundane public works. And, in any event, some would urge, such commonplace stuff, even if positive, was mostly overshadowed by the blindingly negative fiascos.

I know it's easy to feel that way. I've had my moments along those lines myself. I tended that way in my book *The Premiers Joey and Frank*. But the more I have reflected on his handiworks from greater historical distance, the more I have come to appreciate Smallwood's visionary and imaginative and gutsy achievements, among the junk.

One of the best of his early acts was to seek out a superb man to represent this young, emerging province at the cabinet table in Ottawa. Enter Jack Pickersgill.

For years, Pickersgill had been a close adviser to the prime minister of Canada. Federal cabinet ministers of the highest stature were told by the PM to "clear it with Jack." He'd also been a powerful, behind-closed-doors supporter of Newfoundland's Confederation with Canada. As Clerk of the Privy Council, the highest Canadian civil servant, Pickersgill was intimately familiar with all the closets where the skeletons were hidden, and he knew how to dig buried treasure out of the crannies.

It was a great coup, therefore, when Joey secured Jack Pickersgill to run for the Liberal Party in the Bonavista–Twillingate riding in the 1953 federal election. As Joey's man, he won the riding in a walk. The biggest problem, the premier used to joke, was not getting voters to mark their ballots for the candidate; the biggest problem was getting voters to pronounce the candidate's name.

Pickersgill brought many benefits to the province as federal minister. Joey regarded his supreme achievement as the gaining of unemployment insurance benefits for fishermen. Some policy analysts, however, considered that to be a travesty: Fishermen weren't employees, they were self-employed businessmen. The UI, as it was then called (now EI), was not available to other small business owners, they argued, and this extension served only to keep many fishermen in non-sustainable enterprises, who would otherwise find viable employment elsewhere.

I recall discussing all this with Prime Minister Trudeau one time at a function in Ottawa. He told me he used to have negative thoughts himself on UI for fishermen, but after listening carefully to Newfoundland and Labrador MPs, he considered the program to be legitimate. It was an essential income supplement to a crucial Canadian industry in which the productive phase was seasonal, and where fishermen had long months of preparation without compensation for that essential productive season.

On another front, neither Pickersgill nor Smallwood, in the early 1960s, persuaded Prime Minister Pearson to enforce Newfoundland's constitutional right to have its Upper Churchill hydro power transmitted across Quebec. They avoided the issue, reportedly, at Pearson's request. But I had the impression from Joey that the federal minister was able to deploy that discouragement to tap into other sources of federal largesse.

For example, the completion of Newfoundland's Trans-Canada Highway with 90% federal Liberal financing gave Joey the mantra that summed it up: "We finished the drive in [nineteen] sixty-five, thanks to Mr. Pearson" [and Mr. Pickersgill].

In 1970, two or three years after he'd left politics, Jack Pickersgill was made Companion of the Order of Canada, signifying the highest degree of merit to Canada and humanity, on either the national or international scene. That's a good indication of Joey's vision in recruiting that man to his team soon after Confederation.

MY OWN FATHER's great pride and joy in the 1950s, as minister of Mines and Resources, was planning and developing, backed by Smallwood's enthusiasm, a string of provincial parks throughout the province. These pearls of beauty were designed to be held for the benefit of the people, and protected and maintained as public property, in perpetuity.

That government policy survived for decades. Even during Premier Brian Peckford's roughest financial nightmares, he refused to close or sell any of the parks. But the government of Clyde Wells began in the 1990s, as a cost-cutting measure, the dismantling or selling off of many of these scenic and recreational delights. The official vandalism would have broken the originators' hearts.

* * * * *

THE MOST EVIDENT example of Joey's creative building program in the late 1950s, apart perhaps from the visibility of wacko industries all over the place, was the Confederation Building. Its bricks and mortar and cement, and its postwar modern architectural style, were not everyone's cup of tea, but he did succeed for a while in bringing together in one building the widely scattered government departments. He also realized his ambition, with the fancy intercom installed in his office on the eighth floor, of being able to summon ministers and officials into his presence for an audience at the mere push of a button.

He told me he had chosen the site for the building by going up on Signal Hill and scanning northward across the city till he spotted an empty area of land. He ordered a minion to find out who owned it. The acreage turned out to belong to one of the churches, and Joey was so eager to buy it for his edifice that the church, he said proudly, was able to turn a hefty capital gain on the sale.

Built on a cost-plus basis by favoured contractors to the tune of some $9 million (many multiples of that in today's dollars), it opened in 1960. I was attending Memorial University at the time, and some of us students, in the manner of jejune university wits throughout history, called it "Joey's erection." It did strike other observers as demonstrating, in the St. John's landscape of low-rise buildings, a dramatic, vertically thrusting quality. Harold Horwood went Freudian about it: No doubt tapping into a few inadequacies of his own, he said it was a clear indication of the physical, sexual inadequacy of the little man.

One convenience of the building to Joey was his removal of the old historic legislature, the House of Assembly, from the Colonial Building to the Confederation Building. The former House of Assembly on Military Road had been threatened from time to time by rampaging hordes of rioters, but it had a certain dignity. So the move was not to everyone's delight. But Joey placed the new House of Assembly on the ninth floor of the new building as a safeguard: as a young man, he'd helped rescue Prime Minister Sir Richard Squires from a lynch mob that was trying to seize him from the ground floor of the Colonial building. That scene was not an experience he was eager to see redirected at himself.

JOEY LOVED THE whole concept of learning and the company of learned people. He was largely, if sporadically, self-taught as a result of his voracious reading, and he sorely regretted the fact that, as a young man, he hadn't been able to go to university. Listening to him talk as premier about his initiatives regarding Memorial University, I concluded that they were his own vicarious fulfillment. He wanted to have a magnificent university and expansive campus, with many scholarships, grants and bursaries, and low or no tuition—even student salaries at one point—to ensure that no bright young Newfoundlander would ever again be denied, by deprived conditions like his own, of a chance for higher education.

As soon as he became premier, he had the House of Assembly elevate Memorial University College to the status of a full-fledged degree-granting university named Memorial University of Newfoundland. When I entered MUN in the old buildings off Parade Street in 1958, it was a pretty ramshackle place but contained about a thousand highly intelligent students—everyone there seemed to have an electoral district scholarship or centenary of Responsible Government scholarship or some other recognition of merit. They were the smartest kids from communities large and small throughout Newfoundland and Labrador.

But lack of space at the Parade Street campus had forced a cap to be imposed on the admission of first-year students. The need to construct a new, large university campus had become a huge issue by the winter of 1959, when we students marched in demonstration against the Diefenbaker government's curtailment of the Term 29 grant from Ottawa. As we assembled in front of the Colonial Building where the House of Assembly then sat, we chanted, "Diefenbaker, thief and faker." There seemed to be something about our refrain that Joey liked. He came out of the building with alacrity to address us. Thereupon, a student bawled out, "What about the new university?"

Joey twitched mightily, like a frog galvanized by an electric current, as was his wont when he was about to emit something momentous, and he bawled back: Not three years from now, not two years from now, not next year, but this year, right now, right away, this very day, he'd get cracking on the construction of a new university. The new campus, he decreed, would open within three years.

And within three years, in September of 1961, students would move into the spanking new buildings on the Elizabeth Avenue campus in St. John's. I was in my last year, and the official opening erupted into rapture on October 9. It entailed 10,000 placard-carrying school kids from every community in the province, and featured Prime Minister John Diefenbaker, here under a Joey-guaranteed amnesty, together with many presidents of universities from across Canada and the world, plus Eleanor Roosevelt, John Kenneth Galbraith, an effete duke from the UK, and, the most appreciated of all, a Jamaican steel drum band Joey had once listened to on a southern vacation.

Since those years, Smallwood's new Memorial University of Newfoundland, with its admired professional schools and disciplines and institutions, and its many thousands of local, national, and international students and faculty, has grown to become the jewel in the provincial crown and a national treasure.

SMALLWOOD TOLD ME, when medicare came into effect in the late 1960s, that Tommy Douglas, Saskatchewan premier and Member of Parliament, always got far too much credit for bringing it about. Joey himself had introduced a precursor to medicare in Newfoundland for everyone up to sixteen years old and had thereby pointed the way for the rest of the country long before Douglas's plan went into effect in Saskatchewan. When someone told him that *universal* medicare in Canada was the product of plans and actions by Douglas, Diefenbaker, and Pearson, Joey would maintain that it was he himself who had in fact initiated the idea and put it into partial effect. The others had merely expanded on his concept. I have no trouble believing that a publicly funded national health care system was always among Joey's arsenal of progressive ideas.

ONE OF JOEY'S best traits was that he was very receptive to new ideas, wherever they might come from. Some cautious souls thought he was a little too receptive, because often the wackier and more grandiose and expensive the idea, the better he liked it. A case in point was the idea of a medical school in St. John's, combined with a new general hospital.

During the first dozen years after Confederation, the idea of a medical school here was raised from time to time, but the government ministers and top bureaucrats who had to find the money for it did not expect to see such a fanciful thing materialize in their lifetimes. Then, in 1961, Chief Justice Emmett Hall was appointed by Prime Minister Diefenbaker to conduct a Royal Commission on the Health Services of Canada. Hall's main recommendation concerned medicare, but he also suggested that several new medical schools should be established in Canada, including one in the Atlantic provinces. Immediately, the Newfoundland Medical Association formed a committee with Memorial University and the provincial Department of Health to study the feasibility of a med school in Newfoundland.

Speeches and reports pushed the idea until Joey engaged Lord Russell Brain, an eminent British neurologist, to conduct a Royal Commission on Health here. Brain found in 1966 that a medical school was necessary for health care in Newfoundland and Labrador. Just a year later, with the backing of notables like Dr. Ian Rusted and Dr. A. M. House, and Memorial University presidents Raymond Gushue and Lord Taylor, Smallwood committed the money. In September of 1967, the Faculty of Medicine was born.

I recall being invited, as a young minister, by then medical student, later the highly esteemed physician and medical administrator, Dr. Linda Inkpen, to speak to the very first medical school class. The subject of my talk now eludes me, and them, too, no doubt, but the honour, excitement, and fierce intelligence of the questions from the audience remain now, nearly five decades later, emblazoned on my brain.

The existence of the new medical school revived the concept of a brand new general hospital to replace the old one on Forest Road. Several ministers of Health played roles in pushing the project forward, with the university and medical school heads highly involved. Dr. James McGrath, who was minister of Health from 1956 to 1967, played a major part, followed by John Crosbie and Alex Hickman, but their tenures were cut short, casualties of their ambitions to replace Joey. Then, Ed Roberts, as minister of Health, was able to push the matter forward and announce in 1971 that federal government funding for the new hospital had been confirmed.

Ed Roberts and I were in British Columbia at a constitutional conference in the late 1960s and, while there, I'd gone with him to a university where he talked to some key medical people. I recall one of them opining that the trend of medical costs then—medicare, hospitals, treatments, medications, equipment—indicated that, in just a few decades, unless ruthlessly controlled, health care costs would be threatening to consume every single cent of every budget, federal and provincial, in Canada.

Now, these few decades later, his prognosis does not seem to be that far off the mark. Part of our contribution to that expenditure pressure, back in the early 1970s, was the construction of the brand new Health Sciences Centre, which proceeded with the usual political controversies and allegations of graft and corruption, until Premier Frank Moores had the glory of officially opening the realization of Joey's great initiative.

ONE OF JOEY'S grand visions for the province was a hospital for children. He'd always disliked visiting hospitals himself, he told me, and he certainly didn't like the idea of kids staying in hospitals with sick adults.

During the first decade of Confederation, the notion of a children's hospital in a province of our miniscule and scattered population, and poor by national standards, was thought by many in Newfoundland to be foolhardy. A dominant medical viewpoint seemed to be that, for good health care, pediatrics should be included with adult care in hospitals where state-of-the-art equipment was present and specialists were already practising and readily available. However, some leading physicians, local as well as outside, begged to differ.

I don't know definitely, from personal knowledge, what effect this local tragedy regarding children had on the question, but I have the impression from conversations that it may have been decisive: I was away studying law in 1963 when an outbreak of E. coli occurred in the province that caused the deaths of a hundred or more children. I recall from communications from my father, who was in Smallwood's government at the time, that political leaders, the medical profession, and the general population were devastated by the catastrophe. It had happened not in an impoverished third world country but in a province of one of the wealthiest and most advanced nations in the world. It brought home to everyone the absolute need to concentrate frontally and centrally on the health of our children.

One of our own local physicians, Dr. Cliff Joy, had long been a prominent advocate for a separate pediatric hospital. He was elected to the House of Assembly from Harbour Main district in 1962 as a candidate for Joey's Liberal Party, and he would tell me later, as our own family pediatrician, that his overriding impetus for entering politics was to promote, in the House and the government, a kids' hospital in St. John's.

Fortuitously, in 1960, the American forces had closed its base at Fort Pepperrell in St. John's, and all the property was passed over to the Government of Canada. Then, a year or so later, Ottawa transferred many of the buildings to the Government of Newfoundland. One of the structures, containing a bomb shelter in its basement, was the former US Air Force hospital on the base. Although extensive renovation would be required to turn it into a children's hospital, that route would still be far less expensive than a newly constructed building.

Thus, later in the same year as the E. coli outbreak in 1963, Dr. Joy invited Dr. Charles A. Janeway to St. John's to look at ideas for the health care of children. Dr. Janeway, on top of his international eminence in modern immunology, was physician in chief at Children's Hospital Boston and a professor of pediatrics at Harvard Medical School. Dr. Joy arranged for him to meet with Smallwood, where they talked about the necessity of a stand-alone children's hospital in Newfoundland and Labrador.

The upshot was that the provincial government committed the funds and, two and a half years later, in August of 1966, just before he called a provincial general election, Joey officially opened the Charles Alberton Janeway Children's Hospital, henceforth known by everyone, and instantly recognized, as "The Janeway."

ONE OF THE remarkable things about Joey was that, no matter what dire financial straits the province faced, he still had the vision to create public places where the arts could be exhibited, performed, and encouraged to flourish. Some people called this trait of his nothing but mindless extravagance in such a poor province.

In the early 1960s, Joey decided to carry out his vision of creating a chain of arts and culture centres throughout Newfoundland and Labrador, in St. John's, Gander, Grand Falls–Windsor, Corner Brook, Stephenville, and Labrador City. He turned the sod for the St. John's edifice with his famous silver shovel in the spring of 1965.

On the long wooden handle of this shiny tool, many small silver plaques had been affixed, signifying each project for which he had turned the first sod. By then, the premier said, the plaques represented some $250 million worth of projects. (By the time he turned the sod for the Upper Churchill Falls development, the silver shovel was worth well over a billion dollars in good works.) The site he chose for the St. John's Arts and Culture Centre was the former Church of England Boys Orphanage.

A miracle must have occurred during its construction: The contractors didn't level to the ground every living tree growing on the site, which was the usual building practice; instead, they actually preserved some old deciduous trees that lined both sides of the driveway to the orphanage.

In honour of Canada's centennial year, Premier Smallwood opened the St. John's centre on May 22, 1967, to a mild political irony. That same night, the first play in the year's Dominion Drama Festival took the stage there. It was based on the novel *Tomorrow Will Be Sunday* by Joey's former friend but now bitter political enemy, Harold Horwood.

I happened to be there, and everyone I talked to afterwards agreed that the drama was exceedingly tedious. Horwood may have been a pretty good nature writer, but his fiction was preachy and boringly didactic, and his characters were flat and two-dimensional. On top of that, one had to wonder: how can you write a novel set in Newfoundland and make it entirely devoid of wit and humour? Finally, to add to the pain, the story in the play was told once in real action in the first half, and then told yet again by witnesses in the courtroom scenes in the second half. It gave new meaning to Shakespeare's complaint: ". . . as tedious as a twice-told tale/Vexing the dull ear of a drowsy man." So that was a charmless evening. But the building itself was an impressive delight.

It had cost over $8 million to build at the time (probably more than $50 million today.) The Government of Canada kicked in two and a half million dollars because the structure was a centennial project. Two of the provincial government's most favoured contractors, Lundrigans Construction of Corner Brook, and Andrew Crosbie's Newfoundland Engineering and Construction of St. John's (both being Smallwood's generous supporters), built the centre. It included within its walls, at the time, in addition to the main theatre, the province's major art gallery, its main public library, and one of its top restaurants.

From the start, the centre, under the inspired leadership of John Perlin, was a resounding success. Every year the theatre alone has been patronized by 100,000 or more citizens of the province, attracting performers and artists from all over the world. I recall Andrew Crosbie's brother, John, later in 1968, after he first began to take on Joey Smallwood politically, complaining about the cost of the centre, claiming it should never have been built because the province could not afford it.

THE COLLEGE OF the North Atlantic is one of the great success stories in the province, and Joey can be credited with its humble beginnings, which later blossomed into one of the largest and most highly esteemed post-secondary education and training centres in the Atlantic provinces.

In 1963, Joey started by sprinkling some district vocational schools around the province. Within a few years the number had increased to seventeen, one in most major towns in Newfoundland and Labrador. I recall in the late 1960s, as Member for White Bay South district, scrambling for a vocational school in Baie Verte, and succeeding, just as Ed Roberts did for St. Anthony, in his rural district of White Bay North.

Then, over the years, the institutions went through various additions, permutations, and name changes until its seventeen campus locations in the province were joined by partners in China and a technical education college in Qatar.

I was with Joey in England once, when we looked at a polytechnic institution in connection with the programs and infrastructure being contemplated by the Department of Regional Economic Expansion under Pierre Trudeau's vibrant first government. Joey became enthusiastic about the concept of a great polytechnic institution in Newfoundland which would be the envy of the nation and the world.

He would have been pleased with the admired post-secondary institution, which the College of the North Atlantic, starting with his modest district vocational schools, developed into. And he would have been amused by the fact that we had to stop using the acronym "CONA" for College of the North Atlantic because, allegedly, the word turned out to be a vulgar name for female genitalia in the Portuguese tongue.

WHEN FEDERAL JUSTICE minister Pierre Elliot Trudeau entered the race for the leadership of the national Liberal Party in 1968, Joey soon supported him. A number of us younger members of his caucus may have initiated the idea, but from the start, Joey seemed to like the cut of Trudeau's jib.

There was dissension among our Newfoundland and Labrador delegates at the convention, though, over the notion of backing Joey's weird choice. Some thought PET looked and acted androgynous and possessed dubious romantic proclivities. Many of our delegates wanted to support Minister Robert Winters, who had a strong connection with the province as a former chief executive officer of BRINCO.

But Joey harangued us in our caucus room in Ottawa on how Winters had first said he wasn't going to run, before deciding too late to do so. And he rhapsodized on the manifold virtues of Trudeau. As a perfectly bilingual Quebecker, who fitted the Liberal mould of alternating leaders between English and French, he was perfect, coming after Pearson, for national leader. He also appreciated Trudeau's policies, one of which was to use the central government to battle "regional disparity" in economically depressed areas of the country.

So Joey was ecstatic when, within a year after Trudeau won the leadership and became prime minister, he set up the Department of Regional Economic Expansion, better known as DREE. It was Joey's long-time friend and sometime political opponent in earlier days, the great Newfoundland journalist and historian Albert Perlin, who disclosed that "dree" was a Scottish word for "endure" or "suffer." I looked it up and found the Scottish proverb, "You must dree your weird," which may sound dirty but only means, "You must endure your fate."

It turned out to be me who had to "dree my weird." Joey made me minister of the newish provincial department of Community and Social Development, which was mandated to negotiate the province's DREE agreements. But I found that this was a fate not to just endure but to relish. We negotiated agreements for tens of millions of federal dollars to roll into the province. Most of it was for the fancy new bureaucratic term at the time, "infrastructure," including municipal services, roads, and schools. For a while, the term "DREE school" became almost synonymous with educational development.

Like all federal programs for the disadvantaged regions of Canada, DREE may not have been the total salvation envisaged by the Ottawa politicos and bureaucrats. But it certainly improved this province's crumbling or substandard infrastructure and freed up a lot of provincial money for other construction. It also allowed the provincial government to improve on Smallwood's earlier federal-provincial resettlement program with better benefits for families who wanted to move closer to adequate schools and teachers, and hospitals, and services, and generally out of geographical and social isolation, if they wanted to.

PEARSON'S PEAK WAS another political erection of Joey's, located, he said, smack dab at the centre point of the Newfoundland Trans-Canada Highway between Port aux Basques and St. John's. It commemorated the completion of the fully-paved road across the island. In the summer of 1966, only weeks before he called a provincial election, Joey invited all of us candidates and some dignitaries and media to travel to central Newfoundland, just outside Grand Falls–Windsor, for the July unveiling of this monument to Prime Minister Lester B. (Mike) Pearson. As mentioned above, the Pearson Liberal government had increased the federal contribution up to 90% to complete the TCH. Joey gave the substantial contributions of the previous Tory government of John Diefenbaker short shrift.

Prime Minister Pearson's contribution was indeed a lot of money. In dollars of the early 1960s, the amount has been calculated at nearly $100 million, or pushing $800 million in 2017 dollars. Why was Pearson so generous? Was it a payoff to Smallwood as premier to make him go home and shut up about transmitting the Upper Churchill power across Quebec? As I intimated above . . . maybe. Although, in all the time I spent with him before 1972, during which he talked frankly about everything else under the sun, he never mentioned that possibility. Perhaps Pearson had sworn him to absolute secrecy over the bribe/blackmail/hush money, or whatever species of political buy-off the immense sum might have been.

But there would be an interesting parallel later concerning Brian Peckford's dealings with Brian Mulroney. Mulroney's great initiative in concluding the 1985 Atlantic Accord, and his government's later advocacy and huge financial assistance for the offshore oil developments, particularly Hibernia, was compensation for his failure to meet his pledge to remedy the inequities of the lopsided Upper Churchill deal that so favoured Quebec.

The Canadian government seems to be forever obliged to pay us off because they've been so useless in protecting or enforcing our provincial rights.

For all the foregoing reasons, especially his leadership into Confederation and his many progressive deeds as premier, minus the Upper Churchill debacle, and the other deficiencies and mischief noted, I would award Joey Smallwood, as a political leader, a grade of 85%.

Harry Mews

HENRY GEORGE REGINALD Mews took on the job of leader of the Newfoundland Progressive Conservative Party after the electorate had voted for Confederation with Canada in the 1948 referendum.

Mews had been a lieutenant with the Newfoundland Regiment during the First World War and later became a well-known insurance executive in St. John's. He'd been elected as a city councillor during the Second World War.

Mews led his party into the 1949 provincial election in May against the newly appointed premier and Liberal Party leader, Joey Smallwood. Since the Responsible Government League had more or less become the Progressive Conservative Party, Mews was perhaps counting on many of those who had voted for Responsible Government—nearly half the electorate—to vote Tory now. That would mean that he and the new party would make a creditable showing on polling day.

But the blizzard of federal government cheques for family allowances and old-age pensions that hit the province helped to decide otherwise. The political hay that the much superior campaigner, Smallwood, was able to make of the largesse from Ottawa, present and future, allowed his Liberals to easily defeat the PC Party. Of the 28 seats in the House of Assembly, the Liberal Party won 22 with 65.5% of the popular vote, and the PCs got 5 with 32.9%. In fact, the latter figure was a pretty good proportion of the anti-confederate vote. An Independent candidate, Peter Cashin, also won a seat.

Mews himself contested the district of St. John's West but failed to win. He abandoned provincial politics and, six months later, successfully ran for mayor of St. John's. Now he'd found his niche. The citizens of St. John's kept him on as mayor until 1965.

At city hall he gave a pretty good idea of what he would've been like as provincial premier. He was mayor when the city embarked on an ambitious program of slum clearance in the city core and effected a substantial public housing and suburban development plan. He formed the St. John's Transportation Commission to replace the ramshackle private bus system and created extensive water and sewerage infrastructure.

Then, secretly, in cahoots with senior management, without the knowledge of city council, he hoarded a large fund of money for building, after his retirement, a brand new city hall. This surreptitious accumulation of public money, for a purpose that had not been openly debated and voted on, triggered abundant controversy.

As premier, perhaps he would have been a determined activist, but, evidently, rather secretive in his actions.

His son-in-law was T. Alex Hickman, a minister in both Smallwood's and Moores's governments, and a failed leadership candidate for the leadership of the Liberal Party in 1969 against Joey. Later he was appointed chief justice of the Trial Division of the Supreme Court of Newfoundland. Mews's grandson, Sandy Hickman, was elected to the St. John's City Council.

For his contribution to competitive democracy, as first leader of the Progressive Conservative Party after Confederation, intrepidly taking on the triumphantly dominant Smallwood, but deducting his election failures, personally and as leader, and his secretive nature, I'd give Harry Mews a rating of 55%.

Peter Cashin

PETER J. CASHIN was born in 1890 in Cape Broyle, the son of Sir Michael Cashin, a prominent businessman and politician from the Southern Shore of the Avalon Peninsula. Sir Michael was knighted in 1918 for his public service during the First World War and was briefly prime minister of Newfoundland. That had happened in an exceedingly bizarre fashion, perhaps unprecedented in British Commonwealth legislatures.

After Sir Edward Patrick Morris resigned as prime minister and leader of the Newfoundland People's Party to be elevated to the House of Lords in London, Finance Minister Michael Cashin succeeded him as party leader. But despite that, the governor saw fit to appoint another minister, William Lloyd, as prime minister.

Having none of that, Sir Michael moved a motion of no confidence in the government of which he was still Finance minister, seconded by the recently appointed prime minister himself. The government fell, and Sir Michael became prime minister of a new government. Unfortunately, but unsurprising in the extraordinary circumstances, Sir Michael's administration lasted only the few months before the next election was won by Sir Richard Squires.

Meanwhile, Sir Michael's son, Peter, had gone into the Newfoundland Regiment as a private during the First World War and was progressively promoted until he was made a major. Back home after the war, in which he'd been badly injured, he became a restless soul, politically. Some would consider him a loose cannon for his disputes with other politicians, his resignations from parties, and his political positions and actions generally, including crossing the floor of the House. Others considered him a man of integrity for those same views and actions. Whatever the reality of his conduct, Peter was judged by many to be the best speech maker of his era.

In the early 1940s he had used his oratorical ability to take on the Commission of Government, almost single-handedly. He advocated vociferously, especially on radio, the extinction of the dictatorship in favour of a return to a democratically elected regime of Responsible Government.

When the UK government ordered the commissioners and governor here to set up the National Convention to decide upon Newfoundland's future, Peter was elected as one of three delegates from St. John's West. In that forum, he continued to stand for the reinstatement of Responsible Government, and like-minded supporters of that position made him leader of the Responsible Government League.

Despite, or perhaps because of, his long absences away from Newfoundland in Canada, Peter apparently despised the very idea of Confederation. His speeches to the Convention included the claim that a conspiracy existed between Britain and Canada to "sell" Newfoundland to the Dominion of Canada. The conspirators' flowery sales talk, he declared, would tell Newfoundlanders that their only salvation lay "in following a new Moses into the promised land across the Cabot Strait." At one point, the philosophical differences between Peter and this presumed "new Moses," Joe Smallwood, resulted in a fist fight between them on the floor of the Convention.

When Cashin's cause lost by a small margin in the second referendum, he insisted that Responsible Government had in fact won. The result in favour of Confederation, he alleged, had been falsified by London.

He ran as an Independent in his father's old district of Ferryland in the 1949 election right after Confederation, and he won.

After that election, Jack Higgins became head of the PC Party and Leader of the Opposition. Higgins seemed to be a political figure of some consequence. He'd been a Newfoundland Rhodes Scholar in 1909 and studied law at Oxford University. While there he was captain of the Canadian ice hockey team, which played throughout Europe and overwhelmingly won all its games. He served in the First World War in England and France, and then returned to Newfoundland to practise law.

He'd been a leading anti-confederate and campaigned vehemently in favour of Responsible Government in each referendum in 1948. On the day that Newfoundland joined Canada, a moment before April Fool's Day on March 31, 1949, Higgins led other anti-confederates in draping their doors with black crepe to mourn the tragedy.

In the new province's first election in May 1949, Jack Higgins ran for the Progressive Conservative Party in St. John's East. He was elected and replaced the defeated Harry Mews as party leader. He thus became the first Leader of the Opposition in Newfoundland as a Canadian province. He didn't seem to have the stomach for provincial politics, though, especially facing a fired-up Joey Smallwood across the House. He never led his party into an election. When Joey called a snap election in 1951, just two years into his term, Higgins dropped out and did not seek re-election to the House.

He didn't mind a gentler form of politics, however, if it was far away from Smallwood. When Tory prime minister John Diefenbaker invited him to join the Senate of Canada in 1959, Higgins accepted with alacrity and stayed there until his death four years later. It was another "first" for him: the first Tory senator from Newfoundland.

Meanwhile, back to the election of 1951: With the disappearance of Higgins from the scene, the PCs invited Peter Cashin to join their party, become Leader of the Opposition, and spearhead their campaign. He ran in St. John's West again and got re-elected. As leader, he increased the PC Party's percentage of the vote to 35.6% and decreased the Liberal vote slightly to 63.6%. But unfortunately, the Liberals increased their seats by 2 to 24, and the PCs dropped a seat, to win only 4.

Cashin stayed in the House of Assembly as Opposition Leader until 1953 when, following a coup against him in his caucus, he resigned to run as an Independent in the federal election in the riding of St. John's East.

It was rumoured, and widely believed, that he had been lured by Joey to run federally in order to eat into the PC vote in the riding. If that was the plan, it worked. Liberal Allan Fraser beat incumbent MP, Progressive Conservative Gordon Higgins, in that Tory riding. Cashin had attracted over 4,400 votes, most of them, no doubt, at the expense of Higgins. The suspicions of many PCs were confirmed when Joey soon appointed his old sparring partner to the job of director of Civil Defence, where he stayed until 1964.

Peter Cashin's nephew, Richard Cashin, was elected to the House of Commons in 1962 as a Liberal, beating Tory stalwart Billy Browne by some 24 votes. Later Richard would become founder and leader of a new fishermen's union, and would be approached by Joey in 1971, when the provincial Liberal Party was on the ropes, with an invitation to become its leader. The opportunity never materialized.

Sir Michael Cashin, his son Peter Cashin, and his grandson Richard Cashin were all remarkable public persons in Newfoundland's history, and each made a large impact on our politics and policy. Peter's constant demands in the 1940s, nearly a lone voice crying in the wilderness, that Commission of Government be abolished and that the country of Newfoundland return to democratic government, added greatly to our political progress.

For that alone, plus his leadership roles with the Responsible Government League and the PC Party and the Opposition, minus the lack of teamwork that would have allowed his leadership to be more effective, I'd award Peter Cashin a rating of 65%.

Sam Drover

SAMUEL DROVER WAS born in Hodge's Hole, later sanitized to Hodge's *Cove*, Trinity Bay, in 1911. He attended Memorial College and then taught for ten years before joining the Newfoundland Constabulary. He later served with the famous Newfoundland Ranger Force until Confederation.

During my own political travels years later, I would drop in on Sam sometimes, after he had retired to his trailer in Hodge's Cove. Among the subjects of his fascinating chats, he told me how the Commission of Government had asked the Rangers to report back to them on political matters during the lead-up to the referendums in 1948. He and his Ranger colleagues had to go to rallies and public meetings and size up what was going on and who was saying what. During the voting the Rangers helped run the polling stations. "Believe me," Sam told me, "sometimes the strong arm of the law was direly needed."

That exposure to politics helped encourage Drover to run for Joey's Liberals in the first election after Confederation in 1949. He was elected in White Bay district and re-elected in 1951.

In 1955, he left the Liberal caucus and sat in the House of Assembly as a founding member and leader of the Newfoundland Co-operative Commonwealth Federation, known as the CCF. This was the social democratic party that later became the New Democratic Party.

Sam told me he'd become disillusioned with Smallwood when he discovered, painfully, that there was a dreadfully wide gap between the words of the "great socialist" and his actual deeds, especially when it came to the problems of rural areas. Joey, for his part, told me that Sam had bolted because Joey had made it clear to him that, for confidential personal reasons, Sam would never be invited into the cabinet.

Having become the first CCF Member of the House in Newfoundland, albeit not by election but by crossing the floor, Sam organized the new party and managed to run ten candidates in the election of 1956. He himself contested White Bay South, which was so Liberal that the PCs didn't even run a candidate. Sam lost, as did his nine comrades. The new party's popular vote was miniscule, only 0.017%, and it would be nearly three decades later, in the 1980s, before its political progeny, the NDP, would win a seat in the House of Assembly. But Sam Drover had opened a small chink in the Liberal megalith of Newfoundland politics, through which some light would later shine.

He was a declining political force during the rest of his life. He ran in Trinity North in the provincial election of 1959 as an Independent and lost. But he came second to the Liberal, beating the PC candidate. Next he contested the federal election of 1965 as an independent Liberal in Trinity–Conception. He came third, but ahead of NDP candidate Harold Horwood, who came last. In 1972 he ran again as an Independent but came fourth, this time behind the new NDP candidate. Quite apparently, a deep trench of disenchantment had opened up between the NDP hierarchy and this old, original CCFer.

But Sam had carved a mark for himself. I was delighted back in the mid-2000s to see MHA Ross Wiseman rise in the House and pay a handsome, non-partisan tribute to Sam Drover on his ninety-third birthday as "one of two remaining Members of the First Assembly to sit after Confederation in 1949." Wiseman went on "to acknowledge the tremendous contribution that Mr. Drover has made to the history of Newfoundland and Labrador."

For his innovative political role, taking on Joey early on in the House and in the field, albeit without significant success, I would award Sam 45%.

Malcolm Hollett

MALCOLM MERCER HOLLETT was selected as Newfoundland's Rhodes Scholar in 1915, but, having enlisted in the Royal Newfoundland Regiment, he didn't go to Oxford until the end of the First World War.

Appointed afterwards as a magistrate on the Burin Peninsula, Hollett was living there when the earthquake on the Grand Banks in 1929 caused a tsunami that ravaged communities and killed at least twenty-seven people. He helped organize relief efforts in the aftermath of devastation and distress.

Hollett got elected from Grand Falls to the National Convention, where he opposed Confederation with Canada. He became a prominent member of the Responsible Government League during the referendum campaigns.

In 1952, he ran in a St. John's West by-election as a Progressive Conservative. The opportunity had arisen because Al Vardy had resigned soon after his election in 1951. Hollett won and, following the rebellion against Peter Cashin's leadership in 1953, he was made leader of the Progressive Conservative Party and Leader of the Opposition in the House of Assembly.

Rather uninspiring as party boss, he went into the 1956 provincial election with four seats in the House and emerged from the campaign with the same number. Then, before the provincial election in 1959, his party was torn apart by Joey's battle with Prime Minister John Diefenbaker over the federal grant of $8 million to the province under Term 29.

In the House of Assembly, Hollett refused to vote in favour of Joey's motion of censure against Diefenbaker's Tory government in Ottawa. Two of Hollett's PC members left the party as a result and formed the United Newfoundland Party.

Joey Smallwood threatened to remove the PCs from the House entirely as punishment for supporting Diefenbaker; he ran against Hollett in his district of St. John's West and beat him. The PC Party was able to elect only three Members to the House of Assembly, and Hollett quit as party leader.

Hollett's career in provincial politics may have been terminated by his support of Diefenbaker, but his sojourn in political heaven was assured. In 1961, Diefenbaker appointed him to the Senate of Canada, where he peacefully passed the next ten years.

Merely for assuming Opposition Leadership in the days of Smallwood's near-total ascendency, but not for much else, I'd award Malcolm Hollett a ranking of 40%.

Jim Higgins

JAMES DOUGLAS HIGGINS was born in St. John's in 1913 and died in 1974. A practising lawyer, Higgins was elected to St. John's City Council several times, where he served for nearly a decade as deputy mayor.

He got elected as a Progressive Conservative from St. John's East in 1951 and again in 1956. But in 1959, after a falling-out with the PCs over Prime Minister Diefenbaker's handling of Term 29, he formed, with two others, the United Newfoundland Party and became its leader. They supported Smallwood's stance on Term 29. In the provincial election that year, he ran for re-election but was defeated. He passed the leadership of the UNP over to elected MHA Gus Duffy.

In the 1962 election, Higgins switched to the Liberals and ran for the House of Assembly again. He was defeated again. But he was amply rewarded for his pains. The next year, with a change of government in Ottawa from PC to Liberal, Prime Minister Pearson had him appointed, on Smallwood's recommendation, to the Newfoundland Supreme Court.

Throughout his career, Jim Higgins was one of the best-known personalities in St. John's. He was president of the St. John's Regatta Committee, and governor and member of the Sports Hall of Fame, among other athletic organizations. But his greatest fame was as a lawyer. He was frequently in the news for defending clients against all varieties of accusations. In fact, I can confidently state that when I was a preteen boy in the 1950s, Higgins was the only local lawyer that my peers and I had ever heard of. We all agreed that when any of us were framed for murder, we'd hire Jimmy Higgins to get us off.

My later impression of Mr. Justice Higgins grew tainted, though, when I became a lawyer myself. Apart from his propensity to be half-soused in court, and his bully-boy tactics toward lawyers from his lofty bench, he was a racist. Not long after I was admitted to the Bar, I was standing in the Supreme Court registry one day, talking to a lawyer of East Indian origins, when Judge Higgins rolled in. He looked at the other lawyer and turned to me to proclaim—apropos of what I have no idea, unless he was offended by the colour of my companion's skin—"Every goddamned Turk wants his day in court."

I'd grant Jim Higgins, as a political leader, a ranking of 20%.

Gus Duffy

AUGUSTINE MICHAEL DUFFY was born in St. John's in 1905 and died in 1966. A businessman, he was first elected as a PC in Ferryland district in 1951, but his election was invalidated because of irregularities. He ran again in the by-election but was defeated.

In 1956, he was successful as a Tory in St. John's Centre, but in 1959 he left the party, along with Jim Higgins and John O'Dea, to form the United Newfoundland Party. He was re-elected in his district that year and took over as leader of the UNP from the defeated Higgins.

In the 1962 election, Duffy was defeated, and thereafter the United Newfoundland Party sank without a trace.

I'd give Gus Duffy, as a political leader, the grade of 20%.

Ed Finn, Jr.

EDWARD FINN, JR. was a political pioneer. Born in Spaniard's Bay in 1926, he grew up in Corner Brook during the depression. He got a job at the paper mill in 1942 when he was sixteen, and four years later he went to work with the Corner Brook *Western Star* newspaper. Then, in 1953, he took a position with the *Montreal Gazette*. But just two years later, the *Western Star* offered him the job of editor.

He was editor when the loggers' strike under the International Woodworkers of America (IWA) took place in 1958–1959. Joey had the IWA decertified by legislation in the House of Assembly. Finn was to say later, during the emotionally charged labour dispute, that journalistic integrity was simply not tolerated by the newspaper. Allegedly, employees had to toe the company line.

As a result, Finn quit as editor, and a couple of reporters at the paper followed suit. Together they started up their own newspaper, the *Newfoundland Examiner*, which was dedicated to digging up sleaze and wrongdoing in government and commerce. Unfortunately, but not surprisingly, it failed to attract government or commercial advertisers and soon went under.

Meanwhile, the Canadian Labour Congress hired Finn and founded the Newfoundland Democratic Party to confront Joey politically. This new party took over the CCF in the province, and Finn led it into the 1959 general election. It elected no seats, but in Humber West, Finn gave Joey's colleague Charlie Ballam, the provincial minister of Labour, a good scare.

The party as a whole, though, received only a little over 7% of the votes, fewer than the erstwhile United Newfoundland Party under Jim Higgins. The small percentage attracted by Finn's party indicates the relative popularity of Joey's stand at the time regarding the IWA strike. The Liberal Party got 58%.

After the creation of the New Democratic Party across Canada in 1961, Finn's party became the Newfoundland New Democratic Party. He stayed on as leader and ran in the 1962 election, but the party got no seats and a disappointing 3.6% of the ballots cast, only half of the previous election.

He ran federally for the NDP in Humber–St. George's in 1963. He was beaten handily by the Liberal candidate but came in second, ahead of the PC candidate. He resigned as leader of the NDP and took a job with a national union in Ottawa. But he was fired in 1980, along with other members of the staff, for allegedly refusing to open mail during a strike of the union's own staff. Thereafter, he was employed by the Canadian Union of Public Employees until he retired in 1991.

Throughout most of his life, Finn was a prolific writer of articles for many publications. They included a weekly column on labour for the huge *Toronto Star* newspaper. While working for the leftish Canadian Centre for Policy Alternatives, and editing its journal, he had several feisty books of essays published by that research institute. An indication of their no-grey-areas contents could be drawn from the title, *Right is Wrong and the Left Is Right—Cutting through the Neoliberal Bafflegab.*

For his fearlessness, both politically and professionally, in taking on less than popular causes against dominant political forces and insuperable odds, I'd award Ed Finn, Jr., as a political leader, a grade of 55%.

Jim Greene

JAMES JOSEPH LOUIS Greene was a courageous and principled politician and lawyer. He was born in St. John's in 1928 and died in 2014. His father, Joseph, was a Member of the House of Assembly for a term before the advent of Commission of Government. His great-uncle, Daniel Joseph Greene, had been premier for a few weeks in 1894–1895. Jim studied at the University of Notre Dame, won the Rhodes Scholarship, and read law at Oxford.

Back in St. John's, he began building up a flourishing legal practice. But in 1959, he decided to run in the controversial provincial election of that year for the PC Party, which was being demonized as traitorous by Joey Smallwood in his battle against the federal government. In St. John's East district, Greene took on incumbent Jim Higgins, who had been a prominent Tory but was now leader of the breakaway United Newfoundland Party.

By less than 150 votes, Greene managed to defeat the immensely popular lawyer, and following the personal defeat of Malcolm Hollett in that election, the thirty-one-year-old novice to the House found himself leader of the PC Party and Leader of the Opposition.

Greene's personal victory was truly significant. Not only was he elected for the party that Joey had pilloried mercilessly for siding with the great Satan, Prime Minister Diefenbaker, in the Term 29 war, Greene was also lawyer for the Newfoundland local of the arch-fiends, the International Woodworkers of America. This was the union that Joey had decertified by legislation and sent packing from the province during the IWA loggers' strike against the Grand Falls paper mill.

I got an extra idea of those turbulent times when labour activist at the time Steve Neary told me later that, while Jim was meeting with officials of the IWA in a remote shed in central Newfoundland during the strike, a bulldozer, allegedly operated by a company man, ran into and demolished the structure. Greene and the others inside barely escaped out the back, lucky to have emerged with life and limbs intact.

Jim Greene also defended logger Ronald Laing in court against a murder charge for the death, during the strike, of Newfoundland Constabulary Constable William Moss. The fatality had resulted from the riot in Badger on March 10, 1959, of loggers and police. A logger, brandishing a birch junk, had struck Constable Moss in the head. As it happened, Laing had been wielding a piece of wood that night and gave a statement to the authorities which the prosecution considered a confession.

Greene, and a Toronto lawyer who assisted him on the defence, concluded that Laing had confessed to a murder he had not committed. At the preliminary inquiry and trial, Greene was able to obtain eyewitness testimony that Laing was not near Moss when he was struck, but that another logger was close to Moss holding a piece of wood when he fell to the ground. Greene convinced the jury that Laing's so-called confession was obviously incorrect, and they found him not guilty.

Both of his actions at the time—representing the IWA during an atmosphere of great government and public hostility, and representing a self-confessed murderer of a police officer against "open-shut" charges—required considerable mettle and integrity, and Greene demonstrated clearly that he possessed both.

In the House of Assembly, Greene didn't stint in his attacks on Joey's policies or his methods of government. He alleged that he had seen many cases of distress and foreboding coming over Newfoundlanders that kept them from speaking out publicly, or entering public life, or making their voices heard at all, because of fear of repercussions.

Voters in greater numbers seemed to respect his actions and his views. When he led the PC Party into the 1962 election, he not only got re-elected himself, but he increased the number of PC seats in the House from 3 to 7. The popular vote of the party in the province climbed from one quarter of the electorate up to 36%.

Still, he was stuck as Opposition Leader facing the heavy-handed Joey and his domineering majority across the House for another term. By the beginning of election year 1966, his law practice had suffered enough and he knew he couldn't devote adequate time and energy to the political challenge of effective leadership against Smallwood.

To the grief of many who were interested in democracy in the province, he resigned as party leader and declined to run in that fall's general election. Dr. Noel Murphy from Corner Brook took over as leader.

For the courage of his convictions, politically, wed to his professional mettle, which gave a good indication of what he would have been like as premier, I'd grade Jim Greene at 65% as a political leader.

Calvin Normore

CALVIN BECAME LEADER of the provincial New Democratic Party in 1963. He'd been co-leader of the *Newfoundland* Democratic Party with Ed Finn back in 1959. He headed up the Corner Brook Labour Council and served on the executive of the Federation of Labour. A man of solid reputation and good intentions, he had the misfortune of leading his party into the election of 1966, when Joey's popularity was such that he won all but 3 seats in the House of Assembly. Normore got no candidates elected and pulled in less than 2% of the vote.

His lack of success was more a matter of bad luck and terrible timing than any reflection on his abilities. Still, in politics, leaders have to take conditions as they find them, and how they cope with them is a yardstick of their political acumen and abilities.

I'd credit Normore with a grade of 40% as a political leader.

Noel Murphy

DR. NOEL FRANCIS Murphy had St. John's roots, but he was born in 1915 in London, England, while his mother and his father, Dr. John Murphy, were temporarily there. He obtained his early education at St. Bon's in St. John's, but most of his later education and training occurred in England, and he retained a trace of an English accent all his life.

Much later, he and I would talk on the radio a lot, both as Newfoundland commentators on Peter Gzowsky's show on CBC, and on VOCM's *Open Line*. Once he phoned me on the air from a plane flying back to Newfoundland from Bristol, England, during the John Cabot/*Matthew* celebrations. When I asked him where he was, he said he was halfway across the Atlantic. To which I blurted, "So *that* explains the mid-Atlantic accent." He had the good grace to emit a polite chuckle.

When he graduated from the Royal London Hospital with his medical degree in 1942, he joined the 125th Newfoundland Squadron of the Royal Air Force Volunteer Reserve as its medical officer, attaining the rank of flight lieutenant surgeon.

After the war he came back to Newfoundland and headed up the cottage hospital at Norris Point, Bonne Bay, for ten years. Then he moved to Corner Brook with his practice, and also founded there a broadcasting company that soon opened several radio stations. He was often heard enjoying himself on the airwaves.

In the 1962 election he ran for the PC Party in Humber East and defeated the incumbent Liberal Member, Jack Forsey, who'd won the last election without difficulty. After Jim Greene stepped down, Murphy headed the party and led the Tory candidates into the 1966 election.

With Joey riding so high that year, Noel endured a tough battle. He finished by losing 4 of his party's 7 seats, including his own in Humber East. Smallwood had run in the adjoining Humber West district, and from there he'd bolstered Clyde Wells into defeating Murphy.

Thereafter, Murphy was elected mayor of Corner Brook several times, and in 1971 he startled the entire province by accepting an appointment, along with St. John's mayor Bill Adams, to Smallwood's last cabinet. In the general election later that year he ran as a Liberal in Humber West against Tory leader Frank Moores but lost badly. Rumour had it that, in order for Murphy to have undertaken such a forlorn cause, Joey must have promised to get his federal buddies to appoint him either as lieutenant-governor or to the Senate.

In fact, neither position was forthcoming. But a few years later, under his own steam, he was elected mayor of Corner Brook again, the position in which he seemed happiest. He died at the grand age of eighty-nine in 2005.

I'd give Noel Murphy, as a political leader, a grade of 45%.

Frank Moores

FRANK DUFF MOORES was born in Carbonear on February 18, 1933, which was close enough to Valentine's Day, in some people's view, to account for his adult prowess in extracurricular amorous activity. He died in 2005.

His family had sent him off young to St. Andrew's, a private school in Ontario, the same one that John and Andrew Crosbie and Ed Roberts would go to. After that he attended Boston University for two months before giving up on a scholarly career to come back and work in his father's fish plant.

He married very young. Those were the days, he once told a mutual friend of his and mine, "when you thought you had to get married if you wanted a piece of tail." He tore himself away from that constricted mode of thinking in the years to come.

After his father, Silas, died in 1962, Frank couldn't sell the fish plant fast enough, and he found himself wealthy as a young man with some $2 million (worth probably $15 million today).

Charismatic and rich, and energetic when he felt like it, he decided to try his hand at politics. Joey Smallwood used to maintain that Frank's family were good Liberals, but Frank ran federally as a Progressive Conservative in the hitherto Liberal riding of Bonavista–Trinity–Conception. In that 1968 election, Trudeaumania was rampant across much of Canada, but it didn't catch on in Newfoundland and Labrador. Frank Moores and five other Tory candidates here won seats to the House of Commons. The sole Liberal survivor elected was Don Jamieson.

Frank was not an overzealous parliamentarian. After he made his maiden speech in the House of Commons, he was seldom, if ever, seen in his seat there again. Don Jamieson told some of us he didn't see Frank in the House very often pounding his desk, but he certainly *heard* Frank a lot, in the apartment he had next to Don's, pounding the headboard against the wall.

Then he ran for president of the Progressive Conservative Party of Canada and won it. Next, following Gerry Ottenheimer's convenient resignation as leader of the provincial PC Party, he ran for that position in 1970 and prevailed on the first ballot.

Before reviewing Frank Moores's qualities as political leader, a few words are in order about his predecessor, Gerry Ottenheimer, who gave up the leadership before he could lead the party into an election.

Gerald Ryan Ottenheimer was born in 1934. He was a grandson of James Ryan and a great-nephew of Dan Ryan, two brothers who were considered the wealthiest fishing magnates in Newfoundland. The local saying for alleging that someone is filthy rich still prevails in some quarters: "He's got more money than Dan Ryan."

Gerry had to be the most book-educated politician in the history of the province. He studied at Memorial University of Newfoundland, the University of Rome, the Sorbonne in Paris, Fordham University in New York, and the University of Cambridge.

He first entered politics by running as a Progressive Conservative in the 1965 federal election in the riding of St. John's West. He made a creditable showing with over 10,000 votes gained but was beaten by more than 4,000 by Richard Cashin.

The next year he ran in the provincial general election in St. John's East and got elected to the House of Assembly by almost 1,000 votes more than the Liberal candidate. He was one of only three PCs to withstand Joey's nearly clean sweep of all the districts in the province.

Replacing the defeated Noel Murphy as Tory Leader of the Opposition, he stayed in that position only until 1969. Then, out of the blue he resigned from the House of Assembly and took off for Cambridge University to study law. He cited "personal reasons" for his precipitous departure, which caused many skeptics to scoff. But the reasons did turn out, in fact, to be pretty personal.

The Montreal police had raided a whorehouse and found Gerry inside, reportedly helping himself to the comforts therein provided. He was hailed in front of the night-court judge who slapped him with a fine under the Criminal Code.

A lot of people seemed to believe that Gerry had been set up. Some Liberals suggested that the man who wanted to become Tory leader at the time, Frank Moores, had engineered the sleazy coup to clear the decks for his takeover of the party.

Many Tories pushed the alternative scenario, however, that one or other of Joey's more tawdry industrialists in Montreal, probably John C. Doyle, had cooked up the malevolent deed. Joey's story—and he stuck to it—was that he'd had absolutely nothing to do with Gerry Ottenheimer being found in that common bawdy house.

In two years, Gerry was back home, just in time to run in the provincial election called by Joey in the fall of 1971. He ran in the district of St. Mary's against Liberal Michael Maher, winning by only 78 votes.

Gerry's party leadership days may have been over for good, but during the next decade and a half he rose steadily in political office. He became Speaker of the House of Assembly and was appointed to senior cabinet positions by premiers Frank Moores and Brian Peckford. In 1987, Prime Minister Brian Mulroney put him in the Senate, where he stayed until he died of cancer in 1998 at the age of sixty-four. His son-in-law would become PC Party leader and Leader of the Opposition in the House of Assembly, and a cabinet minister, until disaster, in turn, struck him.

Conventional wisdom in the years following Ottenheimer's disgrace and redemption attributed, for some reason, a good part of the later success of the PC Party to him. The Liberal decline after Smallwood's huge election victory in 1966, and Frank Moores's later electoral triumphs, it was said, were brought about by the quietly effective organizing that Gerry had done outside the overpass during his short tenure as leader. I've got my doubts.

BACK TO FRANK Moores: Joey Smallwood talked a good line about Frank's inadequacies. The reality, however, was that Moores's leadership of the PCs gave Joey the jitters, and he held off calling the provincial election until the last legal minute in 1971. This delay left Frank with all the time in the world to campaign, raise money, recruit candidates, and call Smallwood a scaredy-cat.

The election results in October of 1971 have been called a tie between Joey's Liberals and Frank's PCs. But, really, the Tories won that "tie" election with a considerably greater percentage of the votes than the Liberals, just over 51% to just over 44%, and with what looked like one more seat in the House of Assembly. The so-called tie was actually a temporary stalemate caused by Smallwood's refusal to resign until he had properly analyzed some narrowly won Tory seats.

Finally, in January of 1972, following copious finagling and trickery, plus the outright buyout of at least one Liberal Member, Frank Moores was able to form the first PC government since Confederation.

Nothing if not cute, Frank helped to keep himself in power in the 1975 election by providing Smallwood with the wherewithal to field some "Liberal Reform" candidates and split the Liberal vote to the benefit of Tory candidates.

As premier, Moores went through the motions of pushing for rural development, the growth of the fishery, and the expansion of natural resources. He even developed a deal in principle on a hydroelectric project at a Lower Churchill site with separatist Quebec premier René Lévesque. But Moores's own Natural Resources minister, Brian Peckford, scuppered that.

Frank resigned as leader of the PC Party and premier in 1979 to become a "consultant" in St. John's. That career move was unsuccessful, and he relocated to Ottawa to become a genuine federal lobbyist. He nurtured that initiative into a resounding success after 1983, when he helped engineer the downfall of Joe Clark as federal Tory leader and organize the successful campaign of Brian Mulroney for party leadership.

He was close to Mulroney after he became prime minister of Canada, both as a confidant and as a principal of a powerful lobbying firm. There were allegations of conflict of interest on Frank's part and, during and after he retired, evidence of his involvement in the Airbus scandal: In 1995, the RCMP had made allegations in a letter to the government of Switzerland of kickbacks from Karlheinz Schreiber on the sale of Airbus planes to the then Crown corporation Air Canada. Right up to his death from liver cancer on July 10, 2005, in Ontario where he lived, Frank disclaimed any participation in the sordid matter. Some national investigative reporters begged to differ.

In sum, Frank Moores's term as an MP and his tenure as premier were undistinguished and often scandal-ridden, and his days afterwards as a federal fixer were sometimes dodgy. His big claim to greatness was the fact that he ended Joe Smallwood's twenty-three-year rule and was instrumental, especially through some highly effective ministers, in establishing competitive politics and a somewhat more mature democracy throughout the province.

For that one significant thing, minus his assorted weak points as a public person, I'd give Frank Moores, as political leader, a grade of 75%.

Tom Burgess

THOMAS WILLIAM BURGESS was born in Ireland in 1933 and was educated at schools in Dublin. His early working life was checkered. It took him to England, Wales, Africa, Australia, and New Zealand before he landed up in Canada in his mid-twenties and became a resident of Labrador City. Working with the Iron Ore Company of Canada there, he soon became a leading light with the United Steelworkers of America.

Joey Smallwood recruited him as a Liberal candidate for the district of Labrador West in the 1966 election, and he won by nearly 62% of the vote. But by 1969, still languishing in the backbenches of the House of Assembly, despite Joey's promise to make him a cabinet minister, or so he claimed, he bolted from the Liberal caucus and crossed the floor to sit as an Independent. Over there, he displayed considerable oratorical skills, somewhat in the mode of union hall meetings. And soon, he formed the New Labrador Party.

Tom ran in the 1971 provincial election for his new party and got elected again with over half the votes in Labrador West, against three other candidates. And the New Labrador Party came fairly close in the two other Labrador seats.

The 1971 election resulted in a hung legislature, with a virtual tie between Joey's Liberals and Frank Moores's Progressive Conservatives. Because Tom Burgess's seat could determine who would form the government, he went around calling himself "the real premier." There was much vying for his favours. John C. Doyle rented a hotel room next to Tom's in the St. John's Holiday Inn, to use the proximity and perhaps other ploys, opponents alleged, to persuade him that his future lay with Joey.

But Burgess stated, at least at first, that he was siding with the PCs, which helped Moores oust Smallwood. Upon forming his government, however, Frank made it clear that there was no seat in the cabinet for Tom. Declaring that the new premier had reneged on his solemn promise to make him an Honourable Minister, Burgess now rejoined the Liberal Party. One well-founded story was that he did so as a result of Smallwood's pledge that he would make Tom Liberal leader and, subsequently, premier of the province.

Did any politician in Canada ever act on more alleged promises to less positive effect? This "promise" of Joey's turned out to be false, too. During the Liberal leadership convention in the winter of 1972, I can still remember the look of utter shock on Tom's face when the results of the balloting were announced. He actually thought he was going to win. But Joey didn't, or couldn't, deliver. Ed Roberts defeated Burgess, decisively, with 564 votes to Tom's 82.

Then, in the provincial election called by Moores a few weeks later, Burgess ran in Labrador West again as a Liberal and got 31.5% of the votes against the winning PC candidate, Joe Rousseau.

Thereafter Tom Burgess quit politics, left Newfoundland, and, according to a friend of mine who'd been close to him throughout his years in Labrador, he "dropped off the edge of the world."

MEANWHILE, FELLOW PARTY candidate Mike Martin stayed the course and did yeoman service for the movement over several years. Michael Solomon Martin was born in Cartwright, Labrador, in 1938. His ancestry was as wide as the Big Land itself: He once mentioned in the House of Assembly that he was descended from three ethnic groups that have populated various regions of Labrador.

In his early adulthood, he took part in four missions as a United Nations peacekeeper with the Canadian Armed Forces. Then he got interested in politics as it affected Labrador, especially the neglect and exploitation documented in its history. He ran for the New Labrador Party in Labrador South in 1971 but lost to Liberal Joe Harvey by just over 80 votes.

In the 1972 general election he ran for the NLP again in the same district, this time losing by just one vote. When that election in Labrador South was overturned by the Supreme Court, he ran once more in the by-election of the same year and won by 158 votes, thereby becoming the second candidate for the New Labrador Party to have secured a seat in the House of Assembly.

But the legislature was not to Mike's liking. Serious-minded and sensible, he found the antics of other MHAs in the House to be childish and often disgraceful, especially to the eyes and ears of visiting schoolchildren in the galleries.

He didn't run in the election of 1975, and the New Labrador Party disappeared from the political map. But while he'd been a Member, Martin led in the design, in 1973, of a distinctive Labrador flag, which was sewn together by his wife, and became highly popular all over Labrador.

Mike Martin never led the New Labrador Party into a general election, but Tom Burgess did, and although he may have shown some promise at the beginning, Tom ultimately failed the movement and himself through misguided scheming for personal advantage. I'd award Burgess a grade of 25%.

John Connors

JOHN TOOK OVER the New Democratic Party in 1970 and led the party into the 1971 and 1972 elections. As bad luck would have it, the timing was even more inopportune for him than for Calvin Normore before him.

The political battle royal in 1971 was between Joey's Liberals and Frank Moores's Tories, and any other party was doomed to be crushed to death between their collisions. The NDP could attract only 1.8% of the votes cast.

The 1972 election was worse again for them. Following the uncertain election result of the fall before, the electorate was determined to put the Tories decisively in power after twenty-three years of Liberal rule. Anything else, including the NDP leadership or policies, was entirely irrelevant. The party could field only three candidates and received just 0.02% of the popular vote.

I'd rate John Connors at 40% as a political leader.

Ed Roberts

EDWARD MOXON ROBERTS was born in St. John's in 1940. He was the son of Katharine Moxon Roberts and the well-known Newfoundland physician and businessman Dr. Harry Roberts. He was educated at Holloway School and Prince of Wales College in St. John's and at St. Andrew's College, the private school in Ontario. He obtained his undergraduate degree and his law degree from the University of Toronto.

Thus, most of his childhood, adolescence, and young adult school days were spent out of Newfoundland. Some blamed that feature of his life experience for his alleged failure to connect with the greater Newfoundland electorate. Others used it to characterize him as an elitist and, according to some, a rather sardonic one, to boot.

Ed and I have had our serious differences over the years, but the "failure to connect" or "elitist" criticisms are not ones I'd agree with. During all my many dealings with him in politics and through casual chats, I have found him to be small-"l" as well as capital-"L" liberal. Judging by the election results in his own districts, his constituents, wherever he ran, liked and appreciated him. The sardonic, even sarcastic element in his modus operandi, while perhaps somewhat present in him as a young man, mellowed out with the passing years.

Upon graduation from law school, Ed briefly became an assistant to our federal minister, Jack Pickersgill. But soon Premier Smallwood appointed him as his own executive assistant. By all accounts he did a magnificent job there. The premier called him his "boss" and often recounted how brilliant he was. Sometimes, though, he got above himself, according to Joey, and had to be taken down a peg or two by means of a metaphorical "slog in the arse."

Ed got elected to the House of Assembly in 1966 in White Bay North at the age of twenty-six. Joey told me later that Ed had been "hopping mad" at the fact that I was elected in the same election at an age two years younger than him. Ed had wanted to be the youngest Member elected, Joey said, and for that reason, he had urged the premier not to let me run because I was too young.

I never saw or heard a scintilla of evidence of any of that, besides Joey's own say-so, which I took as part of the premier's habitual divide-and-rule tactic. Besides, if anything, Ed's "hopping mad" quota was more than filled when his mentor, Smallwood, appointed the also youngish Clyde Wells as a minister before the 1966 election and kept Ed out of the cabinet. And then, Joey humiliated Ed again after the election by only making him his parliamentary assistant in the House, where he had to sit right behind the premier and jump to it at his whim.

Within a couple of years, though, after John Crosbie and Clyde Wells bailed out of the cabinet, and the disastrous 1968 federal election for Liberals in the province showed that Joey was losing his grip, Ed and a number of us other youngsters were appointed to Smallwood's new and improved cabinet. He first became minister of Welfare and later minister of Health.

Ed would be personally re-elected to the House many times up to 1985, and again in 1992. I'm not aware of his being defeated in any district he ran in, which contrasted with his unsuccessful attempts, twice, to lead the Liberal Party as a whole to victory in general elections.

His first attempt to become premier occurred in 1972. Early that year, after Joey resigned as premier and Liberal leader, and Frank Moores had formed a government, Ed was elected leader of the party and became Leader of the Opposition. A few weeks later, Moores called a snap election for March 24 and cut a huge swath through the Liberal candidates. Only 9 of us managed to win our seats, a drop from the 20 or 21 Liberal MHAs elected just a few months before. The PCs received 60.5% of the popular vote, and the Liberals just over 37%.

A couple of years later, Joey Smallwood attempted a comeback with the idea of ousting Ed Roberts as Liberal leader. The Liberal Party constitution required a leadership convention, and one was scheduled for October 1974. Smallwood threw his hat in, and his fellow MHAs, Roger Simmons and Steve Neary, no doubt sensing a weakness in Roberts's hold on the leadership, also took him on.

Though politically discredited just three years before, Smallwood now came surprisingly close to Roberts on the first ballot. He received 305 votes to Ed's 337. Simmons and Neary got 57 and 24, respectively.

On the next ballot, though, the disillusionment with Joey seemed to break through. Nearly all of Neary's and Simmons's support, and some of Smallwood's, went to Roberts, or abstained. Joey dropped to 298, and Ed won with 403 votes.

But Ed's former political guru wasn't done just yet with tormenting him. The very next year, 1975, just before Moores called a provincial election in September, Joey formed the Liberal Reform Party. Then he ran 28 candidates in the election. This was not nearly a full slate for the 51 districts, but he touted the number as sufficient for him to form a majority government and appoint a Speaker, *when*, not *if*, they all won. And he confidently declared throughout the campaign, having lost none of his chutzpah in his mid-seventies, that he had no doubt they would all win.

The PCs dropped from their 60.5% of the popular vote in the previous 1972 election to 45.5% this time. The Liberals under Roberts got 37.1% of the vote in this election, nearly exactly the same percentage as in 1972. Joey's Liberal Reform Party received nearly 12%.

Opinions differed on the effect of Joey's new party on the outcome of the election. The PCs won 30 seats of the 51 total, down from 33 in the last election, when there'd been a total of only 42 seats in the House. The Liberals got 16, up from 9 in 1972, and Joey got 4 of his Liberal Reform candidates elected.

Some analysts said that Joey's 12% of the votes were at the expense of Roberts's mainstream Liberal Party. Others thought that since Ed's party got a percentage this election that was identical to the last election, you could argue that Joey's percentage came off the PC vote, because he had provided an alternative to the PCs that Roberts couldn't seem to offer.

My own opinion was that the Tories were in serious decline at this time, and there were enough districts where the PC plurality vote was so close, or where the Liberal Reform candidate actually won, that if there had not been a Liberal Reform candidate in those districts, the PC government would have been narrowly defeated.

I didn't run personally in that election, having developed serious issues with Ed's leadership. But, I did campaign for Liberal candidates, mostly outside of St. John's. I saw what was happening in districts where Smallwood had run a candidate. One constituency I spent time in, for example, was Grand Bank district. Powerful PC cabinet minister Alex Hickman ran as the incumbent there. He got elected on only 39.7% of the votes. The relatively unknown Liberal and Liberal Reform candidates got 37.3% and 20.5%, respectively, for a total of what could be considered a Liberal popular vote of 57.8%. I had no doubt that, if it were not for the presence of Joey's candidate, the official Liberal candidate would have been elected there, as in ten or a dozen other districts.

I still believe, in retrospect, that Joey's spoiler act kept Frank Moores and the PC Party in power in 1975, and that, without that intrusion, Ed Roberts, on a balance of probabilities, would have become premier of the province.

IN 1977, I ran against Roberts for the leadership of the provincial Liberal Party. The campaign became a vicious process that I wouldn't wish on my worst enemy. There was no party membership requirement, and therefore anyone could be dragged into the halls and church basements from anywhere to vote for the candidates' slates of delegates. And that's exactly what happened. In more than one case, a leadership candidate hired a taxi company to empty the bars and convey the habitués to meetings to cast their votes. It gave new meaning to the concept of "barroom politics."

It transpired that Steve Neary was backed by Joey Smallwood, and this gave his candidacy substantial impetus, which, in turn, made many Liberal supporters, including large numbers of my own, revert back to Ed Roberts for fear that a split between me and him risked putting Joey's man in the leadership.

The leadership convention was held in the St. John's Arts and Culture Centre on October 15. There were five political luminaries, at least in their own minds, on the first ballot, which yielded these votes for each: Ed Roberts, 356; Steve Neary, 238; Bill Rowe, 159; Roger Simmons, 115; Hugh Shea, 2.

With Shea, Simmons, and Neary sequentially removed from the picture by the fourth ballot, the final voting produced 439 for Rowe and 376 for Roberts. Ed was out and I was now Liberal leader. Wick Collins of the St. John's *Evening Telegram* described what my supporters and I had accomplished as "The Night of the Jackals."

But the gang-up of Simmons and Neary supporters against Roberts was wholly in the nature of political competition, if rather ferocious. So, we all took with a huge grain of salt good old Wick's attempt to seem shocked, especially since it came from the kind of columnist who had said that women should not be allowed on television as news anchors or readers because the sound of the female voice was too irritating.

I'm sure it didn't seem so to Ed at the time, but his defeat in that leadership contest may well have been a blessing in disguise. In the election that followed, in 1979, the PCs under their new leader, Brian Peckford, would increase their popular vote to over 50% and handily defeat the Liberals under my successor as leader, the charismatic celebrity Don Jamieson. Going by that result, Ed Roberts, if he'd continued as leader, would probably have chalked up his third, even more humiliating, defeat.

As for my own political leadership, I haven't graded myself in this book because, for reasons given here and elsewhere, I never did lead the party into an election. But let me stress that, if I had qualified for a ranking here, I would have placed myself, based on the gap between what I had aspired to achieve and what I actually achieved, at the lower end of the scale. I trust that this recognition will be some consolation to any leaders in this book who are smarting and resentful over what they consider the inadequate grade I have assigned to them.

IN BRIAN PECKFORD'S next election onslaught, in 1982, Ed was one of only eight Liberal candidates who were able to cling on to their seats. He didn't run for re-election in the next election, 1985, or in 1989, but concentrated instead on his flourishing law practice.

Then, in 1992, Premier Clyde Wells inveigled him into joining his cabinet as minister of Justice. He didn't have a seat in the House, but he got elected in a by-election, and again in the general election of 1993. He only stayed until immediately after Brian Tobin became premier, which allowed him to say he had served in the cabinets of three premiers.

This time he retired definitively after nearly quarter of a century of active membership in the House of Assembly—a span of time in the legislature about as long as his early mentor, and later nemesis, Joey Smallwood.

In 2002, Prime Minister Jean Chrétien had Roberts appointed lieutenant-governor of Newfoundland and Labrador. In Government House he developed a reputation for widely and frequently opening up the viceregal residence to ordinary mortals.

I consider Roberts to be among the most intelligent and well-read persons I've ever met. But his intelligence seemed to be of a certain type. He had a prodigious memory, an instant comprehension of a point, whether spoken or in a document, and was one of the people most knowledgeable in history that I've known. He had a cutting style of debate, but his overall political oratory was somewhat lumbering, often filled with precious allusions to his vast fund of biographical knowledge, and with quotations of "great men."

His wit tended to be sardonic and sometimes directed toward the person, even an ally sometimes, in an ad hominem fashion. This caused grief to some of his "friends" on occasion. But I wouldn't go so far as to say that Oscar Wilde's dictum applied to him: "He hasn't become prominent enough to have any enemies, but none of his friends like him."

For someone in politics, he did sometimes appear to have an insensitivity to the nuances of a situation or to another person's feelings. I recall one time when Ed was up in the House of Assembly as Leader of the Opposition making a speech, and he noticed that his water glass was empty. He picked it up and motioned it toward Steve Neary, sitting nearby, and asked his colleague to run out and fetch him a glass of water.

At first Neary looked at him in disbelief. Normally, page boys and girls attended to that sort of thing. But then Steve took the glass and jogged out of the House. A few minutes later, he trotted back in with the full glass. Now he mimicked the panting of a faithful dog as he ran over to Ed and delivered his water to him. The House erupted in laughter on both sides, utterly destroying whatever statesmanlike message Ed was endeavouring to impart.

Joey always mentioned Ed's brilliance but characterized it, at least to me, as the brilliance of a first-rate bureaucrat. He'd make an absolutely magnificent deputy minister, Joey would say, a top civil servant of the highest order. But leader? Ah, no. He was lacking the vision, and the dynamic energy that any successful leader must possess.

Still, if Joey, the great man, was correct, he never explained how this same Ed Roberts managed to beat him in a leadership race, and then went on to win far more seats than him as a leader of a party in the 1975 provincial election.

Ed Roberts as political leader I'd rate at 65%.

Gerry Panting

GERRY WAS NDP leader from 1974 till 1977. He had come to Memorial University as a lecturer in history and made a distinguished name for himself there. I recall him from my freshman year as a student at MUN. I would grow to admire him later in life, but I had taken a visceral dislike to the man over an incident on the first day of my first year at university. I all but forgot about it in later years, until I was reminded of it at a recent book signing by an acquaintance who'd been my fellow student at the time in question.

Going around like a hen with my head off like many freshmen on their first morning of classes, looking for the course classes I'd signed up for, I ended up entering Panting's class five minutes late. He chose to make an example of me and berate me for my tardiness, no doubt as a warning right off the bat to all his students that he was not going to tolerate any slackness or general uselessness among first-year idiots. I recall being somewhat humiliated and thinking that this was one needlessly mean bastard. I changed to another history course and never took any of his courses over the next four years.

My fellow student, who'd reminded me of the episode, told me he couldn't believe the totally unnecessary unkindness of the man. He said it had formed his opinion of some NDPers for life, namely that they were the soul of compassion and understanding regarding humanity on paper, but in real life their doctrinaire, self-righteous attitudes made some of them cruel and unforgiving and extremely unlikeable.

I didn't retain the same deep-seated reaction over the years myself, although I confess that I never did warm to Gerry Panting. Yet he and I had some quite interesting conversations on and off the air, during which I admired some of his ideas and appreciated even those I didn't agree with. I recall sincerely saying as much one night years ago, during an event at the Ship, to superb Newfoundland and Labrador musician, singer, and composer Dave Panting.

Among other things that Gerry and I discussed was his passionate advocacy of proportional representation in elections. And well he might advocate that voting method: When he led the party into the 1975 election and raised the NDP vote to 4.35%, a proportional representational system would have given his party at least 2 seats in the 51-seat House instead of none.

Panting ran several times in general elections, without success, but he devoted himself to the building of the NDP here and helped keep the democratic socialist vision alive during the barren years.

I'd award Gerry Panting as political leader a grade of 45%.

John Crosbie

I'VE PLACED JOHN Crosbie here in no particular chronological order. He was never premier and never tried to win a general election at the head of a party, but he did go for leader of the Liberal Party and premier in 1969. And he ran for the leadership of the federal PCs in 1983. He was continuously in the provincial or federal legislatures from 1966 to 1993 and a cabinet minister for well over half that time. So, it's convenient to fit him in anywhere over that period.

John Carnell Crosbie was born in St. John's in 1931. A year later, his grandfather Sir John Chalker Crosbie died, so young John wouldn't have remembered him. But he would have been cognizant all his early life of his grandfather's prominence in the community as the head of the long-tailed Crosbie clan and of his fame and notoriety in business and politics.

Young John was a teenager when the great battle raged in the late 1940s between Confederation and Responsible Government. He helped his father, Ches, campaign for the Economic Union with the US faction of the Responsible Government forces. No doubt he picked up then the spark of the concept of free trade with the US, which he would fan into a flame decades later when he got into federal politics.

He would reminisce, in the 1980s, when he was ushering in the Mulroney government's free trade agreement with the US: "Americans were far more popular in Newfoundland than Canadians, so I was never hung up about the United States. There always seemed to be a hang-up with the Toronto cultural literati about the US. But that's never been the feeling in Newfoundland and Atlantic Canada."

John went to school in St. John's and then attended St. Andrew's College, the private school for boys, in Aurora, Ontario, near Toronto. Aurora has regularly been listed among the ten most affluent municipalities in Canada. The many famous alumni of St. Andrew's have included Group of Seven painter Lawren Harris, novelist Timothy Findlay, publisher Jack McClelland, first Canadian-born Governor General Vincent Massey, Premier Frank Moores, Lieutenant-Governor Ed Roberts, and actor Kiefer Sutherland, the grandson of the great egalitarian socialist Tommy Douglas. Among the school's well-known headmasters was Thomas Hockin, who went on to become the executive director of the International Monetary Fund.

After St. Andrew's, Crosbie graduated from Queen's University with first-class honours and the medal in political science. Then he won the university medal in law at Dalhousie law school and a scholarship from the Canadian Bar Association as the year's outstanding law student. Next he was off to the Institute for Advanced Legal Studies at the London School of Economics, one of the world's most prestigious universities. And finally he was rewarded for all his brilliant academic and professional training by being called to the Newfoundland Bar.

But the practice of law wouldn't engage him exclusively for very long. In less than a decade he was running for St. John's City Council, where he topped the poll in votes and was elected by his fellow councillors as deputy mayor.

Within months after that, in the summer of 1966, he ignored the advice of his savvy late father and accepted Joey's invitation to join his cabinet. In the provincial election that fall, he ran in St. John's West as one of Joey's hand-picked, star candidates. He beat Progressive Conservative stalwart Harvey Cole by over a thousand votes. (Cole would later become Crosbie's assistant in a PC government.)

The kissy-kissy relationship between Joey Smallwood and John Crosbie, two blimp-sized egos, couldn't last. Within a year and a half of trying to occupy the same space in a government too small for both of them, they had a big blow-up. Ostensibly, it was over financing for the Come By Chance refinery.

Opinions differ on whether, in 1968, John was summoned, or forced himself, into Joey's office for the showdown. And once he was in there, accompanied by sidekick Clyde Wells, there's also divided opinion on who was faster on the draw with their respective letters of denunciation.

Some believed the premier when he said he was quicker: He fired Crosbie, he maintained, by launching his letter at the minister first. Others accepted John's version that he pre-empted Joey's letter of dismissal by bawling into the premier's face, "Like fuck I'm fired. I resign!" Whereupon he hurled his letter of resignation at Smallwood.

Knowing both bantam Joey and bulky John, I'd wager that if this had been the gunfight at the O.K. Corral, John would have been in Boot Hill. In those days, it was hard to be faster than Joey. But whatever the resolution of that disputed point of honour might be, John was out of the cabinet. And, right off the bat, there began an unholy war between the two in which honour seldom dared to raise its naive little head. Here, for example, were some of Smallwood's descriptions of Crosbie: "a bagful of hate, a skinful of hate, two hundred pounds of vicious hate," and "a corrupt, diseased mind, turning the august House of Assembly into a beer garden," plus the really unkind "ya big sook!"

To make it look like he was reforming his party as his last noble act, but really to smoke Crosbie out, Smallwood proclaimed in 1969 that he was retiring from politics, and he called a leadership convention. When John jumped into the race for Liberal leader and started to campaign vigorously, Joey decided that his really last noble act had to be saving the party and the premiership from falling into "the wrong hands," that is to say, John Crosbie's heretical mitts. Complaining to the world how heartbroken he was at depriving himself of "toasting his shins by the fire" in blessed retirement, Joey announced his own candidacy for the leadership.

At the leadership convention in 1969, appropriately held over Halloween, Joey won hands down, 1,070 votes to Crosbie's 440. Within a couple of years, John made his political enmity formal. Before the 1971 provincial election, he joined the official Opposition in the House and became a full-fledged member of the Progressive Conservative Party. There he continued to play a huge role in helping newly elected leader Frank Moores totter Joey in the October election and to wrest the premiership from him in January of the next year.

Crosbie became number two man in the Moores government, a position he despised. He possessed a Julius Caesar complex: He'd rather be head man in a village, he'd say, than second man in Rome. Yet here he was, performing most of the heavy lifting for Frank, and almost premier de facto, but, gallingly, not premier in name.

In the provincial election of 1975, he won St. John's West by only 437 votes, a fair number of votes less than the margins of victory that other Tory candidates in St. John's enjoyed over their opponents. His result told him something: You could work your guts out doing everything necessary to put Newfoundland and Labrador's finances on an even keel, and implementing rational government policies, but such laudable effort only brought you unpopularity and public criticism.

In 1976, after holding major portfolios over the past five years—Finance, Economic Development, Fisheries, Intergovernmental Affairs, Mines and Energy—he bailed out of the provincial government to try his luck on the federal scene.

In October of that year he ran for the House of Commons in a by-election in the riding of St. John's West. He won with 11,719 votes. Tom Mayo, the NDP candidate, got an impressive 8,597, which indicated what that party could achieve in the future with a popular and respected candidate. The Liberal candidate, the same man who had given Crosbie a small scare in the provincial district of St. John's West in 1975, Bob Innis, came a fairly distant third. Crosbie's main campaign against him this time consisted of the motto, "*In*nis is going to be *Out*is!"

A Newfoundlander in Ottawa who watched the House of Commons closely told me that Crosbie, upon finding his seat there, straightaway started "crucifying the Trudeau government." As an Opposition critic, he largely made his mark with humorous remarks and semi-witty one-liners.

For example, he directed this suggestion in the House to Fisheries Minister *Roméo* LeBlanc: "He should find his *Juliet* and do to her what he is doing to the fishery." The press gallery ate it up. It was not reported what he and Roméo said to each other at Rideau Hall receptions after LeBlanc became Governor General of Canada.

Because of the high profile Crosbie developed in Opposition, he was greatly esteemed by new PC leader Joe Clark. When Clark took enough seats in the 1979 federal general election to defeat Pierre Trudeau's Liberals and form a minority government, he appointed Crosbie to the most important portfolio as minister of Finance. But Clark couldn't bear to snub the far more senior MP from Newfoundland, Jim McGrath, so he made McGrath minister of Fisheries. They became the "Fish and Chips Boys"—the first and only time this province has had two ministers in the federal cabinet.

On rising in the House of Commons to bring down his budget, Crosbie warned, "With a Polish Pope [John Paul II] and a Newfoundland Finance minister, you mainlanders had better watch your jokes." He went on to shed crocodile tears of self-pity: "Mr. Speaker, the lot of a Finance minister is not a happy one when he succeeds a Liberal government."

At some point in the House, he displayed a document to the Liberal Opposition across the aisle and observed, "By the way, in case the honourable gentlemen opposite have never seen one, this is a tax return." But all the levity in the world couldn't save the poor, benighted Clark government.

John's first and last budget for Joe Clark's Tory administration certainly wowed the business and financial community. They loved his "short-term pain for long-term gain." He was the darling of every board of trade and chamber of commerce and business periodical in the country. Some of them made him Man of the Year. But the ordinary citizens of the land? Not so delighted. For them, one tax increase in particular, announced in John's budget speech, drowned out everything else: "Thus the increase is eighteen cents a gallon for those using gasoline for personal use . . ."

As a result of the Crosbie budget, the Liberals brought in a motion of no confidence in the Clark government. Many didn't expect the motion to pass. But to their surprise and, in some cases, dismay, on December 13, 1979, by a handful of votes, the PC government was defeated. Less than two weeks before Christmas, there had to be an immediate election call.

A lot of commentators ridiculed Clark and his tacticians for not being able to count: They should have stalled the vote until enough of their MPs could get back to the House to allow the government to survive. In retrospect, though, it has dawned on many that perhaps Clark and his spin doctors actually wanted the election.

Joe and his backroom boys apparently figured that, just as Diefenbaker had done in the early 1960s, Joe could turn a minority government into a massive majority because of the electorate's loathing of the previous Trudeau government. And Trudeau himself? Hadn't he confirmed that the Liberals' situation was hopeless by already resigning the party leadership? So the Tories actually courted defeat in the House, which they could then blame on the power-mad, and policy-bankrupt, and much-detested Liberals. It was the pathway to PC triumph for the next four years.

Regrettably for Joe Clark and his brilliant Tory tacticians, if that was their game plan, they had made an asinine public-image error: The cartoonish Clark was no charismatic Diefenbaker, and the magnetic Trudeau, now retreaded as leader, was no lacklustre Pearson. Hence, the Clark versus Trudeau rematch saw thirty-odd seats change hands. After election day, Trudeau was able to rise in the House at the head of his own majority government and crow, "Welcome to the eighties."

Crosbie counted up the length of time that Clark's PC government had been in power in 1979 and came up with a period of just one day less than nine months: "Long enough to conceive," he lamented, "but not long enough to deliver."

Meanwhile, back in Opposition during the first part of the 1980s, he enlivened the Commons with his ridicule of the Liberal government. The press gallery lived for his quips. For example, when Trudeau appointed his buddy Marc Lalonde as Finance minister, after Lalonde had killed the Liberal Party in Alberta with his National Energy Program, Crosbie observed in the House: "The Canadian economy needs a transfusion, and who do they give us? Dracula!"

But hovering over everything for PC members was the big question of Joe Clark's leadership. However long he stayed on as leader, would Joe ever be able to deliver? A sizable minority of party activists didn't think so. Clark himself decided not to resign after the 1980 election defeat, but at the party's convention in 1981, one-third of the delegates voted for a leadership convention.

Still, Clark figured he had enough support to hang on, and his reaction was not to vacate the leadership but to try to broaden the party's base and win the next election by appealing to more women, ethnic groups, and Quebec nationalists. Potential replacements of Clark as leader, though, including Crosbie, started to secretly organize.

The PC Party's next convention was held in Winnipeg in the middle of the winter of 1983. And the huge conundrum was still Joe Clark. Crosbie, while looking to his own future, apparently did not actively undermine Clark leading up to this convention, but Brian Mulroney certainly did. He and his chum Frank Moores, and associated sleazoids like Karlheinz Schreiber, of later Airbus infamy, never stopped stealthily undercutting and sabotaging poor Joe.

They were surprisingly ineffective. They didn't come handy to exterminating Clark. At this convention, only 33.1%, which was even slightly fewer than last time, voted for a leadership convention; 66.9% voted against a competition for a new leader.

But over two-thirds of delegate support wasn't enough for Joe. Although he always seemed to be entirely free of vanity, he had more than his share of pride. He saw his percentage as too small a gain in support among party members. So, he decided to resign, call for a leadership convention, and have himself confirmed as leader by running and winning. Many observers thought he was batty. Obtaining, say, 50% plus one in a divisive leadership race would somehow be better than the more than two-to-one delegate support he'd just received at this convention? Go figure.

Political polls showed the PC Party poised to win the government in the next election. The numbers placed them well ahead of the Liberals. Except for the brief euphoria over Trudeau's repatriation of the constitution in 1982, the Tories were constantly in front of the Liberals by as much as twenty points. The successful leadership candidate was going to become the next prime minister of Canada!

That concentrated the minds of aspirants marvellously. Or as one Newfoundlander said to me at the time, "It drew all the prime minister wannabes like shit flies." Mulroney drooled in anticipation. And all the other hopefuls, including John Crosbie, went to work like mad. The convention was set for June 1983 and looked like a battle between two main contenders.

Joe Clark, MP, the youngest prime minister in Canada's history, still only forty-four years old, had toiled at making himself fluently bilingual, for which many PCs patted him on the head. He appealed to the middle-of-the-road element in the party.

Brian Mulroney, same age, a small-town native Quebecker, fluent in Quebec French, one of the boys, a Newfoundland and Labrador connection as former head of the Iron Ore Company of Canada, had lost to Clark at the 1976 leadership convention. Many voting delegates then, primed by some elements in the media, had perceived him to be too slick and shallow.

That was a surprising perception to me, in view of his brilliant legal and business career to date and his phenomenal political organizing abilities. Exceedingly well-known, and highly regarded by many anti-Trudeau politicos in Quebec, Mulroney's claim to leadership at this current convention was that he'd be able to seduce a lot of seats in Quebec away from their traditional love affair with the Liberal Party.

The other candidates were a mixed bag:

Michael Wilson, forty-six, an MP from Ontario, had been a reputable Toronto banker. But he had no charisma, was a boring speaker, and laboured in French.

David Crombie, forty-seven, another MP from Ontario, had been Toronto's highly popular "tiny, perfect mayor." He was a self-proclaimed "Red Tory."

Peter Pocklington, forty-one, owned the Edmonton Oilers and would become notorious later for trading Wayne Gretzky and for a conviction of perjury and fraud in the US.

John Gamble, forty-nine, yet another Ontario MP, spied a Marxist under every bed. His pitch for leadership was based on a strict anti-Communist policy.

Neil Fraser, forty-nine, railed against the metric system having come to Canada. Plus, he likened the Canadian confederation to a constant blood transfusion to Quebec.

When John Crosbie, fifty-two, threw his hat in the race, commentators were divided. To some, his chutzpah, the unmitigated gall of this guy going for prime minister from a base in little, unimportant, impoverished Newfoundland, was mind-boggling.

To start with, wasn't he the idiot whose budget in 1979 had brought the first PC government in nearly fifty years crashing down? And self-admittedly, the extent of his mastery of Canada's second official language was, "*Avez-vous un scotch*?" Indeed, with that St. John's brogue coming out of him, you were hard put to argue he could speak the other official language, either.

People were bemused by John's pronunciations. In the House of Assembly, we used to listen to him pronounce "the Hebrides" as "the Hee-brides," and "hyperbole" as "hyper-bowl," and Haiti as "high-tee." His accent was edged out only by the caller to *Open Line* who criticized the government for sending seventy RCMP officers to Cuba. When I'd replied to the caller, "No, it was Haiti," the caller responded, "What? H'eighty! Jeez, that's even worse. I thought it was only seventy." When I told John that, he said he'd just have to try harder.

Many deemed him to be the most likeable of the major candidates, which, John figured, said something about his competition. And he was admired as perhaps the best debater in the House of Commons, because his points were leavened with a satirical side that skewered opponents.

His main platform was that Canada should enter into a free trade agreement with the United States. It was as if he was channelling his old man, Ches, from 1948. And he never made any bones about it: "Someday we're going to have a North American continent that's an economic union. That's inevitable. These economic forces are there, and government policy can't stop them. It's only a question of, how do you get into a more secure position?"

At the time of the convention, Brian Mulroney was dead against free trade with the US and, in the campaign, he had opposed Crosbie's free trade line from start to finish. But what surprised me was the number of even non-Crosbie delegates I talked to who agreed that it was time for the PCs to stop being protectionist and to move toward free trade with the US. I think it was an extremely strong plank in John's platform, if somewhat below the surface for many at the time. And it would be remarkable how he changed minds at the very top of the government on that subject just a few years later.

In June of 1983, I was at the PC leadership convention in Ottawa as an observer, and I believe Crosbie would have won it if he'd been able to speak fluent French. That he had no grip on the language was considered bad enough, but his devil-may-care attitude—"I'm not even functionally illiterate in French!"—made his position worse. And his defensiveness added insult to injury: In Quebec during the campaign he told reporters, who were wondering about his English-only deficiency, that his inability to speak French was like not being able to speak German; it would not hamper his understanding of Quebec problems. This in language-obsessed Quebec!

On another occasion, when he was asked if his lack of French would hamper his ability to be prime minister, he blurted out, "No. I don't speak Mandarin Chinese, either." All this gave the impression that he was not sensitive to Quebec's issues, which was unfortunate because it was not true.

I recalled Crosbie's reaction way back in 1969, when Pierre Trudeau brought in the Official Languages Act, making French and English equal in status in the government of Canada, and leading to the country's official bilingualism. John was in the House of Assembly in St. John's at the time, as was I, and he championed the act wholeheartedly, making a speech that displayed great empathy with, and understanding of, the Quebec situation in Canada.

But now in the leadership race, even people's memory of his droll one-liner about Trudeau's bilingualism couldn't help him: "It is better to be honest and sincere in one language than a twister, a trickster, and a twit in two." His reaction to his inability might not have lost him any delegates in Quebec; they were already shared between Mulroney and Clark. But it probably did lose him delegates in the rest of Canada, because it brought dramatic attention to the fact that if he became leader, his unilingualism might defeat the PC Party in the next election.

YOU'D NEVER SAY it to talk to him in a social situation, where he was undemonstrative and often spoke with his eyes closed, but it was John's personality that attracted many zealous and razor-sharp supporters to his causes. That had happened in his 1969 leadership campaign against Smallwood, and it happened again now at the federal leadership level.

People seemed to appreciate his style, or rather his lack thereof. Especially in his public pronouncements, he came across as highly intelligent, witty, right to the point, on top of everything, absolutely fearless in his words and actions, and totally without vanity or airs. One of the graphics in his leadership campaign depicted him as a tortoise slipping by the two rabbits, Mulroney and Clark, who were distracted by their infighting. At the convention itself, even the big Crosbie blimp, which went askew and out of control as it floated high above the crowd at the centre, endeared him to the delegates.

In the backrooms, during the balloting, Mulroney and some other candidates met secretly to put into effect an "ABC" conspiracy—Anybody But Clark. Crosbie wasn't part of it, apparently. He didn't want to polarize support and was hoping Clark would be low enough on the first ballot that some of his supporters, plus those of other candidates forced off the ballot, would come to him as everyone's second choice. John's strategists visualized him slipping up the middle, much as Clark had done in 1976 when he'd unexpectedly won the leadership.

The consensus among listeners seemed to be that Crosbie's speech from the podium was the best of the lot. He even spoke some French and drew praise for promising, if belatedly, to make himself fluent in the second official language within two years after becoming leader.

Joe Clark's results on the first ballot staggered Mulroney and his team. Joe led with over 36% of the votes. No one should have been surprised, though; half the PC caucus of MPs had stood behind Clark on the stage during his speech.

Brian Mulroney was second with a disappointing 29%, and Crosbie third with a little over 21%. All the rest were in the low single digits.

The jest going around during the first balloting was that Pocklington was going to get 99 votes, the same as the number on Wayne Gretzky's jersey. In fact, he bettered that by 3 votes, getting 102, but he was still devastated, both by the weakness of his own showing and the strength of Clark's. Without being required to by the rules, he at once dropped off the ballot and moved his loyal supporters into Mulroney's camp.

Wilson couldn't believe his numbers—144 votes. He and his workers had confidently expected more than double that, at least 300. He dropped off in despair and was wheedled by Pocklington into supporting Mulroney. Spurred more by indecision over who to support than by hopes for his own campaign, David Crombie stayed on the ballot. Gamble and Fraser dropped out and supported Crosbie.

Clark hit a brick wall on the second ballot. At 36.7%, he had much the same result as on the first. Mulroney went up to 34.6%, and this time Crosbie increased to 26.4%. He had gained nearly as much as Mulroney, who had been endorsed by both Wilson and Pocklington. It had turned out that they were able to deliver only about half of their supporters to

Mulroney. Crombie was now forced off the ballot for the third vote. He endorsed Crosbie.

John obviously had far more momentum than Clark, who was essentially stalled. Everyone now realized, including Clark's team, that he was going to lose, especially since, if Crosbie had to drop off the ballot after the next vote, the polls were projecting that two-thirds of his delegates would go to Mulroney.

The only logical way to stop Clark's arch-enemy, Mulroney, was for Clark to drop off the ballot right now and support Crosbie. Premier Brian Peckford inched his way across the convention floor to talk to Clark and his group about that. The Newfoundland premier was picked up by cameras on live television trying to convince them that, rationally, Joe had to abandon all his hopes and aspirations and get behind John.

The numbers and the logic might have been clear, but the whole idea of the first-place candidate, the former prime minister, dropping out to support the man in third place struck the Clark camp as humiliatingly weak and ridiculous. Their reaction was most concisely summed up by Clark's wife, Maureen McTeer, whose response was unencumbered by numbers or political logic. Everyone across the nation read her lips on television replying to Peckford's suggestion with, "Fuck off, you nerd."

On the third ballot, Clark had fallen back a little and was barely ahead of Mulroney: 35.8% to 35.1%. Crosbie's percentage of the votes went up more than the other two to 29.1%. But he was in third and last place and was now removed from the next ballot. Despite probably being the most popular candidate with the rank and file of party membership outside of Quebec, John had lost his spirited leadership bid.

In the fourth and final ballot, Crosbie favoured Mulroney in his own mind. But he would not publicly endorse him, out of respect for Clark as his former colleague and prime minister. However, the earlier prediction that two-thirds of his delegates would go for Mulroney came true.

Clark ended up with 45.6% of the total votes cast. Mulroney's 54.5% made him the new leader. Some political commentators opined afterwards that, if the final ballot had been between John Crosbie and Brian

Mulroney, John very likely would have won because of the deep-seated anti-Mulroney animosity of most Clark supporters.

Those two conventions in 1983 created intense divisions in the PC Party. A lot of the discord had been caused by Mulroney's shameless undermining of Clark after the latter's debacle in the House in 1979 and his lost election weeks later. But nothing succeeds like success: The very next year, in the election of September 4, 1984, Mulroney led the PCs to the largest majority government, by seat count, in Canada's history.

Mulroney's victory had little to do with any of his policies, which were rather weakly etched in his own mind, let alone the public's. It had more to do with his smooth public personality, street-savvy knowledge of Quebec and its players, and his idiomatic articulateness in both languages.

He received a huge assist, moreover, from Liberal leader John Turner's surprising rustiness, compared with the good old glory days when he used to be the media's prime minister in waiting. These modern days, no one could visualize Princess Margaret swooning in his manly, athletic arms on the dance floor and wanting to marry him.

In the leaders' TV debate, when Mulroney confronted Turner with Trudeau's cynical patronage appointments just before retiring, which Turner had implemented without even blushing, Turner's inept public handling of the issue on camera shattered his credibility in the eyes of viewers: "I had no option," he claimed. "You could have said no," said Mulroney.

PRIME MINISTER MULRONEY appointed leadership candidates Clark, Crosbie, Crombie, and Wilson to important government portfolios, evidence to some of an amiable and co-operative administration in the making. But observers were soon disabused of that notion.

His enormous caucus was revealed to be an unwieldy hodgepodge of battling "red" Tory progressives, conservative populists, fiscal traditionalists, and most ominous of all, Quebec nationalists, not to say outright separatists. Added to that, the caucus became racked by scandals, a classic case of too many do-nothing MPs on the government backbenches with time on their hands, some of them of a low-life variety who had been thrown upon the political shore like flotsam on the rising PC tide.

Inept actions in the Prime Minister's Office (PMO) wouldn't help the government's image. And Crosbie, to the delight of the media, was just blunt enough to say so. He was on my *Open Line* show one morning in 1985 talking about some ham-fisted decision in the PMO that had much of the electorate in an uproar. I think it was their maladroit handling of the tainted tuna-recall scandal; allegedly with their knowledge, the then minister of Fisheries had allowed canned tuna judged unfit for human consumption to be sold. I asked Crosbie on air, "Is the PMO staffed by a bunch of dolts?"

He knew the unvarnished truth would hurt too much, but he could not tell an outright lie: "I wouldn't say the PMO is staffed by dolts," he generously allowed, "but perhaps you could say they aren't as astute politically or as politically intuitive as they should be." That was good enough for the media; they had a field day. Members of the Tory caucus might have fervently wished that John would just shut up, but I never heard any of them disagree with his analysis.

MEANWHILE, THE MEASURE of John Crosbie's own extraordinary persuasiveness and influence with the new government, and perhaps an indication of Mulroney's flexible principles, was that he was able to get the prime minister to do a complete one-eighty on the desirability and feasibility of a free trade agreement between Canada and the United States. Indeed, leading up to the next general election in 1988, Crosbie's free trade initiative would become the main lever in lifting the PC Party out of its political abyss.

But in the middle of all that serious stuff, Crosbie was having some recreation helping Sheila Copps advance her political career, not to mention her financial fortune. When notable Rat Packer Copps voiced one of her leather-lunged criticisms of the government in the House in 1985, Minister of Justice Crosbie advised her, "Just quiet down, baby."

That stimulated Copps to bawl back, "I'm nobody's baby!" whereupon she rushed out and wrote her autobiography. It came out the next year, entitled *Nobody's Baby*, and flew off the shelves, quickly becoming a bestseller.

A few years later, at a British Columbia fundraiser, John caused another fuss by reporting that Ms. Copps made him think of the song that goes, "Pass me another tequila, Sheila, and lay down and love me again." Like nothing else he'd ever done or said previously, he marvelled, his comment put him at the top of the national news for two nights running. He did go on to stress, perhaps needlessly, that it was just a song and that it hadn't really happened.

In Copps's follow-up autobiography, *Worth Fighting For*, Crosbie wrote the introduction. In it he said, "She was a constant thorn in my side while she was in Opposition, but her marriage to my fellow Newfoundlander Austin Thorne has made her more serene and has calmed her sometimes volcanic and partisan excesses."

John could never seem to resist causing an uproar among feminists and left-wing women. He would go on, for example, to characterize Copps, New Democrat MP Dawn Black, Liberal MP Mary Clancy, and president of the National Action Committee on the Status of Women Judy Rebick, whenever he could, as the "Four Horse*women* of the Apocalypse." (The original four horse*men* of the apocalypse were said to symbolize pestilence, war, famine, and death.)

One might conclude from all this that Crosbie was nothing but a politically incorrect curmudgeon. But in fact he was very much a social progressive. As minister of Justice he advocated pro-choice regarding abortion, liberalized divorce procedures, appointed more women to Supreme Court benches, supported an apology and compensation for Japanese Canadians interned during the Second World War, amended government policy to stop discrimination against homosexuals in being hired in the public service, and tried to change the Human Rights Code to include sexual orientation.

When the 1988 federal election was called, Ross Reid was selected as the PC candidate in St. John's East. Rumours arose that he was gay, and he simply refused to even comment on them, let alone confirm or deny them. They became a public issue to the point where I kept stating on *Open Line* radio the catchphrase, "It doesn't matter what you do in the bedroom; what matters is what you do in the House." It was somewhat effective in defusing the stupid reaction of some, judging by the fact that years later when Svend Robinson came on *Open Line* as an NDP leadership candidate, he said to me off-air, "Thank you for the way you handled Ross Reid's difficulty."

Still, at the time, some PC supporters continued to oppose Reid's candidacy on account of his refusal to deny, which prompted John Crosbie to convene a meeting of party workers. He proclaimed to them rather pointedly, "I don't care if Ross is having sexual relations with effing cats. He's our candidate, and he's a fine man, and I'm supporting him one hundred per cent." Reid got elected, defeating NDP incumbent Jack Harris.

MULRONEY'S PC GOVERNMENT faced the November 1988 federal election with greatly diminished hopes of winning a majority. Polls pointed to a possible Liberal victory under John Turner. The PC Party tried to focus the campaign on one single issue, the Canada–US Free Trade Agreement.

When the mid-campaign polls suggested a forthcoming Liberal victory, the PC Party upped the stakes and started to spend millions of dollars on pro–Free Trade Agreement ads. Mulroney's political cunning was to turn the election into something of a referendum on the agreement. In that way, the PCs were able to divide the opposition to the agreement between the Liberals under Turner and the NDP under Ed Broadbent, and by election day Mulroney and the Tories had regained the momentum.

John Crosbie, as minister for International Trade, and responsible for negotiating the Free Trade Agreement, was an effective weapon against its opposition. During the campaign, he was reported widely in speeches: "Turner wants to tear it up, and Broadbent wants to tear it down. That's the only difference between these two parties. One is Tweedle Dumb and the other is Tweedle Dumber."

Those rather simplistic tactics combined effectively with the Liberals' continued leadership problems with John Turner. Their troubles had been memorably illustrated by Crosbie in the House when he nailed Turner's alleged Neanderthal attitudes. He reminded the nation that Turner had been caught by the television cameras patting Iona Campagnola on the backside, and he mocked, "The Honourable Leader of the Opposition knows all about butts. He's had his hands on more butts than there are Members of this House."

The Tories on election day 1988 were able to form a substantial majority government of 169 seats. It was much reduced from the 1984 election, but the fact was that, although a majority of Canadians voted for parties who were against the free trade agreement, the PCs with their divide-and-rule campaign gained the majority in the House needed to form a stable government and to implement the negotiated deal.

Within a few years, the Canada–US Free Trade Agreement ultimately led to NAFTA, the North American Free Trade Agreement between Canada, the United States, and Mexico. It was one of the largest free trade zones in the world. It must have been a good agreement, because it has since threatened to drive Donald Trump even nuttier than usual.

DURING CROSBIE'S TENURE as federal minister, he was called upon more than once to save Newfoundland and Labrador's bacon. Despite serious animosities between him and Premier Brian Peckford, he made sure that Mulroney lived up to his commitment to Peckford in 1985 to execute an Atlantic Accord on the federal-provincial management and revenues of our offshore oil. (As a side note, two decades later, when John was out of politics altogether, he would advocate persuasively for improvements to that offshore deal because the province had fallen far short of becoming the principal beneficiary of the resource that had been clearly intended.)

After the 1985 Accord had been put to bed, Crosbie was confronted by an almost insurmountable challenge to save the Hibernia offshore development. One of the partners of the consortium, Gulf Canada, had pulled out of the project, and unless that investment was replaced, the deal would die. In the face of fierce, even vicious opposition from commentators in Alberta and from skeptical members of his own federal cabinet, Crosbie persuaded Ottawa to invest 8.5% in the development to fill the gap. This share in Hibernia would be taken over by the Canada Hibernia Holding Corporation on behalf of the Government of Canada, and it contributed not only to the salvation of the project but to its resounding success.

Then in the summer of 1992, Prime Minister Mulroney appointed John as minister of Fisheries to deal with disconcerting reports on the condition of the Atlantic cod stocks. Straightaway, he had to face what he called the hardest political moment of his life.

He'd already had a couple of nightmarish moments in his dealings with premiers Peckford and Wells over federal-provincial relations. The failure of the Meech Lake Accord, as a consequence of the obstinacy of John's former political ally Clyde Wells, and which destroyed Brian Mulroney's intended constitutional legacy, was one of the worst. But this new nightmare was all but unimaginable.

The total collapse of the northern cod stock forced him, as minister of Fisheries, to close the fishing industry in Atlantic Canada. It was an utter calamity that instantly threw thirty to forty thousand Newfoundlanders and Labradorians out of their livelihood.

When crowds of enraged, shouting fishermen surrounded him at a Canada Day celebration in Bay Bulls, in his riding, he shouted back, "Why are you yelling at me? I didn't take the fish from the goddamn waters, so don't go abusing me."

At his news conference in the Delta Hotel, in downtown St. John's, as he was announcing the shutdown of the fishery, protesting fishermen pummelled and pounded on the closed doors of the room, threatening to break them down. Crosbie said, "They don't need to go berserk, trying to batter on doors to frighten me. In the first place, I don't frighten." (There were reports afterwards that Crosbie's minions had orchestrated the door-battering scenario for the television news, to make sure that Ottawa would be suitably impressed by the volatile enormity of the crisis.)

The federal compensation package for displaced fishermen and plant workers turned out to be hopelessly inadequate. But many of Crosbie's colleagues in the federal cabinet were still resentful over Premier Clyde Wells's destruction of the Meech Lake Accord in 1990, and they held it against the province. They wouldn't hear of contributing any more money to this place.

Reminding them that this catastrophe, the destruction of the greatest protein resource in the world's oceans, had occurred under the watch of successive governments of Canada, including their own, Crosbie prepared to resign. As he moved to do so, even the severely disgruntled Quebec ministers relented and authorized the government to improve the compensation deal substantially.

LARGELY BECAUSE OF their loyalty to the PC cause of stalwarts like Clark and Crosbie, Mulroney was able to keep the party together during his second term of plummeting popularity. But it was very much a rearguard action. The constitutional fiasco over Meech Lake, the formation of the Bloc Québécois, and the surge of the Reform Party out west all added to the impending doom.

The credibility of the prime minister himself tanked, partly because of the electorate's growing distaste for his perceived hypocrisy and glib cynicism. For example, aided by the media's long memory, they recalled Liberal Bryce Mackasey's appointment as ambassador to Portugal by the outgoing Trudeau and incoming Turner governments just before the 1984 election, and Mulroney's reaction: "There's no whore like an old whore." Vaguely amusing at the time, this memory became particularly galling as the scope of Mulroney's own blatant patronage appointments, and speculation on his financial finagling, grew.

Similarly, after Mulroney had denounced Clyde Wells and Pierre Trudeau for engineering the failure of the Meech Lake Accord, it later came out in an interview with the *Globe and Mail* that he had deliberately pushed the gruelling first ministers' conference right up against the deadline. He had brought "the constitutional impasse down to eleventh-hour negotiations," he said. He had rolled "all the dice" on the country's constitutional future. His confession caused citizens to become inflamed and disgusted at what many considered his contemptuous cynicism.

Brian Mulroney's 1988 victory turned out to be the last federal election that the national Progressive Conservative Party would ever win.

WHEN MULRONEY ANNOUNCED his resignation in 1993, his cabinet colleague Kim Campbell ran for the leadership in the June convention. Her initial popularity made the race look like it was going to be a coronation. She had the support of numerous MPs and party brass. But late in the game, Jean Charest was persuaded by Mulroney and Crosbie and others to jump in. Joe Clark and Crosbie and many other MPs and luminaries got behind his campaign. Charest steadily gained on Campbell right up to the second ballot of the convention when she received 52.7% of the votes and was elected leader.

After she was sworn in as prime minister, John Crosbie turned down her invitation to join her cabinet. And although he was still relatively young and vigorous, he chose not run in the October election.

In that 1993 election, under the leadership of Kim Campbell, the PC Party suffered near-extinction. It returned only two MPs. Contrary to earlier polls, Jean Chrétien's Liberals were elected in a walk, and Chrétien became the new prime minister. Kim Campbell lost her own seat in the House.

Crosbie could hide neither his satisfaction at having stayed out of the electoral disaster nor his utter disdain for the campaign Campbell had conducted. She'd spent her time, he claimed, in the back of the campaign bus smooching, snuggling, necking, and more with her brand new boyfriend.

Within about a decade, the PC Party merged with the Canadian Alliance to become a junior fragment of the Conservative Party of Canada under Stephen Harper. Thereafter, it ceased to exist as a viable national entity.

ONCE OUT OF active politics, John managed to stay out, and he concentrated on practising law in St. John's. He had difficulty staying out of the public eye, though. Even in practice with a sedate law firm, he found himself in contentious public situations involving fish plant clients. And he didn't shirk from writing feisty opinion pieces in which he frankly characterized himself as the old curmudgeon.

Even after he accepted Premier Danny Williams's invitation to assume the largely ceremonial and fundraising post of chancellor of Memorial University, he didn't avoid taking part in a public controversy with the government on the structure and organization of the university.

He was even tempted, he said, to run in the 2004 federal election for the newly merged Conservative Party under Stephen Harper, against Liberal John Efford in the riding of Avalon. Too bad he didn't. It would not have been a boring race. Efford was riding relatively high at the time, but the electorate was apathetic: Efford may have won 58.3% of the votes, but the voter turnout was only 49.8%. Crosbie's entry would surely have put some spark in the contest, and the result could well have been different. If so, he might have been able to torment Liberal minority prime minister Martin into granting an improved Atlantic Accord sooner than Premier Williams was actually able to achieve it.

In 2008, Prime Minister Stephen Harper had John Crosbie appointed lieutenant-governor of Newfoundland and Labrador where, as the Queen's representative, he was, by definition, supposed to stay clear of controversy. John didn't get the memo, apparently.

The year after he was appointed, he insisted on wearing his sealskin coat at functions during a Royal visit to the province. When that attracted widespread criticism from the loony British tabloids, Crosbie beamed happily: The coat, he said, was his statement in favour of the province's yearly seal hunt. It was as if he was saying that if the anti–seal hunt gang could use the presence of Brigitte Bardot to attract attention to their cause, then he could damn well use the Royals.

EVIDENCE THAT, AT eighty, his irreverent nature was alive and well—too much so for some tastes—came in 2011 at his swearing-in of Premier Kathy Dunderdale's new cabinet. During his formal remarks to the media, MHAs, and guests, he enlightened everybody with some "jokes" regarding the poor economic conditions. He spoke of a man who got so depressed thinking about the bad economy, with no jobs, and all the wars, and so on, that he phoned a suicide hotline and reached a call centre in Pakistan. When the man told them there that he was suicidal, Crosbie said, they got all excited and asked him if he could drive a truck.

The head of the Pakistani Student Association at Memorial University reacted. The joke was shocking to hear from the lieutenant-governor, he said, and it was insensitive and irresponsible and embedded prejudice and created a stereotype.

Premier Kathy Dunderdale, who'd been sitting in the forefront of the audience during John's remarks, later stated publicly that "The comments of the lieutenant-governor were clearly inappropriate."

It must have been a wild old reception at Government House that day, because Crosbie also joked that the economy was so bad in the United States that ExxonMobil laid off twenty-five congressmen. Moreover, he said, a truckload of Americans were caught sneaking *into* Mexico. Someone told me later that John should go down and supply the Donald Trump campaign with a few crazy new ideas.

Crosbie stated to the *Telegram* at the time that anyone offended was welcome to get in touch with him. He was just trying to give the crowd something to be amused about in the course of his opinions. (He didn't mention if he'd ever heard of a rule of protocol that lieutenant-governors are not supposed to express public opinions likely to cause an international incident.) If people didn't like it, he said, they could write him and say, "You're a terrible fellow, you're ignorant, you're a son of a bitch," or whatever they wanted. That was just the risk you took, he mused, if you said anything in public.

John was heard from again in colourful terms when Stephen Harper's Conservative Party inexplicably turned down his son, Ches, as a candidate in the riding of Avalon in the 2015 federal election. Ches Crosbie was a Rhodes Scholar and a very prominent class-action lawyer in Newfoundland and Labrador. He would seem to have been a desirable candidate for any party in his own right. Add to his profile that he was the son of such a famous political father, and the action of the Harper Tories boggled many minds in the province.

Avalon riding had been won by the Liberal candidate in the 2011 election, but the incumbent had been kicked out of the party for alleged sexual misconduct. With a strong whiff of Danny Williams's "Anything But Conservative" campaign still in the wind, it was not yet thought likely that a Conservative could win there, but someone of Ches's calibre and repute had sparked interest. As national Tory strategist Tim Powers, a relation of Ches's, told *Maclean's* magazine at the time, at least "there was a little hope around his candidacy."

To add to the party's stupidity over the matter, they would not say why Ches didn't suit them as a candidate, citing only "an internal party matter." But rumours swirled. One rumour alleged resentment by the thin-skinned Harper over a satirical play Ches had taken part in; it had spoofed Shakespeare's *Macbeth* with the name "MacHarper" and uncomfortably lampooned the Senate scandal then raging. Another rumour was that the Tories didn't like the class-action lawsuit Ches had brought on behalf of former residential school residents against their federal government. But surely that explanation was too ridiculous to countenance.

A further rationale was bruited about which many observers seemed to accept: Just like John, his old man, Ches Crosbie was too independent. Tim Powers agreed with that one, telling *Maclean's* he thought the concerns were probably really about whether Ches would be a bit like his father, a candidate who would do his own thing to succeed.

If that was really the justification to themselves of the party's backroom boys, they were cutting off their own noses to spite their faces. In the prevailing political atmosphere, no Tory candidate was going to get elected in Avalon on Harper's or the Conservative Party's coattails. As Powers said, "If Ches or anybody else were going to get elected there, they were going to have to do it on their own coattails."

John Crosbie agreed with the accusation that his own Tory Party had quashed Ches's candidacy because he was too independent, but he added that Newfoundland Conservative senator David Wells did it to maintain his control over local patronage. Ches should run as an Independent, John told the media.

"I feel like running myself," fumed the octogenarian patriarch, "and beating the piss out of them." Regrettably, from the standpoint of an interesting election, neither Crosbie father nor son chose to run.

YEARS AGO, JOHN Crosbie worked hard to become premier and didn't make it. But his subsequent career in federal politics was proof positive that a good cabinet minister in Ottawa from here was far more important than a premier—in fact, worth any number of premiers—in effectiveness regarding benefiting the province.

Many people who know John's wife, Jane, have said to me that if I'm giving out marks for John's contributions to the province and the nation, I should award at least half of them to Jane. Without her by his side and tendering advice in times of challenge and crisis, John's effectiveness would have been substantially less.

For all the foregoing positive reasons, including having the wit to marry a remarkable woman, but deducting something for his failure to realize his own ambition to become premier of the province—to become first man in a village rather than number-two man in Rome—I'd rank John Crosbie's political leadership at 85%.

John Green

JOHN BECAME LEADER of the NDP in 1977 and led the party into the election of 1979. I recall thinking during that campaign that he held his own in the TV debate with PC leader Brian Peckford and Liberal leader Don Jamieson.

Against those two heavyweights, his candidates got nearly 8% of the popular vote, the highest return for the party before Peter Fenwick's leadership in the 1985 election. If there'd been a balanced correlation between the popular vote and the districts won, that percentage should have entitled Green's NDP to some four seats in the House of Assembly.

Green received 14.5% of the votes in his own district of St. John's West, which was a remarkably good return in those days, although he didn't come close to beating either of the two "major-party" candidates. He was leader from 1977 to 1980, and I recall that he developed a real political profile in the province, which contributed to the NDP's greater recognition in years to come and some success at the polls.

Fonse Faour, a Corner Brook lawyer, achieved his political success under his own steam, but it did happen on John Green's watch as leader. Faour became the very first NDP candidate from the province to get elected to the House of Commons. He was successful in Jack Marshall's old riding of Humber–St. George's–St. Barbe in the 1978 by-election, and again in the redistributed riding in the general election of 1979. Brian Tobin defeated him in the federal general election of 1980.

Fonse became leader of the provincial NDP from 1980 to 1981, taking over from Green, but he never led his party into a provincial election,

I'd give John Green as political leader a rating of 50%.

Brian Peckford

ALFRED BRIAN PECKFORD was born in Whitbourne in 1942 and grew up there, and in Marystown, and Lewisporte. He received a Bachelor of Education degree from Memorial and pursued further academic studies in English and French literature and other disciplines.

Before helping out John Crosbie in his 1969 Liberal leadership battle against Smallwood and then acting as Crosbie's assistant as John hounded Smallwood in the House of Assembly, he taught high school in Springdale.

Leading up to the 1971 provincial election, Peckford left the Liberal Party and joined the Progressive Conservatives. Then, in the 1972 provincial election, he ran for the PC Party in Green Bay district, one of the most Liberal districts in Newfoundland. The PCs under Frank Moores won a landslide majority government, although some eight or nine of us Liberal candidates were able to hang on to our seats. In Green Bay district, the popular Liberal candidate, Harold Starkes, was expected to win as well, but Peckford pulled off a surprise victory there for the PCs by 135 votes.

After that he left no doubts about becoming an outstanding district man. In the next election in 1975, when the Moores PCs lost seats, Peckford personally defied the general trend and rose from that small majority in the previous election to 70% of the popular vote this time.

In the House, he learned the ropes as parliamentary assistant to Premier Moores and then as minister of Municipal Affairs. But it was when Moores appointed him minister of Mines and Energy in 1976 that Peckford came into his own. There he took on the offshore oil companies to impose new stipulations designed to bring the province greater economic, social, and environmental benefits.

Taken aback by Brian's upstart attitude, the oil companies suspended their drilling operations offshore in a fit of anger and pique. But after a little tweaking of the new rules and regulations, the companies bowed to the provincial government and resumed drilling in 1978. This capitulation to Peckford by the international oil consortium made him a local hero.

In January 1979, Frank Moores announced that he was a fulfilled and satisfied man, after all the good deeds he'd done in these parts, and he could now resign as premier. The PC Party set a leadership convention for March 17, 1979, and ten candidates jumped in. Of the crowd, Leo Barry, Walter Carter, and William Doody were perceived to be the serious rivals of Peckford.

But Brian, by his actions and pronouncements in the Energy department, had made himself a front-runner in the race. He attracted the support of most members of cabinet and caucus, but even so, it took three ballots to decide the issue.

On the first ballot he was only 43 votes ahead of prominent cabinet minister Bill Doody. The close result was attributed by some to the fact that Frank Moores had broken his pledge to remain neutral and, instead, surreptitiously supported Doody.

By the third ballot, Peckford had surged ahead to 331 votes against Doody's 208 and went over the top. At thirty-six, Brian became our second-youngest first minister in Newfoundland's history.

Soon after that, his federal counterpart as PC Party leader, Joe

Clark, beat Pierre Trudeau by a plurality of seats in the national election and formed a minority government in Ottawa. Unsurprisingly, Peckford deemed the moment most opportune to call a provincial election.

On June 18, 1979, his PC candidates won 50% of the popular vote, and 33 seats out of 52 in the House of Assembly, to form a solid majority government. The Liberals under Don Jamieson won 41% of the vote and 19 seats and continued on as the official Opposition.

As premier, a resolute Peckford battled gamely for control of our offshore oil, our hydroelectrical resources, and our fishery, in hopes of greater financial returns for the province. He launched court cases on these matters but without success. Attempted negotiations with Ottawa fared no better, especially with the Trudeau Liberals. At one point, he openly hinted at Newfoundland's separation from Canada.

In 1982, Peckford called an election to gain additional provincial support for his fed-bashing. Of course, he was mostly preaching to an electorate already converted to his cause. On election day, 61% of the popular vote and 44 seats in the House went to the PCs, with 8 seats only to the Liberals under Len Stirling. So Brian certainly got his strong provincial mandate to keep on attacking Trudeau and his minions in Ottawa. But, really, to what avail?

Well, his victory speech that night did allow him to create a mantra for the future. He intoned, ". . . Newfoundlanders and Labradorians speak with one voice when we all say, '*One day the sun will shine and have-not will be no more.*'" It sounded nice, but Prime Minister Trudeau held firm, and within a couple of years, the Supreme Court of Canada got on side as well. They handed down their decision supporting the federal position: The government of Canada, not Newfoundland, owned the resources on our continental shelf.

WHEN BRIAN MULRONEY ran for the leadership of the PC Party of Canada in 1983, he pledged to remedy the inequities to Newfoundland and Labrador of the Upper Churchill power deal with Quebec. But, after winning the 1984 federal election with a huge majority of MPs, many of them from Quebec, some of them separatists, he found himself unable to do anything about the hydro situation, especially in the face of strong nationalist Quebec sentiment in his caucus.

Meanwhile, Peckford had started a political campaign across Canada to advocate federal-provincial joint management of the offshore, with most of the benefits to go to the province. Before the 1984 election, Mulroney had also committed himself to a fair and just agreement with the province regarding the offshore resource. And right after becoming the new prime minister, he hopped to it.

Chagrined over his inability to act on the Upper Churchill shemozzle, Mulroney concentrated immediately on the offshore oil, and within six months after his election, Newfoundland and Ottawa signed the 1985 Atlantic Accord. In it, the federal and provincial governments became equal partners in management and decision-making powers under a jointly run Canada-Newfoundland Offshore Petroleum Board (CNOPB)—the "L" for Labrador would be added later—and the province was to be the principal beneficiary of revenues.

The Accord was a brilliant breakthrough for Peckford after many years of dogged, but futile, legal and political struggles. Though defective in the long run regarding provincial revenues, it was the foundation on which future improvements to the deal could be made, leading to Newfoundland and Labrador becoming the "have province" that Brian had predicted.

Soon after he signed the 1985 Atlantic Accord with Ottawa, Peckford called an election to let voters endorse him as the "Great Negotiator." But many teachers and public service employees were more distressed by the two-year wage freeze he'd imposed on them than delighted by his pie-in-the-sky oil revenues.

On election day, he suffered considerable losses. His Progressive Conservatives won less than 49% of the popular vote, down from 61% in 1982, and dropped 6 seats from the 44 the party had won three years before. The Liberals, who'd won only 8 districts in the previous election, now increased their seats to 15 under leader Leo Barry. NDP leader Peter Fenwick advanced his party's fortunes to an unprecedented 14.4% of the popular vote and got re-elected personally in Menihek district.

Peckford's comfortable (if reduced) majority in 1985 would have made many other premiers jealous. Yet, comparing his lesser results now with the 1982 election, it must have been hard for him not to conclude that he'd reaped more votes in the earlier election by waging a nasty war on Ottawa than by negotiating a good peace. It's no wonder that a lot of political leaders, bright-eyed and idealistic at the beginning, turn into jaded, grizzled cynics by the end.

BRIAN HAD MANY good works to his credit. Upon forming his first government in 1979, he right away appointed Lynn Verge and Hazel Newhook to his cabinet, the first women to become cabinet ministers in the province's history. He introduced a policy of pay equity and created a Status of Women Council.

A year after forming his first government, he brought in a new provincial flag designed by world-renowned artist Christopher Pratt. He established a Department of Environment, added grade twelve to the school system, as urged by Education minister Lynn Verge, and kickstarted initial construction on the Trans-Labrador Highway.

Then in 1987, his positive achievements were dramatically overshadowed. His government entered into a partnership with Philip Sprung's outfit from Alberta to build a hydroponic greenhouse on the Mount Pearl–St. John's frontier. It was supposed to create many permanent jobs in the province by exploiting lucrative international markets. Plus, it was going to pump Newfoundlanders full of fresh, healthy veggies all year long. But after the project had sucked over $20 million out of the provincial treasury for a couple of years, it went belly up.

The Sprung greenhouse has, to my mind, been allowed to cloud Peckford's legacy more than it should have. In our nearly seventy years since Confederation, successive governments have racked up $12 billion in debt, and counting. A sizable portion of that amount has been an utter, out and out, waste of public money. And the horrendous debt doesn't take into account the billions in lost revenues from bungled opportunities like our Upper Churchill project. Looked at in perspective, the Sprung greenhouse fiasco represents a miniscule percentage of the total financial blunders perpetrated by the governments that we in this province have been responsible for electing.

I'm not arguing that Peckford's waste of $20 million on Sprung should be forgotten or ignored. What I am saying is that, stacked up against what he accomplished during his ten years in power, the Sprung farce was small potatoes. (Or perhaps a better metaphor might be "small dead tomatoes.") The project was theatrically ludicrous at the time, for sure, but it should not be allowed, historically, to taint or cloud unduly his otherwise admirable premiership.

Not too long after the stress of Sprung, Brian lamented his loss of the ruthlessness he said he needed in order to do a proper job as premier. He announced early in 1989 that he was resigning and getting out of politics.

Shortly after retiring as premier, he began what, to all appearances, has been a productive, contented life of public service and commentary, and writing, in the salubrious climate of British Columbia.

Brian Peckford was one of our very good premiers, and I'd give him as political leader a grade of 75%.

Don Jamieson

DONALD CAMPBELL JAMIESON was born in St. John's in 1921. His father's untimely death as Don was entering his teens meant that he and his mother and brothers had to struggle to survive. One summer job he got as a teenager was as a bellhop in a city hotel. Later as an adult, during the referendum campaigns, his political opponents sometimes tried to use this schoolboy gofer gig to emphasize and belittle his lowly professional background.

After working as bookkeeper or stenographer with the Commission of Government for a while, he got a job with Crosbie and Company. There, Mr. Ches soon recognized his talents and made him sales manager of their soft drinks division.

During the Second World War, he gravitated toward the entertainment of troops and producing radio broadcasts for servicemen. He was finding what would be his chief vocation in life as a radio, and later a TV, broadcaster with an impressive pipe-organ voice.

During the National Convention on Newfoundland's future, he began giving radio commentaries on the participants and issues. But soon he became an active member of the faction of the Responsible Government group that was advocating economic union with the US.

That was not surprising, since he was still an employee of Crosbie and Company and Ches Crosbie was the faction's leader. Ches himself was hopeless as a public speaker, and Don became his foremost spokesman and campaign manager. Ches's son, John Crosbie, remembered from his youth that Jamieson became known as his father's voice. The chronically overweight Don remembered, also, and once told a group of us, that Ches used to call him Donald Duck, not for his penetrating voice, as many thought, but for the way Jamieson waddled his fat arse when he walked.

Years later, instancing Jamieson's Donald Duck yarn, Joey Smallwood would describe to some of us his take on Don's personality over the years: "Don Jamieson is so great an egotist, so completely a narcissist, so utterly full of himself, that rather than not talk about himself at all, he will say something extremely negative about himself."

Others saw Don's tendency never to shy away from self-effacing humour as a captivating trait that contributed to his considerable professional, business, and federal political success.

Back at the time of the National Convention, Jamieson campaigned so fervently against Confederation during the two referendums that, when it became clear on the night of the final vote that Responsible Government with economic union had lost, he went out for an early morning walk by himself and bawled his eyes out.

He wasn't all that long drying his tears, though. A very silver lining in the cloud of defeat soon became evident and perhaps alleviated his great sorrow.

Within two years, backed by the former great Satan, Joey, now his new best friend, Don and his business partner, Geoff Stirling, were able to secure a licence from the federal government to operate a radio station in St. John's. His grief over losing to Confederation was further alleviated when, a few years later, he and Stirling were also able to receive a federal licence to launch Newfoundland's very first television station.

For years, theirs was the only source of television in the province. The station became a Canadian Broadcasting Corporation affiliate, and for some reason—some alleged Joey's political influence—the national, publicly owned CBC failed to establish its own TV station here until the mid-1960s. Whatever the reason for that convenient delay, in short order, Jamieson developed on his own channel into the best-known and most popular broadcaster in the new province.

Nationally, his talents were recognized as well, as he joined many federal organizations tied to broadcasting. In 1961, he became president of the Canadian Association of Broadcasters and travelled virtually non-stop throughout the country. During this time he became famous for his "minute-torials," his radio commentaries of sixty seconds on every conceivable subject. These were syndicated nationally.

I recall one of his minute-torials in the 1960s in which he decried the terrible state of popular music—all that awful rock 'n' roll—and praised the emergence of a contrasting, charming song recorded by Peter, Paul and Mary in 1963 called *Puff the Magic Dragon*. He wished there were more decent, innocent songs like that.

His commentary drew a howl of derision from certain, perhaps more savvy members of society: Didn't the poor old square know that the song referred to smoking dope? "Dragon" meant taking a drag on a joint, they asserted, and "puff" obviously referred to inhaling the smoke from a marijuana cigarette. Even *Newsweek* magazine had an article speculating on the song's hidden references.

The writers of the song, and its recording artists, denied that the lyrics contained any such veiled meaning. My own perusal of the words would find it a stretch to come up with any marijuana interpretation, but as late as the 1980s, a letter printed by the *New York Times* claimed that the association of the song with toking up was commonly accepted knowledge at the time.

This reaction to Jamieson was part of a more general attitude at the time among many who considered themselves sophisticated and discriminating: namely, that he was a stentorian windbag whose knowledge was a mile wide and half an inch deep.

If that characteristic was in fact true, it certainly didn't hurt him in federal politics. By 1966, Jamieson was ready to go for it. He ran in a by-election in Burin–Burgeo for the Liberal Party of Canada and was elected to the House of Commons by a huge majority. Former prime minister John Diefenbaker was reported to have remarked that Jamieson's first speech in the House was the best maiden speech he had ever heard in all his long years in the Commons.

In the 1968 general election, Don's majority was much reduced, but he still managed to be the sole Liberal elected from this province in the face of a massive anti–Trudeau Liberal vote that put six Tories in the House from here. Thereafter, he got handily re-elected to Ottawa three more times.

Prime Minister Pierre Trudeau first appointed him to significant but relatively mundane cabinet positions: Minister of Defense Production, Minister of Transport, and Minister of Regional Economic Expansion. By 1976, having proved his worth in cabinet and the House of Commons—even the Opposition praised him for actually answering their questions during question period—the PM considered him ready for a prize portfolio, Secretary of State for External Affairs.

Jamieson was a natural for the job, which required a lot of international jet-setting. And the self-confidence and chutzpah of the man was remarkable. Even dour old Leonid Brezhnev, supreme head of the Soviet Union, looked charmed on the television news when Jamieson was shown emerging from an aircraft and greeting him with an embrace that put the legendary Russian bear hug to shame.

I recall a social gathering of Newfoundland and mainland acquaintances of Jamieson at the time where the gossip centred around Don's phenomenal political ascent and his accompanying celebrity status. Many there concluded that the man had risen completely out of their own, fairly exalted, sphere. But, unfortunately, it all had to end.

The 1979 federal general election brought the Trudeau government down, and Jamieson was out of the glamorous cabinet job. But perhaps the greater misfortune, at least for the Liberal Party of Newfoundland, was that Don would find it more than a tough challenge to descend from being Canada's international star to the parochial grubbiness of provincial politics.

When Peckford called a provincial election for June of 1979, right after Clark's national PC victory, most of us thought it was a good idea, owing to the dissension in the Newfoundland Liberal Party, for me to pass the leadership to the famous and now freed-up Don Jamieson.

Initially, he did arrive back to the province like a conquering hero. But regrettably, he seemed to mistake his loud delivery of trite and obvious bromides for attractive policy planks. Those who had earlier characterized him unkindly as a shallow windbag now seemed to be proven correct, at least as far as his unfamiliarity with the provincial scene was concerned. Peckford made mincemeat of him on all important issues. Don continued to bluster, but to little avail. He even lost his voice, which some said became our only salvation in rescuing some seats.

During the election, my mind went back to our visit around 1970, as a provincial delegation led by Joey Smallwood, to Minister Jamieson in Ottawa. Our mission was to plead, hat in hand, for more financial help in aid of urgently needed municipal projects and roadwork in the province. Don, in effect, rebuffed Joey by replying that in this day of modern politics, voters were no longer impressed by politicians who promised to lay pipes in ditches to carry people's shit to the sea.

Over the course of the 1979 election campaign, he did try to show some interest in sewer pipes in ditches and such practical matters, but his heart wasn't in it, and it showed. Peckford walked away with the election.

The next year or so saw Peckford commenting that he thought Jamieson was the best Leader of the Opposition ever, because he was so agreeable and co-operative with the government. That may have been a premier's measure of a good Opposition Leader, but it certainly wasn't the view of the Opposition members. The year after the election, Jamieson gave up and saw fit to resign as Leader of the Opposition and leader of the provincial Liberal Party.

Trudeau appointed him in 1983 to one of Canada's top diplomatic posts as High Commissioner to the United Kingdom. He apparently flourished there. The media reported that he was a great favourite of Her Majesty the Queen. She was enthralled with his vast storehouse of anecdotes and amusing yarns from Newfoundland and the world.

In 1985, the new Tory prime minister, Brian Mulroney, yanked him out of Canada House in London and sent him back home to Newfoundland. The very next year, only in his mid-sixties, while jogging near his home in Swift Current, Don was felled by a heart attack and died. It was a tragedy that he went so young; judging by his memoir writing at the time of his death, he would have had another interesting career ahead of him as an author.

Don Jamieson as political leader, both provincial and federal, with his successes and failures, rates a grade of 65%.

Len Stirling

AN INSURANCE EXECUTIVE, Len Stirling came to St. John's from Corner Brook and got elected as deputy mayor of the capital city. In the late 1970s, he became president of the Liberal Party of Newfoundland and Labrador. As such, he enticed Don Jamieson back from Ottawa with the slogan "Bring Don Jamieson home for good." Brian Peckford had already called an election, and the plan was that Don would beat the newly elected PC leader.

Unfortunately, the plan backfired. Don got clobbered by Brian. Len himself was elected to the House from Bonavista North district, and when Don resigned the next year, he ran successfully for the leadership of the provincial Liberal Party.

As leader, Len was affable, but he was eclipsed by the battle between Prime Minister Pierre Trudeau and Premier Peckford over the ownership and management of the offshore oil. Peckford called an election on the issue for April 1982, and the Liberals were crushed. They won only eight seats, and Stirling was personally defeated in his own district.

Within six months he resigned as leader and went back to his profession in insurance where, by contrast, he continued to have a brilliant career. In 1999, Premier Brian Tobin would put him on the board of Newfoundland and Labrador Hydro.

As political leader, Len Stirling merits a grade of 40%.

Peter Fenwick

PETER FENWICK WAS the leader of the Newfoundland and Labrador NDP when the party produced an important breakthrough in provincial politics.

He was born in 1944 in St. Thomas, Ontario, and received an undergraduate degree from Concordia University (and later an M.A. from Memorial). He came to Newfoundland in 1968 and settled with his wife in Cape St. George, on the westerly tip of the Port au Port Peninsula. They brought up their family there, taking advantage of an early French immersion program in a local school.

I joked with him that I knew he had become a really good Newfoundlander, but did I sense a certain ambivalence from the fact that he had chosen to live about as close as he could to Canada, which was just across the Gulf? Or maybe he'd listened to Newfoundland's anti-Confederate song too much: ". . . her back to the Gulf, Come near at your peril, Canadian Wolf!" But it's a beautiful area to live in, made even more historically resonant by the memory of Bill Keough's famous line from a National Convention speech, about "the last forgotten fisherman on the bill of Cape St. George."

Fenwick's bio says he was a regional director, research director, shop steward, union negotiator, columnist, businessman, and media commentator, among other things, before and after his entry into politics.

Fenwick's first venture into federal politics in 1980 was not auspicious. He ran in Burin–St. George's as the New Democratic candidate and came a distant third to the winner, Liberal Roger Simmons. The next year, he became leader of the provincial NDP, and in the general election of 1982, he contested Humber West. He failed to win the seat, and his party brought in only 3.7% of the provincial popular vote.

But he was not easily daunted, and in 1984 he ran in the Menihek district by-election in western Labrador, far from his home region. This time he had his breakthrough win, thus becoming the very first NDP candidate to be elected to our House of Assembly.

Proving that his exceptional victory wasn't just a by-election fluke, he ran there again in the general election of 1985 and got re-elected. The party secured 14.4% of the provincial popular vote. I believe the percentage was the highest achieved by the party in its history up to then and would not be surpassed for another two and a half decades.

Meanwhile, he was an outspoken and controversial Member of the House, going so far in 1986 as to get himself arrested in solidarity with officers and members of a public service union that was on strike against the government.

Fenwick did not seek re-election in 1989 in the contest between Tom Rideout's Tories and Clyde Wells's Liberals, and he left the leadership of the party. Thereafter he established himself as a provocative article writer and TV commentator. Many people appreciated the content and style of his columns. I especially recall one in which he recounted frankly and movingly a family member's challenges with schizophrenia.

Some other readers, notably his erstwhile NDP comrades, seemed to dislike his often contrarian viewpoint. During those years, many NDP and union representatives remarked to me that he was drifting steadily to the right on the political spectrum. One union leader asked me a rhetorical question of Peter: "How do you suddenly go from the left of Lenin to the right of Attila the Hun?"

In the 2000 federal general election, he would run for the right-wing Canadian Alliance Party in Burin–St. George's riding. He got just over one tenth of the votes of the winning candidate, 1,511 compared to Liberal Bill Matthews's 14,603, and came fourth among the five people running. Ironically, he edged out the NDP candidate in the riding.

Meanwhile, he and I were political commentators together for several years on a TV panel shown weekly on CBC's *Here and Now*. Debbie Cooper was a great host, and our conversations were nice and feisty, with no holds barred, and we had a lot of "fun." Viewers seemed to especially enjoy our jugular thrusts at each other. I will say now what I wouldn't have given him the satisfaction of hearing me say then: He was one of the most knowledgeable and incisive public figures I have encountered in this province.

I frankly confess, though, that Fenwick had a superior talent for getting my goat, and perhaps vice versa, because we both seemed to spend time on camera visibly calming ourselves from each other's exasperating onslaughts. He was also impossible to shut up. I recall achieving that miracle only once.

I had made some point and he insinuated that I was only repeating the uninformed comments of my low-life callers on *Open Line*. I became overly defensive of my precious on-air contributors and responded heatedly that he was a complete hypocrite for making that negative remark: When he used to be in politics and brown-nosing for votes all the time, he hung around, trying to get on *Open Line*, like a blue-arsed shit fly.

There was a moment of silence before Debbie moved on to more edifying issues. But interestingly enough, a little later, Peter himself would agree to sit in as host of *Open Line* for several summers when I was away on vacation. He was good at it, too.

I was sad when he left the CBC panel to take up a research position with AIMS, a highly esteemed think tank. I missed our weekly slugfest.

I've been glad to hear him speaking out from time to time as the owner of the highly regarded "Inn at the Cape B&B" in Cape St. George, and as president of the Newfoundland and Labrador B&B Association, and as the no-nonsense mayor of the town and the chair of the Southwest Coast Joint Municipal Council, and as a provocative letter writer to newspapers. It's refreshing to hear him advance his stimulating, often vexing views.

For his successes and failures, I'd give Peter Fenwick a grade, as political leader, of 65%.

Leo Barry

LEO DENIS BARRY was born on Red Island, Placentia Bay, in 1943, when the community had a few hundred residents. It later resettled, but meanwhile he was growing up in the historic town of Brigus. He graduated from high school and entered Memorial University at fifteen, where he got a couple of degrees. Then he graduated near the top of his class with a law degree from Dalhousie law school and went on to Yale for a Masters in Law.

Leo and I were friends at Memorial, and we both later articled and practised briefly at the law firm of Halley, Hickman, Hunt, and Steele in St. John's before founding our own firm of Thoms, Fowler, Rowe, and Barry in the late 1960s.

Leo ran for the House of Assembly as the PC candidate in the long-time Liberal district of Placentia West in the general election of 1972 and edged past veteran Liberal incumbent Pat Canning. He became Deputy Speaker of the House but was soon appointed by Premier Moores to the cabinet as minister of Mines and Energy. There, years before actual discovery, he started developing offshore oil and gas regulations designed to maximize local benefits to the province. But his flourishing political career was dealt a body blow when, in the next provincial election, 1975, Pat Canning came back and defeated him.

Leo became chair of the provincial Labour Relations Board and then taught at Dalhousie University in Halifax. When Frank Moores announced his resignation as premier and called a PC leadership convention for the spring of 1979, Leo entered the spirited race of ten candidates. By the third ballot, all but three had been eliminated. Barry came third with 80 votes, Bill Doody took second place with 208, and Brian Peckford won with 331.

IN THE GENERAL election that Peckford called soon after, Barry ran in Mount Scio district and got re-elected to the House. Peckford appointed him to his cabinet as Mines and Energy minister, where he had the exhilarating experience of overseeing progress following the discovery of offshore oil. But the euphoria didn't last long. Within two years, following a dispute with Premier Peckford over negotiations with the federal government regarding the resource, he resigned from the cabinet.

A couple of years later, he left the Tory caucus and crossed the floor of the House to become a Liberal. In October of that same year, 1984, he was elected by a landslide as leader of the Liberal Party. When Peckford called a general election the next year, Barry was able to increase the Liberal seats from 8 to 15. There was talk that, with the developing momentum Barry's campaign had shown, if he'd had another week or so, he might have won the election.

Soon, though, the usual disgruntlement with their leader by the Liberal MHAs in Opposition, plus the party's third-place losses in a couple of by-elections, undermined Barry's position. Covert manoeuvring took place to bring perennial white knight Clyde Wells into the Liberal leadership. Early in 1987, his caucus colleagues presented him with a letter insisting on a leadership contest. He assented to a party convention and announced he'd be running. He withdrew later, however, and in June of that year, Clyde Wells was elected leader.

In 1989, Prime Minister Brian Mulroney and Minister John Crosbie had Barry appointed to the Trial Division of the Supreme Court of

Newfoundland and Labrador. In 2007, he was elevated to the Court of Appeal. Around the same time, Ottawa was considering his name for an appointment to the vacancy in the Supreme Court of Canada. But in the end, Prime Minister Harper appointed a candidate from Nova Scotia.

In the fall of 2016, the Liberal government of Premier Dwight Ball and Justice minister Andrew Parsons gave Justice Barry a mandate to hold a commission of inquiry into the death of Donald Dunphy, a man who'd been shot in his home by a Royal Newfoundland Constabulary police officer.

In his report, delivered in June 2017, Barry ruled that Constable Joe Smyth "demonstrated certain errors of judgment and non-compliance with aspects of his training but responded with appropriate force when Mr. Dunphy with no warning threatened him with a rifle." Barry also concluded that the Royal Canadian Mounted Police were correct not to charge Smyth but that their investigation into the shooting contained defects and was "less than robust." He made a number of recommendations designed to prevent such tragedies in the future.

Based on his successes as MHA, minister, and Opposition Leader, and the progressive policies he most likely would have implemented as premier, but deducting his failure to realize that objective, I'd give Leo Barry a grade of 65%.

Tom Rideout

THOMAS GERALD RIDEOUT was born in Fleur de Lys in 1948. He was interested in politics from an early age. When I first met him as a young teenager in the early 1960s on the Baie Verte Peninsula, he told me he was going to be premier. But first he became a teacher in Baie Verte before entering elective politics.

In the early 1970s, Tom was my campaign manager in a couple of successful elections in White Bay South. Then he got elected to the House of Assembly as a Liberal himself from the district of Baie Verte–White Bay in the provincial election of 1975 and served as a bright star in the Opposition.

He was about to cross the floor and join new premier Brian Peckford's PC caucus before the election of 1979 but stopped in his tracks when Don Jamieson came back from Ottawa to lead the Liberal Party. Like nearly everyone else in the party, he thought Jamieson was going to lead the Liberals to victory.

After Peckford beat Jamieson, though, Rideout did move over with the Tories the next year. He claimed he was motivated by Peckford's strong stand against the new Trudeau Liberal government on ownership and control of the offshore resources.

Tom became Peckford's parliamentary assistant before being appointed minister of Culture, Recreation and Youth, and then minister of Fisheries in 1985. When Peckford retired as premier in 1989, Rideout ran for the Tory party leadership against four other candidates, cabinet ministers Len Simms, Neil Windsor, Loyola Hearn, and Hal Barrett. Some of them were leading lights in the government.

On the third ballot, he beat Len Simms 403 votes to 377, and very shortly after being sworn in as premier, he called a provincial election. The results on voting day proved to be peculiar.

In spite of the PC Party languishing under a dark cloud from the Sprung greenhouse boondoggle, and in spite of Clyde Wells having been touted for years as the saviour of the provincial Liberal Party, not to mention of the province itself, Rideout led the PCs to a slightly higher percentage of votes than Wells's Liberals received.

The PCs got 47.6% of the popular vote and the Liberals 47.2%. But the way the votes were distributed determined that the Liberal candidates won 31 seats in the House to only 21 for the PCs. Wells formed the government and Rideout became Leader of the Opposition.

He had been premier for forty-four days.

IN 1991, TOM left as Leader of the Opposition for an appointment to a federal board. When his term of office ran out there, he tried to get elected as a PC in Gander–Grand Falls riding in the federal election of 1993. But he was routed by the popular Liberal incumbent, now senator, George Baker.

After receiving a law degree from the University of Ottawa, he got elected to the provincial House again in 1999 as a PC in Lewisporte district, and later in the district of Baie Verte–Springdale. When Danny Williams won his election in 2003 and formed a new PC government, he appointed Rideout to several positions, including minister of Fisheries, government house leader, and deputy premier.

In 2008, though, after a spat with Premier Williams over some roadwork in his district, Rideout resigned from all his portfolios and the cabinet. A month later, he left the House as MHA, too, and got out of politics altogether.

Taking into account the pluses of his political career, but deducting his unfortunate handling of his political future once he possessed the premiership, Tom Rideout as political leader merits a grade of 55%.

Clyde Wells

CLYDE KIRBY WELLS was born in 1937, in Buchans Junction, and received his schooling there and in Stephenville Crossing. As an adult, Clyde seemed to be a good example of a person who had grown up in a small place where everybody regarded him as the smartest kid in town: It seemed to give him a sense of self-awareness for the rest of his life that he was always the smartest guy in the room and knew better than everyone else.

Whether Clyde in fact felt like that or not, he certainly acted like it a lot of the time. And perhaps the feeling was warranted: A leading educator once told me that, statistically, a child who attended a one-room school in Newfoundland, as Clyde did, had one chance in about 900 of graduating with his grade eleven. So, indeed, he must have been pretty smart.

Wells got an undergraduate degree from Memorial in political science in 1959 and his law degree from Dalhousie three years later.

Joey appointed him, without a seat in the House, to his cabinet in the summer of 1966 and got him elected in the district of Humber East in that fall's general election. Predictably, though, Clyde and John Crosbie found it impossible to serve under Smallwood or to cope with his shenanigans regarding the Shaheen oil refinery at Come By Chance. He joined Crosbie in resigning from the cabinet less than two years later.

By 1971, Wells had helped John Crosbie eviscerate Joey in the House. But then, to the great disappointment of the swelling numbers of Newfoundlanders who wanted Joey out of government after twenty-three years as premier, Wells quit politics to concentrate entirely on his law practice.

When René Lévesque's Parti Québécois was elected to government in Quebec in 1976, widespread consternation reigned across the nation as he continued to advocate, now from a position of power, the separation of his province from Canada. The Canadian Bar Association, encompassing tens of thousands of lawyers, had a high-powered constitution committee which was asked to recommend how, in these new circumstances, the Canadian constitution should be revamped. Clyde Wells's prestige as a legal practitioner was such that they invited him to join the team.

The committee made radical recommendations for a brand new constitution; some elements of their proposals, involving language and legal rights, were actually implemented later. By most accounts, Wells did himself proud on the committee and became well versed in constitutional matters. Not everyone was impressed in a positive sense, though. One of his colleagues on the committee was an actual constitutional expert, and future premier of PEI, Joe Ghiz, who had a graduate degree in the subject from Harvard University. He would claim later, during the Meech Lake crisis in the early 1990s, that Wells had been a prick on the committee back then, and he was a prick now.

In 1987, after an absence more than fifteen years, Wells returned to active politics. His well-honed sense of personal opportunity had detected that the end was nigh for the Tory regime under Brian Peckford and that the position of Leo Barry, then leader of the Liberal Party, was fragile within the caucus.

Wells got elected as provincial Liberal leader, entered the House in the by-election that was opened for him, and became Leader of the Opposition. He told me later that he didn't like being Leader of the Opposition very much. After he'd become premier, I asked him how he liked the new job. He sort of condemned it with faint praise: "It's a hell of a lot better than being Leader of the Opposition." Yet while he was heading up the Opposition, he did seem to be in his element again, savaging the government.

When Peckford defended Newfoundland's right to a hydroponic greenhouse, despite the defeatist naysayers in the Opposition who claimed we had too harsh and inhospitable a climate for it, Wells put one of the last nails in his political coffin. He stated that it was possible to build a Sprung greenhouse on the back side of the moon . . . "if you're prepared to spend the money!" And that was not far from how a lot of Newfoundlanders thought Peckford was spending their money.

Two years later, in April 1989, Clyde led the Liberals into a general election. His party came out with a solid majority of seats but a slightly smaller popular vote than the PCs. Despite all the negatives afflicting the PC government inherited by Tom Rideout, voters still seemed to find it a strain to choose Clyde for premier rather than him.

Some observers attributed the Liberal victory to a fake poll the party put out shortly before election day, showing them a little ahead and creating just enough of a bandwagon effect to win. Others said that, as usual, Clyde was just lucky. But if so, his luck wasn't all good.

Because, amazingly enough, he lost his election, personally, in his own home district of Humber East. Again, opinions on the cause were divided. One school of thought opined that he was known too well there, and the better you got to know Clyde the less likely you were to vote for him. The other school believed his personal defeat could be attributed to his running against star PC Member and minister Lynn Verge, who was extremely popular and highly regarded throughout the province, and especially in her hometown of Corner Brook.

Wells may have ended up on the outside of the House himself, but he was still the leader of the party that had succeeded in terminating more than a decade and a half of Moores-Peckford-Rideout Tory rule. A man who'd led in that achievement had to be put in the legislature.

To get him there, stalwart Liberal MHA Eddie Joyce, who'd had no trouble being elected handily in his Bay of Islands district, stepped down to create a by-election. Liberals held their breath as Wells became their candidate. Fortunately all worked out well: With no competition this time, he was elected by acclamation.

Clyde Wells's perceived lack of personal popularity would never again be an issue in the politics of the province. Just over a year after his election, he would make himself famous across Canada, and extremely popular, at least outside Quebec. It was based on his stand against the Meech Lake Accord. This pact contained a number of constitutional changes which had been agreed to by Prime Minister Mulroney and every premier in the country in order to bring Quebec more happily into the Canadian family.

In the House of Assembly, Wells used his majority to rescind the Meech Lake Accord, which Brian Peckford and the PCs had already ratified there. Then he went to Ottawa to take part in the marathon first ministers' meeting called by Prime Minister Mulroney. For days on end, he stood alone, at first against most, and at last against all, of the other first ministers in Canada. As a result, he became so popular in every province, except Quebec, that polls showed he could probably be elected prime minister without needing to win one seat in that province. But even Wells himself would decry the expressions of prejudice against Quebec in many messages of support he received from the rest of Canada and claimed he wanted to distance himself from them.

Ultimately, Wells came back from Ottawa promising a vote on the Meech Lake Accord in the Newfoundland House of Assembly. That debate was in fact ongoing here when indigenous Canadian Elijah Harper, a Member of the Manitoba Legislative Assembly, prevented unanimous consent there for a vote to take place.

As a result, Wells stopped the debate in his own House of Assembly. His rationale was that the Accord was already a dead issue anyway because of Manitoba's failure to ratify it, and, since it was very likely going to be defeated by the MHAs here, he wanted to spare Newfoundland and Labrador the criticism. A commentator called that a messiah complex, because, as a result of his reneging on his commitment to hold a vote, Clyde certainly drew all the criticism onto himself.

A few years later, in 1995, the separatist cause in Quebec came within a hair's breadth of winning a referendum to leave Canada. Many Meech Lake supporters maintained that separatism had received a tremendous boost from the failure of their Accord, for which they blamed Clyde Wells. But by then, Clyde could not be reached. He was out of politics and safe and secure on the bench of the Supreme Court of Newfoundland.

Meanwhile, back in his days as premier, Wells took, or tried to take, a number of actions that he seemed to believe were positive steps for the province.

He brought in an unbelievably convoluted set of "reforms" to Newfoundland's denominational education system. Though unworkable, the initiative still became contentious, failed a court challenge, and died aborning.

He also crossed the t's on an offshore oil deal negotiated by Peckford, which he stated he would not have implemented if it were not already a done deal. Years later, however, it was noticed that he did not hesitate to take credit for the flourishing offshore oil industry here.

One highly regarded initiative was his government's development and release of a document called *Change and Challenge: A Strategic Economic Plan for Newfoundland and Labrador*. In making it public, Premier Wells stated that the plan would determine the focus and direction of the province's future economic development activity.

Another praiseworthy proposal was announced in the Throne Speech of 1993. There, Wells disclosed the government's intention to develop a Strategic Social Plan for the province. A committee of senior government officials was to put together a comprehensive document, and a public consultation process would take place. The plan would pay attention to income security reform, the fields of education and health, and other important social policy domains. It would not reach completion until after Wells had left office.

While premier as well, he closed down or sold many publicly owned provincial parks and shut down the ombudsman's office. He also tried to sell the publicly owned Newfoundland and Labrador Hydro Corporation. Having stated definitively in so many words that he intended to see that sale through come hell or high water, public pressure made him reverse himself, and he failed ignominiously in the attempt.

Thus Clyde was not very successful in many of his "positive" initiatives. What he was extraordinarily good at, though, was saying "no!" By exercising that formidable talent, displayed to such advantage during the debate on the Meech Lake Accord, he managed to balance the provincial budget in spite of recessionary conditions in our economy. That was a tremendous achievement, but it, too, like the education reform and Hydro sale flops, was executed in a way that also became a humiliating experience.

To help achieve his balanced budget, he cancelled collective agreements already negotiated with the government by public service unions in good faith. Accordingly, he had to endure a vociferous campaign by members of those unions, complete with placards, buttons, T-shirts, and loud shouting, all proclaiming that "Clyde Lied." For a man who wore his self-righteousness on his sleeve, it had to be a devastating experience.

Wells retired as premier in favour of Brian Tobin in January 1996 and went back to practising law. But not for long. In a couple of years, Prime Minister Jean Chrétien, who, with his mentor, Pierre Trudeau, had encouraged Wells's contrary position on the Meech Lake accord, appointed him as a judge of the Newfoundland Court of Appeal, and the next year as chief justice of the province. One reader of my book *No Punches Pulled: The Premiers Peckford, Wells, and Tobin* summed up my description of Wells's career astutely: He never made a false move when it came to his own personal advancement.

Upon retiring from the bench, he has undertaken a number of commissions and studies and other gigs on behalf of provincial and municipal governments. At one point he indicated to an official at St. John's City Hall that he would generously lower his hourly rate from $500 an hour to $300 to do some work for them. This attempt to project an image of self-sacrifice, apparently, from a highly successful man drawing down healthy pensions from his years as minister, premier, and Supreme Court judge, not to mention years operating a lucrative law practice, caused immoderate fits of laughter and head-shaking disbelief among many lawyers and politicos I talked to. One suggested, "Someone should introduce Clyde to the well-known concept of a prosperous retiree offering himself as a dollar-a-year man for the public good and see how he responds. But don't hold your breath!"

It's a wonder to me and to others that Clyde Wells was not a more productive premier. It's a bizarre peculiarity, because he was often brilliant in presenting his cases in court and in the House and other forums. And he had some excellent people around him as premier, including his chief of staff and senior policy adviser, Edsel Bonnell, and his communications director, Judy Foote.

Ed Bonnell had nothing short of a fabulous career in journalism, and media commentary, and as a professional public relations consultant before going with Wells. During his career he received numerous honours, including half a dozen national awards of excellence from the Canadian Public Relations Society. He founded the Gower Youth Band way back in 1973, which, under him as conductor and musical director, has been celebrated ever since. For his many contributions to the public weal he would receive the Order of Canada and an honorary doctor of laws from Memorial University.

Judy Foote, after serving as Wells's communications director, got elected to the House of Assembly and became an esteemed provincial minister for years. Later, she ran for the House of Commons and grew into, under Justin Trudeau, one of the most highly regarded ministers in the Canadian cabinet.

With a couple of powerhouses like them around him, I'd have thought Wells would have accomplished a few more positive deeds. Then someone pointed out to me that there was someone else lurking about the backrooms of Wells's office during his entire premiership by the name of Ed Hollett. He was described to me latterly as a self-glorified Internet troll.

Based on his scribblings on the Internet, he has been as negative in his policy views and criticisms as Wells ever was, but with this added obnoxious trait: Habitually he has snuck out from under his rock on the Internet to squirt his poison at his targeted people personally, and then scurried back to his hidey-hole again until the next piece of mean viciousness occurs to him.

Eddie Hollett has always taken great pride in constantly referring to his association with Premier Wells. He has called himself "special assistant" to Wells. And he was in that "special" position from the time Wells became premier in 1989 until he was let go when Brian Tobin became premier in 1996.

I have only a couple of hazy memories of seeing him skulking about the premier's office whenever I was there during that period—a mousy little fellow not physically constituted to draw very much favourable attention to himself. I could readily perceive why he would be compelled to overachieve in his attacks.

His troll's lair on the Internet is some sort of a blog. It contains mostly long and boring stuff compared to, say, Uncle Gnarly's pieces written by Des Sullivan, which are cogent, to the point, and eminently readable. Hollett also uses his blog to tout his availability to speak. In other words, he uses his own blog to advertise himself for money. You can book him as a speaker, apparently, although he doesn't say how much he charges. But if he has tried to live by his speaking fees in the past, that would no doubt account for his half-starved look in his bio snapshot.

Bob Wakeham, in his must-read column every Saturday in the *Telegram*, has referred to Ed Hollett, accurately, as a former flak for Clyde Wells. He stated that Hollett is a partisan animal, a Liberal stalwart through and through, growling constantly that the Tories are doing absolutely nothing right in his myopic world.

The Atlantic Institute for Market Studies (AIMS), a right-wing think tank based in Halifax, has taken him on as something they call "senior fellow." If Hollett is their senior fellow, I thought when I saw the appointment, I'd hate to have to read their *junior* fellow's blitherings.

When I saw two or three letters Hollett wrote to the St. John's

Telegram in the spring of 2017, on behalf of AIMS, everything about him and Clyde Wells became clear. First, I should warn anyone brave enough to try to read the muck he has been sending in that it is long, meandering, convoluted, and incredibly boring. By coincidence, in one edition of the *Telegram,* there was a letter by Hollett and a letter by Peter Fenwick. They dealt with much the same subject, the provincial budget, and the contrast between them could not have been more stark.

Whether you agreed with its contents or not, Peter's letter was short, punchy, to the point, and readable. Eddie's was long and tedious and dreary and full of wishy-washy insights into the absolutely obvious: "The provincial government spends more money than it collects in taxes and other income . . ." Gosh, what a shock to learn that! "Revenues will indeed rise as the economy grows . . ." Really? The man is a groundbreaking economist! "The pressure on elected officials will only grow as the election draws nearer . . ." Good Lord, the stunning revelation! Who knew?

I did receive an insight, though, into how and why Clyde Wells got himself into such a calamity with his attempt to sell off Newfoundland and Labrador Hydro. It came to me as I read Eddie Hollett's plea on behalf of AIMS to "reconsider the use of the public sector in service delivery." In other words, sell public services to the private sector so that they can make a profit delivering important services to the people.

That suggestion is of a piece with his disrespect and obvious contempt for ordinary citizens of the land. For example, he referred to *Open Line*, which I happened to have hosted, as a "radio forum for any kook in the province with a phone." With an adviser like that, it was little wonder that Clyde found it difficult to connect on a human level with normal mortals.

I couldn't help contrasting Hollett with some of the advisers and assistants other leaders have had the privilege of receiving help from over the years. Just randomly, off the top of my head, and in no particular order, and leaving out many, I could think of Jim Channing, Ed Roberts, Vic Young, Rollie Martin, Debbie Fry, Dave Vardy, Fonse Faour, Malcolm Rowe, Ron Penney, Beth Marshall, Brian Crawley, Elizabeth Matthews, Des Sullivan, Doug House, Rex Murphy . . . the list goes on.

They advised at different levels and were recognized as highly successful in many other professional areas of life.

When I realize that, as premier, Wells was hobnobbing with that unconstructive, off-putting personality of Ed Hollett day in and day out, many of his less commendable actions start to become very clear. But, of course, Clyde has to take full responsibility in history as an out-front premier for his failures and for whom he appointed, including his know-it-all "special assistant," who never put himself forward for election to anything by the public, and who was never elected as so much as dog catcher.

I'd give Clyde Wells as political leader, based largely on his early career in courageously and effectively taking on Joey Smallwood, rather than on much of what his did as premier, a rating of 60%.

Len Simms

LEONARD ARCHIBALD SIMMS was born in Howley, Newfoundland, in 1943. I knew his brother Wes Simms well. He was a big Liberal when I was in politics, and he owned and operated the Simwestco Motel in Grand Falls. Its rooms and coffee shop were favourite stopoff places for those of us who were on the road, politicking.

I only knew Len by reputation, particularly as a past national president of Kinsmen Clubs of Canada, and I didn't know what his political persuasion was. But I recall wondering, when he ran for the Tories in 1979, how we in the Liberal Party managed to lose a man of his reputation to the other side. He got elected in Grand Falls–Windsor–Buchans and remained the MHA there till 1995.

Meanwhile, upon his election to the House in 1979, he became Speaker. I was an MHA myself at the time, and I recall that he ran the legislature in an unruffled and gentlemanly manner. I also recall that he possessed a high degree of non-partisan compassion.

A widow of my acquaintance, a well-known Liberal, was unemployed because of her bad health. She contacted me about her daughter's future. The girl was an intelligent aspiring student, but she was going to have to disrupt her academic prospects because of lack of money.

Her mother thought that, if only her daughter could be appointed as one of the pages in the House, the income from that part-time and flexible work would allow her to carry on with her studies. Who appointed pages in the House? she wondered. I told her I figured the Speaker was the main guy. Her face assumed a look of futile resignation. The Speaker was a top Tory.

I went over to Len Simms's office with no great hopes. I explained the situation and divulged the mother's lifelong Liberal activities. Len listened courteously with a poker face and told me that there was nothing stopping the daughter from applying for the position like anyone else. That sounded rather pro forma, and I left thinking, well, at least he was gentleman enough not to burst out laughing.

I passed on his advice. And a few days later, I watched the bright young woman hustling efficiently around the House of Assembly, tending to the MHAs' official needs. You only had to see her performing her tasks to know that, quite obviously, she'd been hired on her own merits. But equally obviously, Len had not allowed partisanship to act as any impediment whatsoever to her successful application.

In 1982, Premier Peckford appointed Simms to the cabinet, where he would serve as minister of Culture, Recreation and Youth, as minister of Forest Resources and Lands, as president of the Treasury Board, and as president of the Executive Council.

Upon Peckford's retirement in 1989, Simms ran for the leadership of the Progressive Conservative Party, as described in the piece on Tom Rideout. Tom beat Len by only 26 votes. In the general election just a few weeks later, the extremely close popular vote between the Liberals and the PCs that put Wells in power had some PCs muttering that they would probably have won the election with Len Simms as leader.

When Rideout resigned as leader in 1991, the PC Party called a leadership convention, and Simms announced his candidacy. No one else ran against him, maybe because the premiership was not up for grabs this time. He was acclaimed party leader and became Leader of the Opposition in the House of Assembly.

Simms led the PCs into the general election of 1993 called by Clyde Wells, now in his highly popular, post-Meech Lake phase. Wells further polarized the electorate by adding into the mix a big question: Who was going to run the province, the public service unions or the government elected by the people?

The PCs lost, polling worse than they had four years earlier both in popular vote and seats won. The difference in popular vote was not enormous. The Liberals under Wells got less than half, registering 49%. Simms's PCs polled 42%. But the PC Party came back with only 16 seats, 5 less than in 1989. The Liberals won in 35 districts, and Jack Harris won a seat for the NDP.

Simms hung on as leader for a couple more years and resigned from elective politics in 1995.

In 2005, Premier Danny Williams appointed Simms as chair and CEO of the Newfoundland and Labrador Housing Corporation. But two years later he resigned to help manage Williams's campaign in the 2007 general election. Upon the re-election of the Williams government, the premier put him back as head of the Housing Corporation.

The Opposition, such as they were—the Liberals had won only 3 seats, and the NDP 1—howled that Simms's reappointment was flagrant corruption and patronage. But Premier Williams must have been more impressed by Simms's skill in helping him win 44 out of 48 seats and nearly 70% of the popular vote.

I've given Len Simms as political leader, based on the sterling character he would have exhibited as premier, but which he didn't achieve, perhaps because of his too low-keyed efforts, a grade of 50%.

Lynn Verge

LYNN (FISHER) VERGE was born in Corner Brook in 1951 and went to school there. Apart from her own merits, her family name resonated in the area because she was the great-granddaughter of Christopher Fisher, the man considered by many to have been the city's founder.

She graduated in economics and political science from Memorial and got her law degree from Dalhousie in 1973. She articled with Clyde Wells's law firm but went elsewhere to practise law for the next six year after being told there was no future for her with that firm because, being a woman, she might have babies.

Then in 1979, at the age of twenty-eight, she ran for Brian Peckford's Tories in Humber East and got elected to the House of Assembly. Peckford appointed her to his cabinet as minister of Education. She thereby became one of the first two women in history, along with MHA Hazel Newhook, to become cabinet ministers in Newfoundland and Labrador. As Education minister, she introduced much greater Newfoundland and Labrador content in the curriculum of the schools and added grade twelve to the high school program. She also initiated improvements to programs in the schools for children with disabilities.

In 1979–1980, Verge spearheaded a new Matrimonial Property Act to accord greater equality to women regarding marital property rights, and she was designated the minister responsible for piloting it through the House of Assembly.

Peckford appointed her minister of Justice and Attorney General in 1985, and she made advances in child support and maintenance and improved the structure of the courts.

When Tom Rideout became premier, he appointed her deputy premier, and during the few weeks they retained the government, they began the process of appointing the Hughes Inquiry into the Mount Cashel Orphanage child abuse scandal.

In the 1989 general election, Rideout's PCs lost the election and the government, but Lynn Verge defeated Liberal leader Clyde Wells in Humber East, forcing him to seek election to the House in a by-election. Someone said on *Open Line*, "It would make you believe in karma."

In Opposition, she was a constant thorn in Wells's side, including, notably, arguing against Wells's plan to privatize Newfoundland Hydro, and helping to prevent the sale.

In 1995, Verge ran for the leadership of the provincial Progressive Conservative Party. Future premier Kathy Dunderdale was co-chair of her campaign. It turned into a rather vigorous battle between Verge and Loyola Sullivan and was perceived by some as a purely "man versus woman" contest. At the convention she beat Sullivan by 3 votes to become leader. She became the first woman to be elected leader of a Newfoundland political party and the first to be named leader of the official Opposition.

Early the next year, Clyde Wells resigned as leader of the Liberal Party. Some malicious tongues whispered that he could not bear the thought of being defeated yet again by Lynn Verge if he led his party against her in the next provincial election. Brian Tobin took over from Wells as Liberal leader and premier and immediately called a provincial election for February 22, 1996.

By now, Tobin was one of the best-known and most popular politicians in Canada, let alone Newfoundland and Labrador, and he went on to win a huge majority of districts for the Liberals. Although the Progressive Conservatives won only 9 seats in the House of Assembly, it was a credit to Verge's strength of leadership and popularity that her party was able to take 39% of the popular vote against the Tobin juggernaut. Regrettably, Verge lost in her own district by a handful of votes and later resigned as leader of the party.

Not long after, the Alumni Association of Memorial University made her Alumna of the Year, and the university later awarded her an honorary doctor of laws degree.

For breaking new ground, and for her many successes, as well as her disappointments, Lynn Verge rates 65% as political leader.

Cle Newhook

CLEOPHAS NEWHOOK WAS born in 1943 and studied theology at Oxford University in England. After that he worked for several years as an Anglican priest in inner-city slums in the UK, where he headed up education and development programs and was very much a social activist there.

Back home in Newfoundland, in 1986 Cle Newhook became full-time executive secretary of the Newfoundland and Labrador New Democratic Party for a couple of years. Then in March of 1989, the NDP held a leadership convention to replace Peter Fenwick, and Newhook ran against MHA Gene Long. He won by 21 votes.

Almost immediately, new premier Tom Rideout called a provincial general election. Caught in the clash between the Liberals under Clyde Wells and the Tories under Rideout, the NDP dropped from its 14.4% in the 1985 election to 4.4% in this one, and they lost their 2 seats.

But the next year, there was a rebound. Under Newhook's leadership of the party, Jack Harris ran in the St. John's East by-election and won. But, not long after, when Cle ran in the Trinity North by-election in 1991, he wasn't so successful. He did put up a good fight, though, coming second to the Liberal candidate and attracting over 29% of the votes. The next year, he ran in another by-election, this time in Ferryland district, but he came third. Soon after that, his fifth attempt to get elected, he decided to resign as leader of the NDP, and Jack Harris, with his seat in the House, took over.

Cle has made substantial contributions to the well-being of whatever cause he's been associated with. Some examples:

Back in the early 1980s, after the *Ocean Ranger* oil rig disaster, in which eighty-four men perished, he became the director of the Ocean Ranger Families Foundation. That organization was set up to assist families of the victims with counselling and financial aid and to sit in on hearings. It also advocated for better safety offshore. The foundation's chair was Lorraine Michael, who would herself become NDP leader over twenty years later.

When the NDP held a federal leadership convention in 1989 in Winnipeg, there were at least seven candidates. The perceived front-runners were former BC premier Dave Barrett and MP Audrey McLaughlin. Cle supported McLaughlin. The race was fairly close through the first three ballots, with only a couple of percentage points separating Audrey from Dave on the second, until McLaughlin finally won with 55% on the fourth ballot. She became the first woman in Canada, with Cle's help, to head a major federal party.

In the summer of 2014, Newhook, who was then president of the Newfoundland Pony Society, undertook the complicated process of bringing back to Newfoundland some twenty ponies that were stranded and in dire straits well over 4,000 kilometres away, in British Columbia.

Cle Newhook, as a political leader, receives a ranking of 45%.

Ed Byrne

ED BYRNE WAS born in 1963. His university education was at Memorial, where he picked up undergraduate degrees in arts and education. While there he was elected president of the council of the students' union.

He entered a career in adult education, and administration, and as a management consultant. He married a daughter of former PC leader and cabinet minister Gerry Ottenheimer, who had been elevated to the Senate of Canada.

In the provincial general election of 1993, Ed got elected to the House of Assembly from Kilbride district and was re-elected there in 1996, 1999, and 2003.

In 1998, he ran for the leadership of the PC Party. Loyola Sullivan was serving as interim leader at the time, having taken over from Lynn Verge, who had lost her seat by a few votes in the 1996 election. With Brian Tobin as the popular Liberal premier, the Tories seemed to be demoralized in 1998, and nobody else would run for the leadership against Byrne. He took the position by acclamation, although the word "acclamation" may give a distorted impression of his reception.

I saw him on a television news clip right after the convention as he entered the Opposition offices in Confederation Building, and the place looked and sounded like a morgue, with little if any "acclaim" or even best wishes from the MHAs. I don't recall many MHAs emerging from offices to greet him. Of course, there were only nine of them to draw on at the time.

That soon changed. Byrne led the party into the 1999 general election against the Brian Tobin Liberals and the NDP under Jack Harris. Toward the end of the campaign I asked Tobin—Captain Canada—during a commercial break on *Open Line* if he was going to win every seat. I was only half joking. He replied that he'd be lucky to win the election. And he too looked like he was only half joking. The nurses' union under Debbie Forward was giving him grief: demonstrating, rallying, protesting the government's inadequate wage offer, and dogging him wherever he went in the province.

On election day, Byrne came back with 14 victories, a gain of 5 seats from the last election. Harris's NDP gained a seat for a total of 2, and Tobin's Liberals dropped from 37 seats to 32. That number would easily enough form a substantial majority government in the 48-Member House, but it was a sobering result nevertheless: There was a difference of less than 9% in the popular vote between the Liberals and the PCs.

Tobin was soon gone as premier. He resigned abruptly in October 2000 to join Chrétien's government in Ottawa as minister of a top portfolio, Industry, and to run in the federal riding of Bonavista–Trinity–Conception.

Leading up to that 1999 election and afterwards, Ed Byrne never got the credit he deserved as an effective leader who improved the prospects of the PCs. Then, in 2001, he "voluntarily" resigned as leader to allow Danny Williams to waltz into the position. Byrne had been acclaimed as leader of the party in 1998 because, at that time, no one else wanted the thankless job. Danny Williams was acclaimed as leader in 2001 because, although the future of the party now looked bright for anyone who wanted to be premier, no one else dared to take on the celebrity lawyer and magnate.

Upon leading the Tories to majority government in 2003, Premier

Williams appointed Byrne as government house leader and minister of Natural Resources. He was generally regarded as the number-two man in the government.

After Premier Williams invited me to go to Ottawa as his representative there, I asked one of his advisers about the perceived strengths and weaknesses of the provincial cabinet ministers. When we came to Ed Byrne, the adviser grimaced and made the gesture of bringing a half-clenched hand like a glass up to his mouth as if he were taking a drink. Byrne had been convicted of impaired driving back in 1991. And in 2009, he would plead guilty to failing the Breathalyzer after blowing three times over the legal limit.

In between, on June 21, 2006, in a news release issued at 6:15 in the evening, Premier Williams announced that he had asked Minister of Natural Resources Ed Byrne to resign from the cabinet, effective immediately. Williams had taken the action as a result of an examination by the Auditor General's department and conveyed to the Speaker, in which concerns were raised over the financial records of the House of Assembly. On the advice of the Auditor General, Premier Williams referred the matter to the Department of Justice.

Lack of public transparency and accountability regarding the financial operations of the House had opened the way for corruption among some MHAs. A body called the Internal Economy Commission was, by law, supposed to govern all matters of financial and administrative policy affecting the House of Assembly, its offices, and staff. The commission consisted of the Speaker and some MHAs from both sides of the House.

In 2000, under a Liberal majority in the House, this commission had banned the Auditor General from having access to the accounts of the House. The phony reason the commission gave was that it was inappropriate for the Auditor General, a servant of the House, to audit the accounts of his or her employer. Evidently, that specious claptrap led some MHAs and staff to go wild at the money trough, before new premier Danny Williams overturned the decision in 2004 and forced the commission to invite the AG back to audit the accounts of the House.

The day after Byrne's forced resignation from cabinet, the Auditor General, John Noseworthy, made public his report on Byrne's constituency allowance claims for the fiscal years 2003 and 2004. Byrne had been entitled to about $31,000 during those years, but he had in fact claimed over $300,000 more than that. Further probing by the Auditor General indicated that Byrne had received well over $400,000 more than he was entitled to.

Other MHAs were also implicated, including a Liberal Member, a New Democrat Member, and a former Liberal Member. A senior member of the staff, Finance Director Bill Murray, the alleged enabler of the frauds, was suspended. Following criminal investigations by the Royal Newfoundland Constabulary, the four MHAs and the public servant were charged under the Criminal Code. In November 2006, Byrne announced his resignation from the House as of January 1, 2007.

In 2009, he was convicted in provincial court after pleading guilty to the fraud charges. On sentencing, the judge cited the aggravating factors—that the fraud and bribery were committed by a person in a high position of public trust—but the judge also noted a couple of mitigating elements. Byrne's marriage had fallen apart as a result of the scandal, and he would effectively be barred forever from employment in the public service anywhere in Canada. He was sentenced to two years less a day. The judge also ordered him to repay over $100,000. The government has sued him for the remainder deemed by the Auditor General to be due and owing.

Four and a half months after starting his nearly twenty-four-month sentence at a minimum-security facility, Byrne was released wearing an electronic monitoring device around his ankle.

It was a sad case, and made more poignant by the fact that Byrne had been such a good district man and continued to enjoy the support of some loyal former constituents. One of them, incensed by my frequent mention of the case on *Open Line* when it was a big story on the news, complained to the Law Society that as a lawyer I should be stopped from criticizing Mr. Byrne. The Law Society dismissed the complaint out of hand as groundless, of course, but it caused me a pang over the fact that many good people were heartbroken over his fall.

As a political leader, Ed Byrne merits a grade of 25%.

Brian Tobin

BRIAN VINCENT TOBIN was born in 1954 in Stephenville and grew up there and in Happy Valley–Goose Bay. He went to Memorial University for a time but did not graduate. Instead he worked in radio, and in television news for a short while in the late 1970s before he applied to become my executive assistant when I was Leader of the Opposition. He got the job and quickly demonstrated that, in his early twenties, he was already an extraordinary political creature.

In the 1980 federal general election, because no one else wanted the candidacy, he ran as cannon fodder for the Liberals in Humber–Port au Port–St. Barbe, He was up against the popular incumbent MP, New Democrat Fonse Faour. A well-known PC candidate was also running in the riding which, for years before Faour's election, had been a stronghold of the Tory party. In his mid-twenties, and against all odds, Tobin got elected there to the House of Commons.

After the short interval of PC power under Joe Clark, that 1980 election had put Trudeau and the Liberals back in the saddle. But the initial euphoria of victory soon wore thin. Brian Tobin now had to endure four long years in the dull and tedious government backbenches.

Like his seatmates in those remote reaches of the House, he was mostly irrelevant to Trudeau and the government as long as he voted properly. As Canada's leader, PET was focused almost exclusively on leaving a constitutional legacy and adding to the lustre of his international name during this, his last prime ministerial kick at the can.

Tobin was able to get re-elected in 1984 in spite of the Progressive Conservative Party's landslide victory under new leader Brian Mulroney. Now in the Opposition, with the Liberal ranks in the House drastically depleted, Brian came into his own. He swiftly developed into a leading member of the notorious "Rat Pack." This was a cluster of young, brazen-faced, Grit MPs who gained notoriety for their daily vilification and abuse of the Tory PM and ministers across the House.

The press gallery seemed to express little but contempt for them. But in the process of making the ministers' lives miserable day after day from the low blows they delivered, the Rat Pack probably saved the Liberal Party from extinction.

TOBIN WAS STAUNCHLY in favour of the Meech Lake Accord and keenly against Clyde Wells's position on it. But even though Chrétien was right behind Wells in that constitutional battle, wherein the Meech Lake agreement was wrecked, Tobin played a large role, immediately afterwards, in getting Chrétien elected as national Liberal leader. Brian was nothing if not a flexible pragmatist.

In the 1993 federal general election, the Liberals under leader Jean Chrétien dealt the PC Party a trouncing from which they never recovered. And Brian Tobin's time had come at last. Now, after a decade and a half of, first, suffering the weary ennui of the government backbenches, and, next, navigating the sometimes entertaining but ultimately empty wasteland of Opposition, he found himself front and centre in the new Liberal government. Chrétien appointed him minister of Fisheries and Oceans, a controversial portfolio still struggling with the recent devastation of the northern cod stocks and the shutdown of the entire Newfoundland and Labrador cod fish industry. To some, the portfolio looked like the kiss of death.

But under Tobin, the Fisheries ministry was only superficially unpromising; he exploded into activity. He soon became one of the best-known ministers in Canada for his aggressive campaign against foreign overfishing on the Nose and Tail of the Grand Banks, just outside Canada's 200-mile limit. No other minister of Fisheries, not even the forceful John Crosbie, had been able to take such a hard-line position, because none had been fully backed, as Tobin now was, by his own prime minister.

Tobin's actions on the Fishery file culminated in the 1995 "Turbot War," during which his enforcers arrested a Spanish trawler, the *Estai*, by firing across her bow in international waters. Spain and the European Union called him a pirate and Canada a rogue nation. Any truth to their claim that Canada's fishery problems had been caused by this country's own mismanagement was lost in Tobin's rhetoric and dramatics.

He held a news conference for the international media aboard a barge on the East River in New York near the United Nations. There he excelled himself in histrionics by displaying from a crane high in the air the closely woven, illegal meshes of the twenty-storey net cut from the *Estai*. And he introduced a tiny turbot, less than the size of his hand, to the audience, while proclaiming, "We are down to the last, lonely, unloved, unattractive little turbot clinging by its fingernails to the Grand Banks of Newfoundland, saying, 'Someone reach out and save me in this eleventh hour, as I'm about to go down to extinction.'" Some commentators in Canada cringed, but the international media ruckus was phenomenal.

The EU accused him of engineering a conspiracy to falsely incriminate their fleets—a complete frame-up—by manipulating the media. The United Kingdom's government, although at first sympathetic to the EU position, ultimately supported him to the hilt after he became a superhero there and in Ireland. Back home he became a national icon from St. John's to Victoria and gained the moniker "Captain Canada."

It was probably his fame from the Turbot War that made Tobin so successful in organizing, later that same year, 1995, a monster rally in Montreal just before the Quebec referendum on separation. Thousands of citizens from outside Quebec were bused, flown, and conveyed by train into the province in order to wave a gigantic Canadian flag and sing the praises of a united country. Many Quebeckers claimed Tobin's actions were not legal and had in fact backfired, but others, including savvy Québécois like Jean Chrétien and Jean Charest, seemed to believe that the rally had a positive effect on achieving the razor-thin referendum victory that kept Canada whole.

Within a couple of months, early in 1996, Tobin used the glory from his Turbot War and his salvation of Canada as a springboard to catapult himself out of federal politics into the political leadership of Newfoundland and Labrador.

He hustled Clyde Wells off the scene, ruffling the man's considerable self-esteem, and became leader of the Liberal Party by acclamation. And upon being sworn in as premier, he called a snap election. The Liberals won 37 seats out of 48, and Tobin formed an immensely strong majority government.

He invited lawyer and federal government adviser Malcolm Rowe, a Newfoundlander, to become the top civil servant in the province as Clerk of the Executive Council and secretary to the cabinet. Rowe had the talent and nerve to use whatever draconian measures were necessary to balance the provincial budget, while Tobin's charisma and his slogan, "Ready for a better tomorrow," somewhat eased the pain in the public mind.

In 1998–1999, the Newfoundland budget showed a surplus for only the second time since Confederation. Malcolm Rowe was later appointed to the Newfoundland Supreme Court, and in the fall of 2016 he would be appointed to the Supreme Court of Canada, the first Newfoundlander, after some sixty-seven years of Confederation, to achieve that distinction.

IN AMONGST THE cuts and the economic pain, Tobin resorted to his dramatic flair to inspire the populace with pride in our history, and he caused his government to develop a number of highly theatrical celebrations. They included, in 1997, the five hundredth anniversary of

John Cabot's discovery of "Canada," and in 1999, the fiftieth anniversary of Newfoundland's Confederation with Canada.

Then, in the year 2000, he had the province celebrate the thousandth anniversary of the landing of the Vikings on the tip of the Great Northern Peninsula at L'Anse aux Meadows. And he planned for the hundredth anniversary in 2001 of Guglielmo Marconi's reception on Signal Hill of the first transatlantic wireless radio transmission, which had been sent in Morse code from Cornwall, England.

Meanwhile, on July 31, 1997, Tobin made a no-nonsense, hard-nosed speech to the province announcing his intention to abolish denominational education. Over the electronic media, he declared that he was going to ask the people by referendum to remove the churches completely from the education system. He would leave no room for any ifs, ands, or buts in the decision, such as existed in Clyde Wells's incomprehensible, hybrid half-measures.

On referendum day, after a vigorous, often emotional campaign on both sides, the electorate of the province voted by 73% to get rid of the denominational system of education, completely.

WHEN THE CHRISTIAN Brothers kept playing hardball regarding the claims of victims of the Mount Cashel Orphanage abuse, the Tobin government made a financial settlement with some forty male survivors of the appalling scandal. Then the province spent the next six years getting the money back from the Catholic religious order, which was a good indication of the endless time and distress the former orphanage residents had been spared.

A number of other actions introduced by Tobin while premier included the creation of a film development corporation, the amendment of our Human Rights Act to ban discrimination on grounds of sexual orientation, the bringing of the Morgentaler abortion clinic under medicare, the move toward changing the province's name, constitutionally, to Newfoundland and Labrador, and initiating the erection of a $40 million cultural facility, The Rooms, to bring the archives, the art gallery, and the museum securely under one roof.

He also completed the development of a Strategic Social Plan, earlier set in motion by the Wells government, with widespread public consultations, to evaluate the government's social policies and programs and to decide on the future direction of social development in Newfoundland and Labrador. According to Tobin, it would combine with Clyde Wells's release of a Strategic Economic Plan in 1992 to create an overall policy framework for the economic and social development and well-being of the province into the twenty-first century. Its results were met with high regard by interested parties across Canada.

In the field of resource development, Tobin both made progress and set a certain tone. He concluded deals with Petro-Canada and Husky Oil to exploit the Terra Nova and the White Rose oil fields, and he established a new simplified generic royalty regime for offshore oil projects.

Regarding the massive Voisey's Bay nickel deposit in Labrador, he held firm against the attempts of mining giant Inco Limited to smelt ore outside the province. "Not one spoonful" would leave Newfoundland and Labrador unprocessed, he maintained, bringing negotiations to a grinding halt.

Roger Grimes as premier would later make an accommodation with Inco on moving ore out temporarily, to be replaced later when the local plant was built, but Tobin had established an attitude against any exploitation of our resources at less than full advantage to the province.

Tobin raised great hopes of entering into a massive $12 billion hydroelectric deal with Premier Lucien Bouchard of Quebec on the Lower Churchill in Labrador, combined with other rivers in Quebec. That was constantly in the news as a going concern for months, but then, within a year after he'd won another general election in 1999, the big hydro project fell through. A month later, October 2000, Tobin resigned as premier, suddenly and unexpectedly, to be appointed to Jean Chrétien's cabinet as minister of Industry. The abrupt move was an unpleasant, even hurtful jar to many supporters, and an opportunity for critics to assert that the man was only out for himself.

But Tobin's prestige was still high enough, when Prime Minister

Chrétien called a snap federal election, to easily put him over the top in the riding of Bonavista–Trinity–Conception against well-known political stalwarts Jim Morgan for the Progressive Conservatives and Fraser March for the New Democrats.

Thereafter, he continued the campaign he'd clandestinely started as premier, to run for the leadership of the Liberal Party of Canada. He seemed to be flourishing in that race, but Chrétien let him down by permitting Finance Minister Paul Martin, in his budget, to squeeze out Tobin's pet project of a Canada-wide broadband Internet. As well, Chrétien appeared to be favouring John Manley's leadership bid, by appointing him as deputy prime minister. These actions made Brian look and feel like he was being left twisting in a cold wind.

He came to believe, contrary to some observers, including myself, that Paul Martin had an unbreakable stranglehold on the Liberal leadership, and Brian gave up his own campaign. Within months, in January 2002, he suddenly resigned from cabinet and the House of Commons in order to pursue a private life.

Since leaving politics, Tobin has engaged in a highly successful business career but has caused a few double-takes in the process. Appointed as CEO of a couple of Frank Stronach's enterprises, he resigned mysteriously after a few months, with little comment from either side, but with a substantial golden handshake that made eyebrows shoot skywards.

Tobin and one-time Ontario Liberal premier David Peterson smoothed the way for Tory MP and former PC leadership candidate Belinda Stronach to cross the floor of the House and join the Liberal Party and be welcomed into Prime Minister Paul Martin's cabinet.

Brian also joined the so-called think tank, the Fraser Institute, an organization which, as premier, he'd called "Loony Tunes." He performed on the media as well, doing some economic pontificating, but got a few cracks from critics for superficiality. One commentator acquaintance of mine from the mainland said to me at the time, over a beer, "Brian Tobin? He's as shallow as piss on a plate." Really? You sometimes got the idea there was a little jealousy on the go.

In recent years, Tobin has been hugely successful as a senior adviser with one of the largest law firms in Canada and as an officer or director with some top Canadian corporations.

On Christmas day, 2010, his son Jack was charged with impaired driving causing death when his best friend was killed as a result of "doughnuts" Jack was executing in a parking garage with his pickup truck. In the aftermath of the terrible tragedy, and the trial and sentencing, many observers were moved by the dignity shown by Brian in reacting on the media to the appalling heartbreak of loved ones.

As a political leader, provincially and federally, I'd rate Brian Tobin at 80%.

Roger Grimes

ROGER D. GRIMES was born in Grand Falls–Windsor in 1950 and grew up there. He graduated with degrees from Memorial University and embarked on a successful career in education; he was elected president of the teachers' association in 1985 and became a member of the board of directors of the Canadian Teachers' Federation.

He created a public profile in those positions, and when newly elected PC leader Premier Tom Rideout called an election in 1989, Grimes ran under Liberal leader Clyde Wells in Exploits district. He managed to get himself elected to the House of Assembly against the PC candidate, Paul Cooper, by 49 votes.

Wells appointed him as his parliamentary assistant, and within two years he was invited into the cabinet as minister of Employment and Labour Relations. Although Grimes was not a flamboyant politician, he was in the news a fair amount because, from the start, he never shied away from contentious issues.

One of the first things he did was tackle union voting procedures, whereby the show of hands favoured by the unions was replaced by the secret ballot. Next, he helped overhaul the procedure associated with the workers' compensation system under which some injured workers could actually take in more net income while injured than he or she could earn while working. The labour movement loudly voiced their discontent with the changes, but Grimes, backed by Wells, prevailed.

Premier Brian Tobin also valued Roger as a point man when he appointed him successively as minister of the senior portfolios of Education, Mines and Energy, and Health.

As minister of Education, he led the way with Premier Tobin in completing the education reforms shakily begun by Premier Wells. Grimes could see that the changes made under Wells, which he described to me as denominational subcommittees within a non-denominational board, were totally impractical and unworkable.

He backed Tobin in launching the new referendum in favour of intelligent, forthright changes; their straightforward campaign helped gain overwhelming support of the public. Grimes assisted in drafting the constitutional amendment and the new Schools Act that would rid Newfoundland and Labrador of the benighted medieval system. He told me on *Open Line* that it was a proud period in his career as a lifelong educator.

Upon Brian Tobin's hasty resignation as premier late in 2000, Deputy Premier Beaton Tulk took over as interim premier while the party set a Liberal leadership convention. Grimes and two of his colleagues, Paul Dicks and John Efford, ran for the top job.

Efford became Grimes's main competition. He was an outspoken populist, or, as some of the Liberal caucus characterized him, an unpredictable loose cannon. A couple of years earlier he'd given ammo to the anti–seal hunt gang by ranting to the House of Assembly that he "would like to see the six million seals, or whatever number is out there, killed and sold, or destroyed or burned. The more they kill, the better I'll love it."

And just a year before that, he'd blustered publicly that, if his federal Liberal colleague and counterpart, Fisheries Minister Herb Dhaliwal, didn't revoke licences to Prince Edward Islanders to fish shrimp off Newfoundland, Efford was going to "lead riots in the streets." The licences stayed in PEI, but Efford's perceived defence of sealers and fishermen, exceedingly passionate if wholly ineffective, made him the darling of what Joey Smallwood used to call "the ragged-arsed artillery."

The leadership campaign became an extremely nasty process, and although Grimes had the support of the Liberal caucus, Efford's appeal to the "grassroots" of the party made it a neck-and-neck race. At the convention in February 2001, Efford came within 14 votes of beating Grimes and taking the premiership.

After the convention, both Efford and third-place finisher Paul Dicks announced they could not work with new premier Grimes. They both resigned from the House of Assembly, Dicks to practise law, and Efford to run and get elected in a federal by-election, the next year, to the House of Commons.

Grimes had not long been sworn in as premier early in 2001 when he put into effect an initiative begun by Tobin: The name of the province was constitutionally changed to Newfoundland *and Labrador*. The alteration was not to everyone's taste on the Island, but it resolved a long-term grievance felt by many Labradorians.

Grimes also set out to make the government more open and accountable. He reinstated the office of ombudsman, or citizens' representative, earlier abolished by Clyde Wells. He put the proceedings of the House of Assembly on television. He initiated an office to regulate fuel prices. And he created the position of child and youth advocate. One criticism by the Opposition, though, was his failure to bring the Auditor General back to audit the books of the House and the financial activities of MHAs. That had to wait till Danny Williams became premier.

Grimes had said that he had no objection whatsoever to such auditing, but the issue was not raised during his premiership, to his recollection. It had been a huge issue under Brian Tobin while Paul Dicks was the Finance minister, he said, and they were both adamant that the Auditor General, Beth Marshall at the time, not be given access, as an employee of the House, to the books of the House. Tobin apparently cited the federal model to maintain that it would be inappropriate. And, Grimes also felt, the fact that the matter was not raised as an issue in the House while Ed Byrne was Opposition Leader might be relevant.

AT THE BEGINNING of Grimes's tenure, he announced a 25% decrease in tuition fees at Memorial University. This was implemented in the three budgets he presided over by way of 10% reductions in each of the first two years and 5% in the third. Grimes was gratified that it has resulted in students enjoying, since 2003, one of the lowest tuition rates in Canada.

Advances in offshore oil development should have benefited the Grimes government more in popularity than they did. He was able to announce the third big project in March 2002, when Husky Oil gave their go-ahead on White Rose at an estimated value of nearly $2.5 billion. The Terra Nova project, at $3 billion, started producing at the beginning of the year, adding to the huge Hibernia project, which had begun producing its first oil in 1997.

Grimes reopened and ratcheted up talks with Inco regarding the enormous nickel deposits in northern Labrador's Voisey's Bay. Negotiations had stalled some two years before, when Premier Brian Tobin vowed that "not one spoonful" of nickel ore would leave the province to be processed elsewhere. It all had to be refined in Newfoundland and Labrador, he insisted, or not at all.

But Grimes announced a deal with Inco in June of 2003. The government estimated his Voisey's Bay project to be worth $20.7 billion to the province's gross domestic product during its predicted thirty-year life, with thousands of jobs during construction and several hundred once operations began.

Discussing the deal with me one time, Grimes gave full credit to Minister Lloyd Matthews in helping him find a way to overcome Brian Tobin's rhetoric. His government allowed Inco to ship ore elsewhere for processing, but on the condition that the company would return at least an equivalent amount to the province once the Long Harbour processing plant was up and running. The deal appears to have been an outstanding success overall. Roger Grimes in retirement has taken satisfaction, in his understated way, by declaring that the fears expressed by the naysayers have been shown to have no substance. (I recall Danny Williams as Opposition Leader being the most vociferous of the naysayers.)

MEANWHILE, IN 2002, Grimes established a Royal Commission on Renewing and Strengthening Our Place in Canada, consisting of chairman Vic Young and commissioners Sister Elizabeth Davis and Judge James Igloliorte. A year later they reported their findings and recommendations.

After detailing the province's familiar weaknesses and challenges—the destruction of the cod stocks, our Labrador hydro chiefly benefiting Quebec, the highest unemployment in Canada, the lowest per capita income in Canada, the highest tax rates in Canada, the largest provincial out-migration in Canada—the report went on to make some valuable recommendations.

They included the need to revise the Peckford-Mulroney Atlantic Accord of 1985 to ensure that offshore oil and gas royalties would, in fact, primarily benefit this province. Grimes tried to persuade Prime Minister Paul Martin, his fellow Liberal, to agree to such a revision. There was a narrow window of opportunity, Grimes argued, for Newfoundland and Labrador to stand on its own two feet economically by gaining access to the oil revenues without the crippling equalization clawbacks. But Martin dug in his heels and wouldn't act.

Ultimately, Martin had to be politically bludgeoned into doing it. When Danny Williams became premier in 2003, he made this Royal Commission recommendation his early top priority, triggering the famous "war" between him and Paul Martin in 2004–2005. A great deal of needless national acrimony and venom from both sides ensued before the prime minister capitulated.

Grimes has lamented how Paul Martin disregarded the fairness of the province's case until he found himself in political jeopardy later. The prime minister, instead of putting himself in a position where he had to be forced to recognize the justice of it, should have just done it a couple of years earlier, as simply the right thing to do. The Atlantic Accord amendments that Premier Danny Williams and Minister Loyola Sullivan finalized with Paul Martin, Grimes has stated, mirrored the case presented in the Royal Commission report and argued by Grimes as premier.

The Royal Commission report also recommended teamwork between Canada, Quebec, and Newfoundland and Labrador to develop the Gull Island hydro site on the Lower Churchill River. Grimes entered into talks with Quebec and has stated that his government was on the cusp of doing a major export-based development.

It would have seen the province own 100% of the project with a guaranteed floor price and an inflationary clause to capture any upsides for this province rather than for Quebec. A Gull Island project was the chief consideration, he has said, whereas Muskrat Falls was always regarded as a non-viable add-on that could really be contemplated only if some island link-up occurred after 2041.

Dissent on the board of Newfoundland and Labrador Hydro Corporation and resignations over Grimes's deal led to its failure to go ahead. Grimes has said that the parties were close, but he ran out of time and lacked political capital to sanction the deal before calling an election. He has remained convinced, I believe, that his arrangement would have benefited the province greatly but, unfortunately, time and circumstance led to other outcomes.

Those other "outcomes" are Grimes's reference to how Danny Williams, after he formed the government, emphatically did not follow the recommendation of the Royal Commission. Williams opened instead, just before he resigned as premier, the Muskrat Falls initiative. That deal, which went ahead to the absolute exclusion of Quebec, has since been threatening, in the view of many, to bankrupt the province.

The Liberal Party's diminished political capital, as cited by Grimes, had been caused partly by Brian Tobin's hasty disappearance as premier and the resulting vicious infighting for the Liberal leadership. The bitterness and rancour outlived the leadership convention. Those elements, plus the fact that Grimes possessed no election mandate from the voters, widened his party's credibility gap among the public as time went on. The emergence of a popular new leader of the PC Party exacerbated the Liberal malaise.

Already, at the beginning of 2001, two disastrous by-elections had taken place in formerly Liberal districts: Tobin's abandoned provincial district, The Straits and White Bay North, which had been powerfully Liberal for fifty years, was lost to Progressive Conservative candidate Trevor Taylor; St. Barbe district, previously held by senior Liberal minister Chuck Furey, also went Tory when Wallace Young won it by 23 votes.

Then, by-elections held in June of the same year, to put MHAs in the districts vacated by Liberals Paul Dicks and John Efford, painted a clear political picture. The PC Party's new leader, Danny Williams, won in a walk in Humber West, and although the Grit candidate managed to hang on in extremely Liberal Port de Grave district, it was by only 98 votes. Meanwhile, in public opinion polls, the Tory lead over the Liberals was escalating in most districts throughout the province.

The Liberal decline was also driven by labour difficulties with public sector unions. Just over a month after Grimes became premier, negotiations with the Newfoundland Association of Public Employees (NAPE) and the Canadian Union of Public Employees (CUPE) hit a wall. The unions wanted a 15% increase in wages over three years. The Liberal government dug in at 13%.

At once, some 19,000 government workers walked out on strike. Most were health care providers and winter road maintenance crews. As chance would have it, a big blizzard descended on the Island. With roads smothered in unplowed snow, some people were cut off from food and fuel and access to already severely reduced medical care. I took calls on VOCM *Open Line* during that period, and I never heard callers so angry. Grimes bounced around the possibility of back-to-work legislation, but ultimately the government said yes to the unions' demands. The settlement more than doubled the province's budgeted deficit for that year alone.

As the time for a provincial election approached in 2003, the government in Ottawa put the last nail in the cod fishery coffin by announcing a moratorium on the remaining fishery in the Gulf of St. Lawrence. Thus, the federal Liberals added to the pall of gloom surrounding Grimes's prospects.

The provincial Liberals had been in power for fourteen years, and many of the electorate were well and truly sick of them. Grimes could try all he wanted to distance himself from previous leaders with his impressive menu of progressive ideas and actions, but the fact remained that the party had placed itself, irreversibly, on the skids. And it was ushered to its demise by the fresh dynamism of the PC leadership.

In the election of October of 2003, the Liberals went down from the 32 districts they'd won in the 1999 election (27 held at dissolution) to 12 seats after voting day. Roger became Leader of the Opposition, and Danny Williams, supported by 34 seats in the House, became premier.

A year and a half later, on May 30, 2005, Grimes left the House of Assembly, where he'd sat for sixteen years, and resigned as leader of the Liberal Party.

During the years since then, Grimes has been a fairly regular commentator on the political scene. During the past couple of years he has been critical of the Muskrat Falls hydro project and, although considered a nice guy himself, has complained that Liberal premier Dwight Ball's responses have been far too kind compared with the shots being taken at him by former Nalcor chair Ken Marshall and others.

That comment provoked the brother of Ken Marshall, lawyer Steve Marshall, to send Grimes an email banning him from the skating rink that Steve owned. Roger Grimes would never, ever, be allowed to play hockey there again.

That was certainly a cruel and unusual punishment, because, from his youth, Roger had dearly loved to give those elbows a good workout in the corners of a rink. His reaction now, understandably, was that he thought the ban was a joke. But no, Steve Marshall was perfectly serious. In an email to the CBC, he wrote, "Mr. Grimes saw fit to take a public cheap shot at my brother Ken, so there will be no hockey for Mr. Grimes at our rink. He should now realize that in saying negative and untruthful things about my family that I will do something about it without hesitation."

The CBC reported Grimes as responding that this was an example of immature and childish bullying by Marshall: "It's a bullying tactic that he gets from his close friend Danny Williams. That's an approach they take. If they don't like what you're saying, threaten you with something. . . . I've taught kids in school that when you feel you're being bullied or intimidated in any way, you have to confront it. My way to confront it is to expose it for what it is and let everybody see what it is, and people can judge for themselves."

Steve Marshall had been a partner in the former law firm of Danny Williams, and his brother Ken had been an executive at Cable Atlantic, which Williams used to own.

Evidently, cooler heads prevailed by that fall. Roger had chatted with the brothers Marshall at the end of summer, and while they were still a little upset with his commentary, it was acknowledged that things had been said "in the heat of the moment." Steve agreed that Roger would indeed be allowed to skate on the ice in his rink.

When Roger went to play his customary hockey at the rink just after Thanksgiving of 2016, he reported that Steve Marshall greeted him at the door and helped him carry his hockey equipment up over the stairs to the dressing room. Roger told me that Steve Marshall was the most relieved person in town, and very glad to have this embarrassment come to an end.

Roger has continued to criticize the Muskrat Falls deal and to suggest that power be bought from Quebec. When I appeared on CBC's *Radio Noon* with Ramona Dearing in the winter of 2017 to take calls on "burying the hatchet with Quebec," he told me afterwards he'd been surprised to hear a few ardent Danny Williams fans on air buying into the nationalist "anyone but Quebec" rhetoric, despite the tremendously increased costs to ourselves.

To my mind, Roger Grimes was a good, activist premier during the short period he had the job. He has not been accorded the kudos he deserved for his deeds which, I believe, indicate the thoughtful, progressive actions he would have continued to take as premier over a longer span.

But from the positives must be subtracted, even if the circumstances were difficult, his failure to receive the mandate he sought from the electorate.

I'd grade him at 70% as a political leader.

Jack Harris

JOHN JAMES HARRIS was born in 1948, one of a family of eight kids. While not well off, his parents made no bones about expecting him to go to university. I saw and heard some enlightening background on him from the television program on CPAC called *Beyond Politics*, hosted by superb interviewer Catherine Clark.

Catherine was in Newfoundland years ago, campaigning with her father, Joe Clark, former prime minister and at the time leader, for his second go-round, of the PC Party. They called up *Open Line*, and I fear I was a little unkind to him: "Listen, Joe, b'y," I said, "I don't mean to hurt your feelings, but seeing and hearing Catherine on the media, I have to say you should get out of politics yourself and start campaigning for her instead." I wasn't joking.

Jack Harris mentioned on her program that he'd gone to Memorial University, had become president of the student union, and graduated with a degree in psychology. His family was anti-Joey, and his father was a big Tory who'd met Diefenbaker at the airport and brought him to a rally in St. John's in the late 1950s. Yet, Jack didn't hesitate to give credit to the enlightened post-secondary education policies in Newfoundland in the 1960s, initiated by Joey, including free tuition, for easing his way to university.

After that, he spent a number of years kicking around at various jobs, including a spell as a labourer with a pick and shovel, digging ditches somewhere on the mainland. Then, in his late twenties, he went to law school at the University of Alberta in Edmonton, and after being admitted to the Bar of Newfoundland, he travelled across to the famous London School of Economics and got an M.A. in law.

One of the reasons he wanted to be a lawyer, besides liking the subject, was that his mother, before marriage, had shown such promise and intelligence, as a secretary at a law firm, that a partner there wanted her to read law at the firm and get admitted to the Bar as a full-fledged lawyer. Her parents discouraged her from doing it. The good old days!

Jack has practised law in St. John's, and during some of that time he was a partner of future Tory premier Danny Williams. In the 1990s he was prominent in representing victims of abuse at the hands of the Christian Brothers in Mount Cashel Orphanage.

But already, back in the 1980s, he'd succumbed to the allure of politics. A seat opened up in Newfoundland because newly elected prime minister Brian Mulroney had disappointed his good friend, MP Jim McGrath, in 1984, by passing him over as cabinet minister. Mulroney had appointed instead the more junior John Crosbie, and he tried to make up for it a couple of years later by selecting the long-time Tory MP as our lieutenant-governor.

This opened up a by-election in St. John's East, and in 1987 Jack Harris ran there as the New Democrat candidate. His opponents were well-known for their years of success in politics: Tom Hickey for the PCs and Steve Neary for the Grits. Jack beat them both and thus became only the second NDP candidate, after Fonse Faour, ever to get elected from the province to the House of Commons.

A year later, though, in the 1988 federal general election, the PC candidate in St. John's East this time, Ross Reid, exploited the lyrics of the song, "Hit the road, Jack, and don'tcha come back no more, no more . . ." to defeat him.

But Jack did come back. First he turned to provincial politics. When Tory MHA Shannie Duff, daughter of prominent former Liberal minister Alain Frecker, decided to seek the mayoralty of St. John's and resigned from the House of Assembly, Harris ran in her St. John's East seat in the 1990 by-election. He won, taking more than 49% of the votes, and within a couple of years the provincial NDP made him leader of the party by acclamation.

Then, in the 1993 provincial general election, he fielded a full slate of NDP candidates, a feat unprecedented, I believe, in the history of the party. In the face of the onslaught by new Tory leader Danny Williams, Jack Harris's NDP were able to more than double their popular vote from last election to 7.4% this time. Still, he was the sole NDP candidate elected to face the large PC majority in the House.

I always appreciated Jack Harris's compassionate but pragmatic, left-of-centre point of view. He would call *Open Line* occasionally, but only when he had something weighty and well-considered to say. And I found it unusual to attend any event or public place in his district without running into him and having an interesting and amusing gab. I can remember going through only one little squabble with him.

Talking one morning on *Open Line* to an organization that wanted to attract more women into politics, I advanced an idea of George Bernard Shaw's: Every single district should be changed by law to elect two Members each, a man and a woman. That would ensure representation in the legislature of 50% men and 50% women, roughly equivalent to the population breakdown. And it would automatically overcome the systemic difficulties women were having in organizing, raising money, and getting nominated against men. A lot of people liked the idea on the air, except for some men who expressed grave anxiety over the way I was becoming a wussy feminist.

That afternoon in the House of Assembly, Jack Harris was reported as putting the identical notion forward to the MHAs, and without any reference to either Shaw or myself. On *Open Line* next day I kidded about Jack filching the brilliant idea of two great political philosophers, me and Shaw.

Then a little later, when I appeared on Peter Gzowsky's *Morningside* to give one of my regular provincial reports, Peter asked me about Jack Harris pinching my proposal and presenting it as NDP policy in the House. We laughed about it, especially the part where Premier Wells, the dreaded "Dr. No," rose in his place in the legislature to characterize the concept as "just silly" and to assert that people of all sexes should be elected on their merits alone.

A few days later, I was at Fred's Records looking for an album when I heard a familiar voice right behind me proclaiming rather testily that he certainly had not stolen my idea. It was in the public domain; he had merely heard it somewhere and had passed it on to the House as a creative suggestion. He sounded and looked more than a little peeved at my public insinuations, and I didn't blame him. We had a few words but then settled down and concluded with a few laughs, especially about Clyde Wells's reaction.

JUST BEFORE THE 1996 general election, Brian Tobin replaced Clyde Wells as Liberal leader, and in the face of Tobin's snap election call and campaign bulldozer, Harris was able to place NDP candidates in fewer than half the districts. Tobin led the Grits to a big victory, reducing considerably the number of Tory MHAs and defeating their leader, Lynn Verge, in her own district. The NDP popular vote dropped to 4.45%, their worst return in over a decade. Unsinkable Jack got personally elected again, though, in Signal Hill–Quidi Vidi district.

The next year, Harris took it into his head to run for mayor of St. John's. He may have been inveigled into it by his former law partner, Danny Williams, who had revealed a visceral dislike at the time for then mayor Andy Wells. ("What Andy Wells needs is a good shit-knockin'.") Or perhaps Jack was simply sick of being a loner in the House of Assembly.

Whatever the case, some of the top brass in the NDP, angrily and publicly, decried Jack's abandonment of the party leadership to move to municipal politics. But the polls at first showed him as the distinct favourite to win. With Danny Williams running his campaign, he looked like a shoo-in. Then something happened.

If I remember correctly, Jack alleged that Andy Wells ran his mayor's office out of his cellphone from the deck of a George Street eatery-cum-bar. The negative reaction by voters to that statement seemed to be out of all proportion to its degree of nastiness. After all, Andy was by no means a shrinking violet when it came to heaving out unpleasantries at opponents. Yet Jack went into a serious decline in the polls.

One of his organizers told me afterwards that his drop in popularity vis-à-vis Andy Wells was in fact caused by one of Jack's unfortunate traits: He was as lazy as a cut cat. You couldn't get him off his arse to campaign, the organizer alleged, or stop him from shooting the breeze with already converted cronies for hours on end.

I disputed that contention as totally preposterous. Jack had gotten himself elected against insuperable odds in past federal and provincial contests by his own efforts alone. His problem in the mayoralty contest was that he was up against a superb campaigner and media-savvy mayor in Andy Wells who possessed a sizable core of fervent supporters. They could be used to foment that disproportionate reaction against Jack.

Whatever the case, the battle was a close-run thing. On election day, September 30, 1997, the result was a near tie. The end of October would arrive, after a recount of the ballots, before Andy could be definitively declared the winner and sworn in as mayor again.

In the general election of 1999, Jack resumed his provincial political career and ran again in Signal Hill–Quidi Vidi. Well-known actor, comedian, and later talk-radio host Pete Soucy, also known as the popular character Snook, came close to toppling him. Pete ran as the Liberal candidate and approached to within 169 votes of Jack's winning results.

In the 2003 general election, Harris managed to withstand the Danny Williams onslaught, but he was elected by only 235 over a relatively unknown Tory candidate. Perhaps during the next couple of years he saw the handwriting on the wall: There was no realistic hope of ever arriving at a policy-implementing position, even if he did manage to keep getting elected personally. He must have been good and tired by now of third-party status in the House.

In 2005, he resigned as NDP leader, after a length of time there, I believe, second only to Joey Smallwood's tenure as leader of the Liberal Party. Lorraine Michael replaced him at the top of the party. Because Jack didn't resign immediately from the House, his former law partner and mayoralty campaign manager Premier Williams accused him of deliberately delaying his departure so that Michael would have time to build up her profile as leader. Most observers had difficulty seeing that as a nefarious crime, or as anything but normal, in the world of politics.

When Harris did resign as MHA in 2006, he publicly asked the other parties to let Lorraine Michael run in his Signal Hill–Quidi Vidi seat unopposed in order to provide the by-now traditional and much-needed presence of the NDP in the legislature. Liberal leader Gerry Reid said he'd be happy to oblige on principle, although Liberal organizers divulged that the party was broke and needed every cent it could raise for the coming general election. Danny Williams declared, though, that his Tory party intended to run a candidate in the by-election.

Jerome Kennedy became the PC candidate and campaigned tirelessly with Danny by his side. On by-election day, despite Danny's unprecedented popularity in the province, Lorraine Michael beat Kennedy, his hand-picked candidate. Perhaps the Tory leader had been on to something earlier when he accused Jack Harris of a Machiavellian delaying tactic. Judging by the low turnout, though, it seemed more likely that many traditional PC voters just stayed home in the belief that there was no harm to democracy, or Danny's majority, in having a highly regarded social activist in the House.

TWENTY YEARS AFTER Ross Reid told Jack to hit the road and not come back, Jack was back federally, running again in St. John's East in the general election of 2008. And he was back with a vengeance. He reaped over 74% of the votes cast, among the top five highest percentages in Canada.

He was elected there yet again in the election of 2011 with some 71% of the votes. During his tenure in Ottawa, *Maclean's* magazine lauded his performance in the House of Commons by listing him more than once among the "Backbench Top Ten."

Then came the 2015 federal election. All in all, it looked like another walkover for Jack. The Liberals did plead with the electorate, though, that voters should not split their ballots between the parties of the two good guys, NDP Tom Mulcair and Liberal Justin Trudeau, because that would only put the bad guy, Conservative Stephen Harper, back in. Choose one, the Grits urged, and make the choice the Liberal Party with Justin Trudeau.

That Liberal posture was a little unnerving to the NDP nationally, owing to the lack of charisma of their leader compared to the appeal of the Liberals' glamourpuss. But the tactic wasn't expected to have any impact on Jack Harris's election, because he'd personally entrenched himself so solidly in the riding.

That's what I was thinking when I made statements to Jack that anyone superstitious might reproach me for. On September 9, a little over a month before federal election day in 2015, the esteemed writer Susan Chalker Browne launched her beautiful new book, *The Story of the Basilica of St. John the Baptist.* There was a huge crowd present, including Jack Harris and myself. (An aside for political junkies: Susan was the daughter of Barbara Chalker, the Liberal candidate in the 1990 provincial by-election whom Jack had defeated.)

During our chat at Susan's book launch, I kept telling Jack that he was going to walk away with the election. I lived in his riding, and I could see it clearly. I even told him I wouldn't be surprised if he became a senior minister in a new NDP government. Admittedly, my latter point was a bit of a stretch, but it was of a piece with my positive feeling for Jack's candidacy. As I was saying all that, though, I saw a distraught look on the face of someone there very close to him. After my third or fourth time saying it, she whispered to Jack, "I wish he'd keep quiet. He's going to jinx you!"

Election night, everyone was surprised, including Jack and his Liberal opponent, Nick Whalen. Jack had lost to the Liberal by just over 600 votes out of nearly 45,000 cast. A few days later, I ran into Jack at a restaurant having lunch with some campaign organizers. He didn't say anything about my jinxing him, but he did voice his full expectation that I had voted for him. "I trust you lost your vote," he laughed.

I'd accord Jack Harris as a political leader the grade of 70%.

Danny Williams

DANIEL E. WILLIAMS was born in St. John's on August 4, 1949. He was the eldest child of lawyer Tommy Williams and Teresita Galway of the highly regarded city family of that name. Both his parents had actively supported the Progressive Conservative Party and candidates since Confederation, long before it was cool to do so. Tommy and I used to joke that, under early Smallwood, the only thing protecting the Tories were the small-game laws. Danny recalled putting up posters as a boy to champion the PC Party during the elections that made Joey's arch enemy, John Diefenbaker, prime minister of Canada.

Danny got a degree in political science and economics from Memorial University and was awarded a Rhodes Scholarship in 1969 to read law at Oxford. While there he was an ice hockey star. Then he went to Dalhousie University for his Canadian law degree.

Even before graduating from law school, Danny put together an eclectic local consortium of business people and social activists and entered it in a vigorous competition for a Newfoundland cable television licence. His group won.

Over the following decades, as major owner, he built the enterprise into a telecommunications business and a cable TV franchise that he was able to sell separately in 2000 for well over $200 million. As a result, some St. John's wags tried to dub him "Danny Millions," mainly for the benefit of the mainland media, but I never heard locals seriously call him that, and the contrived nickname was too ridiculous to stick.

On top of his business successes, Williams conducted a flourishing law practice during the 1970s, 1980s, and 1990s, breaking new legal ground in his representation of accused murderers and advocating for many survivors of the physical and sexual abuse they'd endured as boys under the Christian Brothers during the Mount Cashel Orphanage scandal.

In the early 2000s, Danny purchased the naming rights to the big, newly built sports complex in downtown St. John's for $600,000. Some expected him to commemorate himself by naming it the Danny Williams Centre. But he surprised many by commemorating instead the building's location near the eastern starting point of the drive across Canada. He called it the Mile One Centre. He was required to put up with a lot of ribbing about the name: To avoid breaking the law under Canada's metric system, local jokers advised, he had to change the name to Kilometre 1.609 Centre.

Danny now revived his long-smouldering interest in active elective politics. Even back in 1989, during the run-up to the leadership convention that elected Tom Rideout as PC leader and premier, he'd seemed to be tempted to enter the race. At least, he publicly expressed his disgruntlement that he'd somehow been squeezed out of contention by party brass and organizers.

This time, though, the office up for grabs was Leader of the Opposition, not premier, and nobody was tempted to even run, let alone squeeze him out. He was welcomed as the party's saviour, and he won the Tory leadership in April 2001 by acclamation.

Just over two months later, he ran in the by-election in Paul Dicks's old seat of Humber West and got elected to the House of Assembly. It came out that he would be donating his salary as MHA and Leader of the Opposition to charity. Critics opined that such generosity might have more merit if it had it been done anonymously instead of in a great big glory-seeking proclamation by "leak." He also declared that he would be placing his extensive business holdings in a blind trust, but when the transition seemed to take a long time to accomplish, dubious critics speculated about his sincerity there, too. He was being clobbered with the problems of being exceptionally successful in real life before entering politics!

But the PC Party went up in popularity as soon as Danny became leader. In his nearly two and a half years as Opposition Leader, his party's candidates won several by-elections, and a Liberal MHA crossed the floor to join his caucus.

Meanwhile, Roger Grimes, as premier, was governing on the say-so of a mere handful of Liberal delegates at a party get-together, but with no mandate from the electorate. He clung on to the government for about two years and eight months—a time span that was pushing into the length of a normal government term between elections. The long wait frustrated Williams exceedingly.

The Opposition clamour that Grimes go to the people was loud and incessant, and his failure to do so until nearly the last minute helped undermine Liberal credibility. Williams pledged to bring in legislation requiring general elections to be held every four years on a fixed date, and compelling any premier elected to that post by a party leadership convention to call a general election within a short, specified time frame afterwards.

Finally, Grimes did call an election for October 21, 2003, with public opinion polls showing Williams's Progressive Conservatives enjoying a wide lead over the Liberals. Election day put an end to over fourteen years of Liberal governments. The Tories won nearly 59% of the popular vote and elected 34 Members to the 48-seat House of Assembly. Danny Williams had become the proud premier of a province drowning in debt.

The budget deficit for the 2004–2005 financial year was estimated at nearly $850 million. Danny went into alarm mode and appeared on province-wide media to announce the dire news: He was forced to slash spending and freeze the incomes of government workers and lay off thousands. Cancellations and delays were declared in several health care and education and other projects, including The Rooms, then under construction. The announcement soon sent some 20,000 public sector employees out on strike.

Late in the night of the day that Williams announced cuts of 4,000 public service jobs over four years, his son was attacked and badly beaten in the nightclub area of downtown St. John's. He had to be hospitalized with serious injuries to his head and face.

Williams issued a warning in the media: "Let me just serve notice right now on anybody out there who is in a union: Don't go near my family, or my home, or the homes of our ministers, or anybody else in our caucus, because I can tell you right now, they will be out until the cows come home, if they go near any members of our families."

Williams conceded that he didn't know if the injuries were associated with the labour unrest but that his son had probably paid the price "for having a father who went into politics and is trying to do something to straighten this province out."

At first the unions were outraged by the insinuation, but before long they were exhibiting inflatable cows at their rallies and picket lines and chanting, "The cows have come home."

Later, a young man in his early twenties would be arrested and charged for the injuries to the son, but a judge would find him not guilty.

Meanwhile, the public service strike went on for nearly a month of nasty name-calling, huge, loud crowd scenes in front of entrances to government buildings, and the need to have government members and management police-escorted in.

On at least one occasion, the premier and the powerful, plain-speaking union leader, Leo Puddester, met clandestinely, under cover of darkness, in a parking lot, in an effort to end the struggle and settle the thing. People were laughingly asking which one of them was "Deep Throat." But it was all to no avail. Ultimately, Danny broke a campaign commitment and called the House together to legislate the nearly 20,000 public servants back to work.

Further labour disgruntlement and much public criticism ensued when, that same year, his government consolidated health boards and education boards to cut costs and, allegedly, to produce greater efficiencies.

All of which sent the new government's popularity plummeting in the polls. A survey done in June 2004, just over half a year after Danny's election return of nearly 60% of the vote, showed the PC Party and the Liberal Party practically tied, within the margin of error, at about 40% each. Danny's own popularity as leader had taken an even greater hit, down from 65% then to about 39% now. Very clearly, it was time for Premier Williams to do what a couple of his forerunners, likewise beleaguered by domestic problems, had done in the past: declare a just war on Ottawa.

Prime Minister Paul Martin had called an election for June 2004. During the campaign, polls showed that he and the Liberals were losing the momentum to Stephen Harper and the Tories. As part of his effort to stem the tide, Martin phoned Williams just after seven one morning and promised that he would accept Danny's demand regarding the offshore revenues.

That meant that 100% of the provincial revenues would go to the province with no "clawback" for equalization payments. Soon after, Martin announced to the media, "What we've really got to do as a government is make sure that Newfoundland and Labrador is the primary beneficiary of its resources." He went on, "I have made it very clear [to Williams] that the proposal that he's put forth is a proposal that we accept."

Luckily for Danny, at least on the surface, Martin came out of the election with a shaky minority government. But if the premier figured he had the prime minister right where he wanted him, he was soon disabused of that notion. A battle royal ensued as he tried to make Martin live up to his commitment, or even to get the PM to put his oral commitment in writing. The feds kept fabricating new ifs, ands, and buts and dragging them into every letter and every meeting.

The times grew interesting to media and the Canadian populace:

Near-fisticuffs were reported between the two leaders, a dramatic walkout was staged by Danny at a federal-provincial summit meeting, a daily media war raged in which the premier mostly made mincemeat of the prime minister, and the destruction of the political career of the province's minister in the Martin federal government, John Efford, progressed.

The fury of Newfoundlanders, inside the province and out, probably reached its peak when Martin proposed a deal wherein the provincial government would keep 100% of oil revenues until they reached the tax revenue per capita of Ontario. Then the clawback would kick in. Apparently, it was unthinkable in Ottawa and Toronto that lowly Newfoundland could be allowed to be a richer "have" province than mighty Ontario. So, naturally, in the eyes of the prime minister and the premier of Ontario, a cap had to be applied to our oil revenues, which would have the effect of depriving this province of billions of dollars during the life of offshore exploitations.

In spite of attempts by the Prime Minister's Office to drive a wedge between Nova Scotia premier John Hamm and Danny Williams, the two provincial premiers stuck together during and after many failed meetings with the feds.

Two days before Christmas, 2004, Danny went on television to announce that, by way of protest against federal non-co-operation and reneging, he was taking down all Canadian flags over provincial government offices. Sensationally, he pointed behind him at the maple leaf flags he was going remove from the premises—"That's gone! And that's gone!" They would be politely folded up, he said, and stowed away in a drawer somewhere.

Many in the national media went off their heads. This was "traitorous" disloyalty to Canada. Most, but not all, of the residents of his own province seemed to be okay with Danny's flag flap, though. It would be nearly three weeks later, in January 2005, after an agreement was reached to resume negotiations that Danny allowed the national flag to fly again over government buildings.

That month, he and Premier Hamm made a deal in Ottawa with

Prime Minister Martin. Danny flew home with over $2 billion, climbed up on a piece of furniture in the St. John's airport, raised fists in the air, and bawled out, "WE GOT IT!" A few weeks later, a political poll taken in the province showed that popular support for the Williams government had shot back up, this time to 86%.

Next year, Danny's approval ratings remained high when he took on Beatle Paul McCartney, and his wife, Heather Mills, on television with Larry King over the seal hunt. It has always been an uphill battle, defending what many in Europe and the US deem indefensible, but he did himself proud, helped by the obnoxiousness of Ms. Mills and the geographical ignorance of both: They were speaking from Prince Edward Island, but they actually believed, and argued the point, that they were in fact in Newfoundland.

IN NOVEMBER 2006, a by-election was held in Signal Hill–Quidi Vidi district as a result of the resignation of NDP leader Jack Harris. As mentioned earlier, the PC Party ran well-known lawyer Jerome Kennedy, and the newly elected leader Lorraine Michael ran for the NDP. Danny Williams and his party were high in the polls, but Lorraine Michael, aided by federal NDP leader Jack Layton, who came down to campaign for her, hung on to the seat for their party by a good majority of the votes. It was as if the PCs stayed home to read their Shakespeare and apply it to their esteemed leader: "It is excellent to have a giant's strength, but it is tyrannous to use it like a giant."

Meanwhile, in the fall of 2005, a vote of no confidence in the House of Commons had caused the fall of Paul Martin's government, and a federal election was set for January 23, 2006. Leading up to it, on January 4, 2006, Premier Danny Williams cajoled federal Conservative Opposition Leader Stephen Harper into sending him a letter stating that a Conservative government would "remove non-renewable natural resource revenue from the equalization formula to encourage the development of economic growth in the non-renewable resource sectors across Canada."

The election put Harper in power with a minority government.

Right off the bat, the new prime minister had a serious attack of "election-promise remorse" over his written commitment to Danny. Criticism of what he'd done came from federal financial advisers and some provinces. Harper's commitment, on top of the 2005 Atlantic Accord, was especially unpopular with Ontario's Liberal premier, Dalton McGuinty. Hence, the federal budget of 2007, while pretending to meet Harper's promise, in fact cut the guts out of it.

Among other changes, the budget said it would allow each province to exclude natural resources from the equalization formula but capped the amount of equalization the province would then receive. Danny's famous Atlantic Accord of 2005 was effectively emasculated.

Ontario's Dalton McGuinty was elated. He had achieved through the Tory PM what he couldn't pull off with fellow Liberal Paul Martin. The Grit premier couldn't gush enough praise for the Conservative budget. The political hugs and kisses between the Ontario premier and the national prime minister, made all the more startling by one being a Liberal and the other Tory, represented a first in federal-provincial relations.

These restrictions in Harper's new formula, Danny raged, had shafted his province. He launched an anti-Conservative campaign. That spring, he spoke to a mainland business audience and detailed how Harper's reneging on his pledge would cost his province billions of dollars. He was going to urge Newfoundlanders and Labradorians and Canadians to vote ABC—"Anything But Conservative"—in the next federal election. Newfoundland Liberal leader Gerry Reid said that Williams's action were damaging to the province's investment climate.

In the middle of the renewed war with a different Ottawa enemy, Danny signed a memorandum of understanding in 2007 with oil corporations involving the Hebron field, and, among other things, the provincial government acquired some equity in the offshore project. Then, in September of the same year, he called a provincial general election. Many thought he was going to win every seat in the province.

On election day, October 9, the PCs received nearly 70% of the popular vote, the highest share ever attained by a party in the province.

It was an even higher percentage, apparently, than when Liberal leader Frank McKenna had won every seat in New Brunswick in 1987. While Danny did gain an extra 9 seats, his final count was not a clean sweep, however, but "only" 44 districts out of 48. The Liberals won 3, although leader Gerry Reid was personally defeated in his own district, the Isles of Notre Dame, by just 12 votes. Amazingly, NDP leader Lorraine Michael was able to hold on to her seat.

Harper called a federal election a year later, and Danny's ABC campaign went into high gear. He did not place his provincial party officially behind either the federal Liberals or the NDP, but some individual local PC politicians did campaign for their normally rival candidates. The "ABC Campaign" was registered with Elections Canada to comply with election expenditure rules, and apparently the provincial government itself paid for some of its advertisements.

The campaign set up a website and, reportedly, Danny expected all his caucus to take part in the anti-Harper crusade. I believe that only Elizabeth Marshall, Danny's former Health minister, bucked his command. She had resigned or been dismissed from cabinet over an earlier clash with Danny and made it clear now that she was not going to support a Liberal or NDP candidate in this federal election, or even campaign against the federal Tories. Harper appreciated her loyalty and courage so much that he would later appoint her to the Senate.

Danny's "Anything But Conservative" campaign did not appear to be very active in the rest of the country. He did a few interviews on mainland media and had a big billboard erected on a major Toronto traffic artery, but he did not stump across Canada as he'd earlier indicated he would.

Harper made a brief campaign visit to Newfoundland. While here, he stated that the decision by Newfoundlanders and Labradorians on what candidate and party to vote for should be based on "your own best interests." This was described by ABCers as both a thinly concealed bribe and a veiled threat.

On election day, the federal Conservatives lost the 3 seats they'd held in this province before the election was called. They didn't even come close to winning 1 seat out of the 7. The party's popular vote dropped to 17%. The Liberal Party elected 6 MPs and the NDP elected 1.

Nationally, many pundits thought Williams's ABC campaign had had no effect in the rest of Canada: Harper in fact elected more MPs than before, including additional wins in Ontario, where criticism of Danny's stand on the Atlantic Accord and equalization was loudest. Harper was able to form a stronger minority government than he'd had going into the election. Others thought, however, that the lack of any Conservative seats in Newfoundland and Labrador, plus Williams's negative views on Harper nationally, may well have kept him from forming a majority government.

After the election, Danny kept on maintaining that Harper's equalization amendments were going to damage Newfoundland to the tune of $1.5 billion in just three years. He lobbied for support from the other provinces, but only one premier got behind him, PEI's Liberal Robert Ghiz. The others seemed bored by yet another attack by Williams on yet another federal government. There seemed to be a collective sigh of, "Oh no, not you again!"

Williams asked the Liberals in the House of Commons, under Opposition Leader Michael Ignatieff, to vote against the federal budget. In response, he only got the back of Iggy's hand. "I'm not in the business," the Liberal leader said, "of carrying Premier Williams's water." In fact, Ignatieff laid on the whips to make his Liberal MPs *support* the Conservative budget, although he did allow the six Newfoundland and Labrador Liberal MPs the freedom to vote against it. Thus, Harper's minority government budget, including the equalization changes that so perturbed Danny, passed into law with Liberal Opposition help.

That prompted some observers to ask if, next time, Danny was going to lead an "Anything But Liberal" campaign. But no such action turned out to be necessary. In the 2011 federal election, Ignatieff would lead the Liberals to the worst election return in Liberal Party history. He even lost the party's official Opposition status to the NDP. Defeated in his own seat by a Conservative, he would quickly resign as leader and hasten back to the groves of academe that appeared to suit his persona a good deal more.

Meanwhile, Danny expressed his displeasure with the apathy and lack of support from other provinces. "The country disappoints me," he said, "when we don't rally to protect each other." I didn't hear the country apologizing for disappointing him. But, as the months went by, both he and Harper started to make conciliatory noises in the media indicating that it was time to work together again. Even in Newfoundland and Labrador, a growing feeling emerged that the only thing Williams had accomplished with his ABC campaign was to cut off his nose to spite his face.

That criticism was countered by the argument that Danny's ABC had motivated the Harper government to get back in Newfoundland and Labrador's good books by later agreeing to guarantee part of the funding for Danny's hydroelectric project at Muskrat Falls. But the more money that project has drained out of the provincial economy ever since by its massive over-expenditures, the larger the number of people here who have fervently wished that Harper had never made amends with Danny by agreeing to the enabling guarantee.

Danny's disenchantment with Quebec seemed to have pushed him into a hydro deal that may well end up tarnishing his whole political career. Williams had always been rather forthright in his criticisms of Quebec and Hydro-Québec regarding Labrador hydroelectric developments. He reached a crescendo of denunciation, however, when Quebec premier Jean Charest and New Brunswick premier Shawn Graham executed a memorandum of understanding in October of 2009 to sell most of the multi-billion dollar assets of NB Power to Hydro-Québec.

Danny launched a campaign in New Brunswick to prevent it. He claimed that Quebec was trying to foil the Lower Churchill development in order to maintain and build on its own pre-eminence in power markets. His robust allegations that Quebec's selfish interest was injuring other provinces and the nation were thought to be influential in ultimately causing the Quebec–New Brunswick scheme to collapse.

MEANWHILE, DANNY WAS striving to get the best possible deals for the province from the offshore oil. One example occurred in June of 2009, when he reached an agreement with the consortium to enlarge Hibernia and allow Newfoundland and Labrador to gain 10% of the equity in "Hibernia South." Government estimates of the value of the transaction indicated the province stood to reap an additional $13 billion.

Critics asked, What the hell was the government doing, tying up scarce tax dollars in a private enterprise operation? What were they going to do next, invest tax dollars in pork bellies? Proponents of the deal said, however, that after successive provincial governments had perennially lost their shirts putting money into linerboard mills, oil refineries, phosphorous plants, and cucumber greenhouses, it was about bloody time we invested in something viable and profitable for a change.

EARLY IN FEBRUARY 2010, Danny Williams flew to the United States to undergo serious heart surgery. Deputy Premier Kathy Dunderdale stated that the option to have the operation performed in Newfoundland was never offered to him. She wouldn't say whether he could have had it done somewhere else in Canada, or where payment for the procedure in the US was going to come from.

The cryptic nature of the disclosed information made some people wonder publicly whether the Canadian health-care system was up to scratch, or even good enough to do such an operation in a timely fashion. Opponents of public health care in the US had a field day: They used Canadian "Governor" Williams's rush to avail himself of American surgery as proof positive of the inferiority of the Canadian system.

It came out that he was at the Mount Sinai Medical Center in Miami Beach. Patients treated at the famous hospital had included "Prince" Louis Alphonse, the pretender to the throne of France, Muhammad Ali, Jackie Gleason, Michael Jackson, Dwayne Wade of the Miami Heat, and Maurice Gibb of the Bee Gees, among other celebrities. On February 8, 2010, news was received that the surgery had gone well and Danny was recovering nicely.

The premier brooked no complaints about his choice of hospital. He told the Canadian Press: "I did not sign away my right to get the best possible health care for myself when I entered politics." Notwithstanding his "utmost confidence" in Newfoundland and Labrador's health care system, he said, he had decided to go where surgeons were doing his very specialized surgery three or four times a day, five and six days a week.

Later in the same month, February 25, the highly esteemed medical columnist in the Toronto *Globe and Mail*, André Picard, tore into Danny's explanation, or lack thereof. Picard's newspaper piece was headlined: "Williams's heart surgery choice was based on ignorance." In it, he stated that the ignorance and arrogance Danny Williams displayed in making the decision to get heart surgery in Miami Beach was staggering.

"As the Premier of Newfoundland and Labrador," wrote Picard, "he is one of the stewards of the medicare system. The least we can expect from a political leader is some leadership and sound reasoning. What we got instead were inanities like: 'This was my heart, my choice and my health.'"

The clear implication of Williams's statement to the Canadian Press, Picard went on, was that the surgery he sought in the United States was not available in Canada, and that health care in this country—and cardiac surgery in particular—was inferior.

"That is utter nonsense on both counts," Picard wrote.

Williams had an obligation to explain his actions: "Skulking off to Miami, then petulantly refusing to detail why, just doesn't cut it." The surgery that Mr. Williams wanted, claimed Picard, was available in at least seven Canadian cities. His sin was not in going to the US for surgery; it was in acting on partial information, uttering untruths about the availability of care, and smearing—however inadvertently—Canada's health system in the process. Health care in this country is good, Picard concluded, but it would be better if we acted more often with our heads than with our hearts.

Within a year, Danny resigned from politics. At the time, one of his big supporters said to me, referring back to that *Globe* piece, "Christ, is there any wonder the man got out, after having to read the like of that about his own life-saving *heart* operation?"

But I doubt that that was the reason Williams left politics. I believe he got out because he thought he had completed his legacy as premier. On top of the 2005 Atlantic Accord, and putting the province back on the financial rails with oil revenues—making it a have province—and getting a piece of offshore equity, he had announced a power deal toward the end of 2010 that, ostensibly, had eluded all premiers before him.

In November, Danny Williams and Darrell Dexter, the premier of Nova Scotia, held a breathless news conference to announce a $6.2 billion pact to develop power at Muskrat Falls on the Lower Churchill River. The Newfoundland and Labrador Crown corporation Nalcor Energy partnered with Emera Inc. of Nova Scotia on the development; 824 megawatts would be produced and transmitted from Labrador across the Strait of Belle Isle to Newfoundland, where 40% of the power would be consumed. The project would allow, as its prime rationale, the retiring of the oil-burning generating plant, and its three towering smokestacks, at Holyrood. That was said to be equivalent to removing 300,000 cars and their emissions off the roads.

The rest of the power would be transmitted across the Gulf of St. Lawrence to Nova Scotia in a line constructed by Emera Inc. at a cost of $1.2 billion, for which they would get 20% of the power for provincial customers, with the remaining 40% to be sold by Nalcor to outside markets.

Later that month, looking very much as if his work in the Premier's Office was done and his esteemed reputation intact, Danny proclaimed that his resignation as premier was effective December 3, 2010. Deputy Premier Kathy Dunderdale would serve as caretaker premier until a new PC Party leader could be elected.

A few days after his resignation, Corporate Research Associates (CRA) put out their political poll for November. It showed that 90% of the voters in the province were completely or mostly satisfied with the

PC government; 75% said they supported the Progressive Conservatives, and 76% thought Danny was the best choice for premier.

Except for his first year as premier, when cutbacks and layoffs and a rancorous public service strike lowered his approval ratings, Danny had been continuously and wildly popular throughout the province. A couple of years after becoming premier, once he'd bludgeoned Prime Minister Martin into a deal on equalization, his government was favoured by 86% of the province. Thereafter, he remained by far the most popular premier in Canada. His percentage approval ratings ranged constantly in the 70s and 80s and even higher throughout his tenure.

But popularity was evidently no guarantee of respect from one's peers. Joey Smallwood used to say that there was nothing deader than a retired politician. Not long after Danny's own retirement, he was heard to complain that Premier Dunderdale and her staff were distancing themselves from him. One allegation was that her ministers and caucus had been ordered to change their mobile phone numbers and not to give them to Danny. Ouch.

At the Progressive Conservative leadership convention in the spring of 2011, during which the new leader was to be crowned, a dinner was planned for April 1 to pay tribute to Danny Williams and honour his legacy. Before it could take place, though, Danny announced he would not be attending.

A month later, in May 2011, Danny, who'd been the driving force to bring an American Hockey League team back to St. John's, supported a request to the provincial government for a multi-million dollar subsidy of the operation. He expressed absolute confidence that a cost-benefit analysis would confirm the public benefit of the subsidy.

But Kathy Dunderdale, the woman he'd placed in the premier's chair, and all the former colleagues he'd made ministers turned him down in scarcely disguised scorn. Some callers to VOCM *Open Line* thought the government should say yes to Danny's request. But many expressed disgust at the very idea of feeding millions of provincial tax dollars into the maws of a few thousand fanatical supporters of second-rate, come-from-away hockey.

Danny was publicly flabbergasted and dismayed at his former colleagues' negative reaction. However, the project did manage to go ahead and thrive for a good while without taxpayers' money.

In December of the same year, Danny declared his interest in developing a 2,400-acre site for housing and business operations on the outskirts of St. John's. He called it Galway, after his mother's family name, and touted it as amounting to some $5 billion in value over the next couple of decades.

The following year, 2012, he associated himself with a company conducting mining explorations in Labrador. Not long afterwards, he and the company sued the Sierra Club of Canada, plus an environmental activist, and a political blogger, for defamation stemming from allegations of conflict of interest made on radio and social media.

THE ACTUAL LEGACY, as against the intended legacy, left by Danny Williams is ambivalent. His "No More Giveaways" mantra was politically appealing and raised the consciousness of the electorate regarding our resources. His take-no-prisoners approach to negotiations with the international oil companies secured better revenues and equity stakes in the offshore developments. He negotiated a better Atlantic Accord with the federal government, resulting in a more than $2 billion upfront cash benefit to the province.

He saw Newfoundland and Labrador become a have province for the first time since Confederation. Scoffers have attributed that to the pure dumb luck of astronomically high international oil prices, over which he had no more control than the man on the moon. But the fact was that he had positioned the province to take full advantage, if, as, or when the pure dumb luck occurred.

He got a portion of the Lower Churchill going and avoided entanglement with Quebec in doing so. He reduced the provincial debt and brought in nationally attractive personal and corporate tax measures. A strategy to reduce poverty and a beneficial student aid program, plus some settlements of aboriginal land claims, were also part of his arsenal of progressive advances.

But in tandem with revenues pouring in from the temporary windfall of high international oil prices, he took the lid off government spending during most of his tenure as premier. As a result, he's been blamed, at least in part, for the financial disaster caused by unprecedented provincial deficits since the oil prices plummeted. And, perhaps as a result of his passionate zeal to avoid that entanglement with Quebec, Muskrat Falls has turned out to be a chapter of budgetary and management fiascos—almost farcical if the doubling of its costs weren't so menacing to the province's very future.

During a media briefing on June 23, 2017, Nalcor Energy CEO Stan Marshall stated, "I think this project is a hell of a lot worse . . . deal than the Upper Churchill." Earlier, upon his appointment in April 2016 as new CEO of Nalcor, Marshall had called Muskrat Falls "a boondoggle." Now Williams characterized Marshall as "a boondoggle buffoon."

As of this point in history, taking the good and the bad with the uncertain, Danny Williams merits a grade of 70% as a political leader.

Gerry Reid

GERRY REID WAS born in Carbonear in 1954. His father died when he was twelve, leaving his mother to bring up half a dozen children. He overcame challenges to reach Memorial University, where he obtained undergraduate degrees in arts and education and an M.A. degree.

He became executive assistant to the provincial minister of Fisheries in 1989. Before the general election of 1996, he took on his own boss, Minister of Fisheries Walter Carter, for the Liberal nomination in Isles of Notre Dame district and won the candidacy. He got elected to the House of Assembly and thereafter served successively as government whip, parliamentary secretary to the premier, and minister of Education.

When Roger Grimes left the party leadership, after the Williams Tories defeated the Liberals in 2003, Reid was appointed interim leader of the Liberal Party. He declined to run in the leadership convention early in 2006, and Jim Bennett was acclaimed. But when Bennett was forced out by the Liberal caucus within months, the party executive elected Reid.

He was the very popular choice of the party, but it was not a position he coveted. He would quote Michael Corleone of the Mafia from

The Godfather movie: "Just when I thought I was out . . . they pull me back in." Danny Williams was riding high after negotiating the Atlantic Accord and its two billion plus dollars from Liberal prime minister Paul Martin. And offshore oil revenues were astronomical. The public opinion polls showed Williams with unprecedented popularity.

The general election of October 2007 confirmed the polls. The Tories got nearly 70% of the popular vote. Reid's Liberals emerged on polling day with only 3 of the 48 seats. He himself lost in his own district by just 12 votes. A month later, he resigned as party leader and left politics altogether. Yvonne Jones, one of the 3 Liberal MHAs elected, became leader of the Liberal Party and Opposition Leader, the first woman to lead the provincial party.

The same day that Gerry Reid resigned, Premier Williams put out a cordial news release commending Reid and wishing him well. In it, he said that individuals like Mr. Reid, who have served the public with such dedication for so long, deserve the recognition and appreciation of the people of Newfoundland and Labrador.

Gerry Reid might have been an excellent premier and entitled to high marks, if he'd reached the post. But having to take the unfortunate facts and deeds as we find them, with the bad luck and the poor timing, I'd award him 45% as a political leader.

Ern Condon

IN 2003, LABRADOR guidance counsellor Ernest J. Condon revived the concept of a party dedicated to the proposition of Labrador getting its fair share. He named it the Labrador Party and led it into the provincial election of that year, with candidates in all four Labrador districts. He personally finished third, receiving nearly 13% of the votes in Labrador West. Candidate Brandon Pardy got 32% of the votes for the party in Lake Melville district, reaching second place there.

The next year, in the federal general election, Condon ran in the riding of Labrador, as an Independent candidate representing the Labrador Party, and lost. But he earned over 10% of the votes and beat out the NDP candidate.

In 2005, he ran federally in the same capacity in the Labrador riding by-election and came fourth out of five candidates, with fewer than 600 votes.

THE NEXT LEADER of the party, Ron Barron, deputy mayor of Wabush, ran in a provincial by-election in Labrador West in 2007 and came third with about 16% of the votes. In a strategic decision, the Labrador Party did not contest all four of Labrador's districts in the general election of that year, so as to avoid splitting the anti–Progressive Conservative vote. Jim Tuttauk ran in Torngat Mountains and received 109 votes.

If the past is anything to go by, the future of a Labrador Party looks sporadic and problematical. Meanwhile, I'd give Ern Condon, who led the party into a provincial general election, and then maintained the struggle for his cause, federally, for a while, a grade of 35%.

Kathy Dunderdale

KATHLEEN MARY MARGARET (Warren) Dunderdale was born in 1952 in Burin, and grew up there, in a family of eleven children. After high school, she went to Memorial University to study social work. But back home in Burin, she met Captain Peter Dunderdale, a master mariner from the UK, and married him. She devoted her early adult life to a variety of activist volunteer undertakings while looking after their two children.

Dunderdale was a member of the committee that advocated against Fishery Products International's decision to cease operations at the Burin fish plant. Their lobbying succeeded, and the plant remained open. She also served on the local school board and with the Status of Women Council.

She got elected to the Burin town council in 1985 and later served as deputy mayor. She became the first female president of the Newfoundland Federation of Municipalities and served as director of the Canadian Federation of Municipalities. As well, she was elected as president of the provincial PC Party.

I recall first seeing her on a television panel during that early period—I think an election was on the go—and being most impressed with her thoughtful, level-headed comments.

Professionally, she did social work with the Department of Social Services and, in the early 1990s, after the cod moratorium was imposed, was appointed to an appeals board for inshore fisherfolk.

When Premier Clyde Wells called the 1993 provincial election, she decided to run as a PC candidate in Fortune–Hermitage district against Liberal cabinet minister Oliver Langdon. She lost by more than two to one.

A couple of years later, she became co-chair of Lynn Verge's campaign for the leadership of the Progressive Conservative Party. It was extremely close—only 3 votes separating first place from second—but they won.

In the 2003 general election, having moved to St. John's several years before, Dunderdale ran in Virginia Waters district against Liberal cabinet minister Wally Noel. She won by 58% of the vote. New premier Williams brought her into the cabinet as minister of Innovation, Trade and Rural Development. A couple of years later, he appointed her to the senior portfolio of Natural Resources.

Dunderdale got re-elected in the general election of 2007 with 73% of the popular vote. Premier Williams recognized her competence and status as minister of Natural Resources a year later by adding to her tasks the position of deputy premier, as well as Minister Responsible for the Status of Women.

In the summer of 2008, Dunderdale and Premier Williams and a consortium of oil companies signed the second-largest deal on Newfoundland's offshore, the Hebron oil field. The development was touted as bringing in, over its life, some $20 billion in royalties for the province. The following June, the "Hibernia South" extension to Hibernia with its additional billions in royalties was proclaimed.

The next winter, during the month and a half in February and March of 2010 that Danny Williams would be undergoing, and recuperating from, heart surgery in Florida, he appointed her acting premier of the province.

In the fall of the same year, Premier Williams and Minister Dunderdale and Nova Scotia premier Darrell Dexter, along with Nalcor Energy and Emera Inc., held a news conference in St. John's to announce the multi-billion dollar "first phase" of the Lower Churchill project at Muskrat Falls.

Within days, Danny announced his resignation and, on December 3, 2010, had Dunderdale sworn in as interim premier, pending a party leadership convention. She was the first female premier in the history of the province. She announced that she would not be running for the leadership of the PC Party. It was widely understood that her intention not to run was the reason Danny had named her as temporary premier and that she was there on a purely caretaker basis.

Once she held the reins, Dunderdale became her own person. She made it clear that she was going to end a bitter little strike concerning just fifteen home care workers on her home territory, the Burin Peninsula. It had been festering for more than a year. The government under Danny Williams had been urged to settle the differences but would not get involved.

Just a few days after moving into the premier's office, Dunderdale oversaw a settlement offer, which the strikers accepted, and ended the dispute. Her action was generally interpreted as showing a wide contrast between Danny's hard-nosed approach and Kathy's compassionate concern.

The irony would be that by the end of her short reign she'd be harshly criticized in at least two serious cases for having a tin ear when it came to sympathetic and empathetic understanding of difficult situations facing people.

Meanwhile, she'd taken over as interim premier while the Medical Association and the provincial government were at loggerheads over doctors' income negotiations. The government's offer of a 31% increase was not enough. More than a dozen doctors had announced they were leaving their practices as a result.

Having publicly stated that she was working toward a solution to the dispute before Christmas, she held a news conference on December

15, 2010, along with the president of the Newfoundland and Labrador Medical Association, John Haggie, and Finance Minister Tom Marshall, and Health Minister Jerome Kennedy. They disclosed that a tentative agreement had been reached that included parity with Atlantic Canada within two years. All but one of some fourteen doctors who had resigned came back.

While that was going on, everyone was waiting for the PC Party's plethora of talented Members to announce they were running for the leadership. The speculation included Minister Joan Burke, Minister Jerome Kennedy, MHA Steve Kent, Minister Darin King, Senator Elizabeth Marshall, Minister Tom Marshall, Minister Kevin O'Brien, national and local media commentator Tim Powers, Minister Shawn Skinner, and even former chief of defence staff Rick Hillier.

Two weeks after being sworn in as interim premier, Dunderdale announced that she was undergoing a change of heart and reconsidering running for the PC leadership. The word leaking out of the Confederation Building was that she was coming under intense pressure from her caucus colleagues to go for it. Party heavyweights started dropping out of the running like flies. One after another, as if it were plotted by a choreographer, Jerome Kennedy, Darin King, Tom Marshall, Kevin O'Brien, and Steve Kent all announced that they would not be running and encouraged Kathy Dunderdale to throw her hat in.

On December 30, 2010, Dunderdale declared that she was now indeed a candidate for the Tory leadership, and her whole caucus jostled to proclaim their endorsement of her. Although she had said earlier that she would resign as premier if she ran for the leadership, now she stated that she would leave the premiership only if someone else also jumped in and contested the leadership against her.

For ten days, it looked like clear sailing. The entrance fee of several thousand dollars and the requirement of fifty signatures of support from party members seemed to be doing a good job of precluding the emergence of nuisance candidates.

Enter the fly in the ointment.

Just before the deadline for nominations on January 10, 2011, one

Brad Cabana filed his papers. Cabana was a former mayor of a town in Saskatchewan, and was now a blogger in Newfoundland and a frequent caller to St. John's open line radio shows. At this turn of events, the squawks of dismay from the Tory caucus room threatened to lift the roof off the Confederation Building.

The very next day the credentials committee of the PC Party ruled that Cabana was unqualified to be nominated. They claimed that he hadn't provided the required fifty signatures from party members. Cabana thereupon alleged that an assistant to Minister Ross Wiseman had tried to scare him out of running with a threat, and he appealed to the rules committee.

More than two weeks later, the committee upheld the decision barring Cabana from being a candidate. Hence, Dunderdale remained on as premier and became leader-designate by acclamation. On April 2, 2011, at the party convention that Danny Williams boycotted because he felt disrespected, Dunderdale was officially sworn in as leader.

In September of 2011, Dunderdale called a general election for October 11. The PC campaign slogan was "New Energy." As will be seen, the part of that catchphrase that pertained to Muskrat Falls would later develop more negative ramifications than she'd bargained for at the time. But going into the election, the party was flush with cash, the buzz was good, and the political polls showed her way ahead of her opponents.

On election day, the Tories won 37 of the 48 seats, which was a drop of 7 districts from the last election. That was still an enviable majority, but, in retrospect, the decline in seats may have been a harbinger of events to come for her and the party.

The big surprise was that the NDP under Lorraine Michael had won in 5 districts and that her party's popular vote was greater than the Liberal Party's. It was a record return for the NDP, both in seats and votes. But, because of the distribution of the votes, the Liberals under new leader Kevin Aylward picked up a couple of seats, for a total of 6. By the skin of their teeth, the Liberals remained as the official Opposition, but Aylward lost personally in his own district.

At that point in history, Kathy Dunderdale was only the second female party leader in a Canadian province, after Catherine Callbeck in PEI, to win a general election.

Dunderdale had hitched her wagon squarely to the Muskrat Falls development. Before becoming premier she'd been front and centre with Danny Williams and Nova Scotia premier Dexter in the signing of the partnership deal. Then, in a get-together with Prime Minister Stephen Harper early in February 2011, she had requested a loan guarantee from the federal government for the project, which would reduce costs a little by lowering interest rates on the financing and give the thing a huge vote of confidence.

In her maiden Throne Speech that March, delivered in the House by the viceregal John Crosbie, she gave great significance to Muskrat Falls. Then leading up to federal election day on May 2, 2011, she got up on a stage in St. John's with Harper and supported his campaign. Danny's ABC initiative was well and truly dead and buried. For her personal risk in publicly hugging Harper up there—some said she had exposed herself to frost burn—the new premier received the prime minister's loan guarantee commitment.

In August 2011, Harper's recently elected majority government proclaimed a memorandum of agreement for the loan guarantee. But you had the impression that more than a few Ottawa mandarins must have been muttering to the boss, "Prime Minister, just what the hell do you think you're doing?" Because well over a year would pass before the federal backing was concluded.

But finally, just before Christmas in 2012, the Newfoundland and Nova Scotia principals scrambled to launch synchronized news conferences in St. John's and Halifax where they declared the Muskrat Falls hydro project officially sanctioned. With great fanfare, the province had crossed the boundary between economic vitality and threatened insolvency.

BURTON WINTERS WAS a fourteen-year-old boy who lived in Makkovik, Labrador. On January 29, 2012, he failed to return home on his snowmobile and was reported missing. The Canadian Forces claimed that bad weather kept them from launching a search before forty-eight hours had elapsed. Later they would admit that their two helicopters at Goose Bay were down for maintenance reasons.

On February 1, three days after he'd gone missing, young Burton's body was found far out on the sea ice. He had frozen to death after abandoning his stuck snowmobile and walking nineteen kilometres over the snow and ice. Residents of Makkovik stated that he must have missed a turn on the snowmobile trail and mistakenly headed out to sea on foot, thinking he was walking home. His family, and some politicians and members of the public, protested the unacceptable lack of action by officials responsible for search and rescue.

Demands were made by the family and others to have a public inquiry into the tragedy. Burton's grandmother also arranged for a meeting with Premier Dunderdale, which the premier agreed to on a "grandmother to grandmother" basis. But when the family planned to have a retired search-and-rescue coordinator attend as well, Dunderdale withdrew from the intended meeting. This was a man already outspoken on the lack of official response, so the congenial "grandmother to grandmother" chat she'd agreed to had evolved into something else, she claimed, namely some big public relations stunt. Hence, the family should meet instead with the provincial minister responsible for emergency services.

The premier may have been strictly correct in her response to the grandmother of the dead boy. But politically speaking? She definitely did not come out of the incident looking good. It was one of the situations where even supporters were wondering how such a smart and empathetic person could have allowed herself to come off appearing so tone-deaf as premier.

NATIONALLY, DUNDERDALE WAS given credit for showing leadership over an energy plan for the country. As minister of Natural Resources, she had pushed for an electrical power grid to span Canada. When she became premier, the Council of the Federation, a congress comprising the first ministers of Canada's provinces and territories, appointed her to a committee of three premiers to help draft a national energy strategy.

At their meeting in 2012, contrary to the reticence of most other premiers, she didn't hesitate to pass judgment on the fracas between British Columbia and Alberta over the Northern Gateway pipeline. This was a project to construct a twin pipeline from Bruderheim, in northern Alberta, to Kitimat, on the coast of British Columbia.

Comparing that situation to the conflicts between Newfoundland and Quebec over Labrador power, she stated that provinces should not be able to "use their geographic location to hold off economic development for their sister provinces . . ." Her forthrightness was admirable, but its impact turned out, at least in the short term, to be negligible.

WHEN DUNDERDALE'S 2013 budget announced that the remaining four English school boards in the province, already drastically reduced in 2004, would now be amalgamated into just one board, the criticism, especially from education administrators, was loud and vociferous. At the same time, the budget cut money from the Department of Education, which added to the strident criticism. But the minister of Education, Clyde Jackman, maintained that this province still enjoyed the best student-teacher ratio in the entire country.

Also in the same budget, there was a cut in funds to the College of the North Atlantic, accompanied by the abolition of its adult basic education program. This was the high school equivalency program for men and women who had not finished high school, and it was to be taken out of the college curriculum and privatized. Already, the program was provided by private colleges and non-profit institutions to some 60% of the ABE students.

The minister of Advanced Education and Skills, Joan Shea, stated that it was costing about $5,000 more per student to administer ABE at the college than at the private institutions, and that the average cost for each student here was three times that of other Atlantic provinces. Despite the rationale and fiscal logic behind the change, Dunderdale's government came in for serious public disapproval from those concerned.

WHEN DUNDERDALE HAD been a minister under premier Danny Williams, Newfoundland and Labrador enjoyed unprecedented economic growth, largely because of the godsend of high international crude oil prices. Big budget surpluses started to pile up, and while much of it was applied to the provincial debt, the government also set out on a spending spree. After decades of austerity and cuts, it was hard to blame them. Early in Dunderdale's premiership, the Auditor General's report stated that government spending had gone up by nearly 50% over the past five years since 2006.

Minister of Finance Tom Marshall was unabashed. Not only did the province have to play catch-up after our years of poverty, he maintained, we had to do our bit to fight the then intense global recession by accelerating spending. It's not recorded in the cabinet minutes if the picture he painted of little Newfoundland staving off international financial collapse by flinging its oil money out, left, right, and centre, caused titters around the cabinet table.

Dunderdale's own first budget as premier recorded an increase in spending of nearly 5%. She was truly a socially conscious Red Tory; the upturn in expenditure covered the gamut of government activity, including construction and social and health programs. More ominously, though, was a financial contribution to Nalcor Energy.

A small surplus of less than $60 million was forecast in the spring budget for that fiscal year of 2011–2012, but when the government put out their fall update, the projected surplus had grown to over $750 million. This was a government that, financially, could do no wrong. Or so they thought.

Even the right-wing conservative Fraser Institute was impressed. For the 2011–2012 financial year, it awarded Premier Dunderdale's policies in taxes, debt, deficits, and government spending the best score of all the premiers in Canada. In passing, the think tank did comment that her good score in spending was mainly because of strong economic growth rather than any restraints in actual spending. They were on to something.

Dunderdale's antennas were out, though, and she sensed trouble ahead. Early in 2012 she announced that the unrestrained government spending was going to stop. There was to be no new spending in that year's budget, and all government programs were going to be audited. In the Throne Speech a month later, she continued her expressed intention of conservative restraints: Everything in every department was under financial review. Cuts totalling $100 million had to be found.

But when Finance Minister Tom Marshall read his 2012 budget speech a few weeks later, the government was seen to be making less than $40 million in savings, and only a handful of temporary positions were to be eliminated. Spending was increasing by nearly 2%. Startlingly, a deficit of over $250 million was projected. This was all founded on an estimated oil price for the fiscal year of $124 a barrel. Thoughtful observers didn't know whether to laugh or cry at such unsupported optimism.

Three months later, Dunderdale held a news conference to announce further cuts. That day international oil prices stood at a little over $100 a barrel. The drop was causing the deficit to rocket upwards. It was estimated that for every $1 decrease in oil prices, the provincial coffers were being deprived of $20 million. When Marshall finally released a delayed "mid-year" update about ten days before Christmas that year, the government was forecasting a deficit for 2012–2013 of $726 million.

Early in the new year, Dunderdale shuffled Marshall out of Finance and put in Jerome Kennedy. He'd been Finance minister during the tough 2008 negotiations with the unions, and his reappointment now was seen by some as a scare tactic directed at public-sector negotiators.

They were right. One of the first things Kennedy did was alert the province that unless spending was controlled, we would be staring at a deficit of over $1.5 billion next fiscal year, with multi-billion dollar increases in the provincial debt over the ensuing few years. By the time the budget was brought down in late March of 2013, Kennedy and Dunderdale had partially saved the day. At a cost of some 1,200 government jobs and cuts of more than $300 million, the forecast deficit had dropped to "only" $564 million.

THE FISHERY WAS not a source of glory for Dunderdale as premier. Over three years or less, she appointed four ministers to head the Department of Fisheries. That would make seven ministers in ten years. You certainly got the idea that successive governments had no idea how to cope with the problems in the fishery.

At the beginning of February 2011, an independent report on the fishery recommended an enormous scaling-down of the industry at a cost to government of nearly half a billion dollars. Even with its relatively flush treasury at the time, the government could not reject the recommendation fast enough. The price of rationalizing the fishery was way too high. This caused the union and the Opposition to criticize premier and minister. Resignations were demanded.

During and after the election of October 2011, Dunderdale stated that there were too many people chasing too few fish and that she was going to implement long-overdue hard decisions.

In February 2012, she announced that the government would be cutting off funding to the Fish, Food and Allied Workers Union. During the past five years the government had provided the FFAW with well over a million dollars for marketing, research, and technology. The new minister of Fisheries, Darin King, gave a politically controversial reason for the chop: No matter what the government did, the union was only concerned with its own self-interest and not that of the industry. Some lauded his bluntness, but many interpreted the cut as the action of a government that was penalizing the FFAW for daring to speak truth to power.

On top of this was an ongoing dispute over minimum processing requirements in provincial fish plants. These requirements were designed to keep employment in the province by adding value to the resource right here. The union wanted to maintain the requirements in place; a fish company wanted a break from them, and its local plant workers took a stance against their own union to support the company. The government dithered in the middle. At length, after another bout of Fisheries ministers' musical chairs, the government ultimately granted exemptions, right before Christmas, to the minimum requirements, that seemed to satisfy no one.

Minimum processing requirements were also caught up in Prime Minister Harper's negotiations of the Canada–European Union Comprehensive Economic Trade Agreement (CETA). Dunderdale claimed in May of 2013 that the feds were trying to blackmail her into eliminating minimum processing requirements in the trade deal. If she didn't bend, the feds were intimating to her, their loan guarantee for Muskrat Falls would collapse.

Dunderdale declared that she was refusing to tie the two unrelated items to each other. Remembering those hugs with Harper on the stage a couple of years ago, she must have kicked herself now for having been so kind to the Machiavellian PM.

By late October of the same year, Dunderdale was delighted to announce that the federal government was going to invest $280 million in the Newfoundland and Labrador fishery, with the province throwing in $120 million. The federal money was supposed to be compensation for the province agreeing to drop minimum processing requirements in order to satisfy the European Union.

Afterwards, though, the federal portion of the fund was the subject of a quagmire of disputes and accusations between the province and the feds over who agreed with whom to spend what money where.

BILL 29 BECAME one of the most painful political thorns in Dunderdale's side. In June of 2012, her Tory government brought the legislation into the House. It amended the Access to Information Act to allow the government to keep briefings to ministers confidential, and to allow ministers to deny "frivolous" requests for information, and to obstruct the Auditor General's access to certain records. Fees were raised and time limits lengthened.

A Canadian-based international human rights organization, the Centre for Law and Democracy, claimed that Bill 29 would place the province below some Third World countries regarding the rights of citizens to information. The Liberals and the NDP in the House conducted a filibuster on the bill for nearly a week, prompting Dunderdale to bring in that "anti-democratic" bane of every opposition known as "closure" to end debate and pass the legislation.

Bill 29 might have had scant relevance to the daily lives of most normal mortals if the Opposition and the media had not kept criticism of it alive for months on end. By their constant dinning, they succeeded in making it part of the electorate's consciousness. The negativity was helped along by the resignation from the caucus, in September 2012, of prominent MHA Tom Osborne. He blamed Dunderdale's leadership for his move, especially over Bill 29, and he would sit as an Independent for less than a year before joining the Liberals.

Ever the activist politician, a month later, Premier Dunderdale took the progressive step of setting up the Office of Public Engagement, which covered the operations of the rural secretariat, the voluntary and non-profit secretariat, the Youth Engagement Office, the Strategic Partnership Initiative, plus the Access to Information and the Protection of Privacy Office. Unfortunately, this positive step was somewhat overshadowed by continued criticism in the media over the content and the actual operations of Bill 29.

The public-opinion polls showed that support for Dunderdale had gradually gone down almost from the start of her premiership in December 2010. The popular vote of her Tory candidates in the October 2011 election was still a highly respectable 56%. But by November of 2012, a Corporate Research Associates poll showed only 36% agreeing that Dunderdale was best choice for premier.

Less than six months later, in March, the CRA poll indicated that the PC Party and the NDP were neck and neck in public support, at 38% and 39%, respectively. The Liberals languished at 22%. In the category of who would make best premier, NDP leader Lorraine Michael, at 33%, was slightly ahead of Dunderdale's 32%.

Next month, an Angus Reid poll put Dunderdale and BC's Liberal premier, Christy Clark, in a photo finish for most unpopular premier in the nation, each with a 25% approval rating. (Incidentally, to prove how unreliable polls can be in predicting election outcomes, Clark would overcome the NDP's 20-point lead, as registered by the polls, and lead her party to election victory in May of 2013.)

Another CRA survey in May 2013 reported Dunderdale at 21%

as best choice for premier. She trailed both Michael and new Liberal leader Dwight Ball. By the end of the year, she had moved ahead of Michael but was still behind Ball. The Liberal Party had surged ahead, with over half the voters saying they'd vote Liberal if an election were held then.

Into this already dismal scenario dropped "Dark NL." Newfoundland and Labrador Hydro's capacity at the beginning of 2014 was already strained to the limit in the extremely cold conditions. The frigid temperatures and strong winds, together with inadequate hardware and generation, caused ominous rolling blackouts. Then a fire at the generating station in Sunnyside piled challenges on the system which it was unable to meet. The whole shebang crashed.

Many Newfoundland homes were entirely without power in the icy cold for several days. At first, Premier Dunderdale seemed to have gone underground. Then she emerged to state that the widespread outage was "not a crisis." Besides, she added, she had propane heat, so she'd been quite comfortable throughout. Meanwhile, the media were reporting that elderly citizens had to be removed from their glacial homes to warm shelters for their own safety.

The outcry was savage. Many could not believe the political tin ear the premier seemed to be afflicted with. The disgruntlement in her caucus was palpable, with scarcely concealed whispering that she had to go. One of her staunchest supporters on earlier talk shows, Mount Pearl South MHA Paul Lane, left her caucus in disgust and walked across the House to the Liberals.

Dunderdale came back from a shortened January vacation to speak from the lobby of the Confederation Building: "Just as you know when it's time to step up," she said, "you also know when it is time to step back, and that time for me is now." And she announced that two days hence, on January 24, 2014, she'd be resigning as premier. She took no questions and remained largely mute on the subject thereafter.

Finance Minister Tom Marshall would become interim premier until the party held a leadership convention. At the end of February, Dunderdale resigned as MHA for Virginia Waters, bringing to a close her political decade of both impressive feats and increasingly troublesome public-opinion woes.

Basically, at the end, she'd been stabbed in the back by the very supporters who, in the election just a little over two years before, had practically danced in the streets over being dragged into government on her skirts.

I was sorry she didn't stay the course and run in the next election to see if she could turn the political situation around, just as Christy Clark had done a couple of elections ago in BC. Perhaps, when the chips were down, Kathy's straight-from-the-shoulder honesty and frankness with the electorate, instead of being condemned as "political tone-deafness," would have been appreciated at the ballot box as integrity.

Early in 2016, Dunderdale began volunteer work with the Gathering Place in St. John's, an organization that helps people in need with meals, clothes, and a variety of social and other services. That summer she was hired by the not-for-profit association as a coordinator of its hundreds of volunteers.

I'd award Kathy Dunderdale, as a political leader, a grade of 65%.

Kevin Aylward

KEVIN AYLWARD WAS born in Stephenville Crossing in 1960. He was first elected to the House of Assembly in the general election of 1985 at the age of twenty-four, one of the youngest on record, and he was a Member of the House for some eighteen years. He didn't run for re-election in the 2003 election that produced the Williams Tory victory.

While he was in the House, he was appointed to the cabinet in various portfolios by Clyde Wells, Brian Tobin, and Roger Grimes. Aylward is a member of the Qalipu Mi'kmaq First Nation Band.

When Liberal leader Yvonne Jones announced her resignation in August of 2011 to deal with her breast cancer, less than two months remained before the next provincial election. There was no time for a regular leadership convention, so the night she resigned, the executive of the Liberal Party met to devise a method for putting a new leader in place, quickly.

The next morning, party president Judy Morrow announced that nominations for leader would open at noon that day and close two days later. Anyone interested could write her a letter of interest enclosing a $500 fee. Seven candidates dived in. Notables included businessman

Brad Cabana, who had attempted unsuccessfully to run for the PC leadership earlier that same year; St. John's lawyer Bern Coffey; businessman and former party president and MHA Danny Dumaresque; and Kevin Aylward.

For the next forty-eight hours, the nineteen men and women on the party executive consulted with Liberal supporters across the province. Then, they brought in each candidate to make a speech to them for half an hour. After that, only five days following Yvonne Jones's resignation, the executive voted for their choices by secret ballot. Aylward's previous experience as MHA and minister was evidently decisive in their minds. Only one ballot was needed: Aylward won the leadership.

There seemed to be some disgruntlement among the other candidates. A front-runner, Bern Coffey, who had earlier indicated he'd be seeking the Liberal nomination in St. John's East, ended up not running in the election. Another candidate said he'd have a tough time running under Aylward's leadership. A third candidate, who already had the Liberal nomination for Terra Nova district, bowed out because he didn't agree with Aylward's direction for the party.

The Liberal Party's slogan for the upcoming election was "We can do better." The electorate seemed to have no problem believing it, but perhaps not in the way Liberal strategists intended.

In that election of October 2011, Kathy Dunderdale's Tories won a majority government with victories in 37 districts. That was not unexpected, but what did come as a surprise was that the Liberals came third in the popular vote, with only 19%, behind the NDP's 24.6%. By a fluke, the Grits managed to cling on by their fingernails to their status as the official Opposition, with 6 seats compared to 5 for the NDP.

Aylward lost to PC Joan Shea in his attempt to get elected again in St. George's–Stephenville East. Shortly afterwards, he resigned as leader.

I'd give Kevin Aylward, as a political leader, a ranking of 40%.

Lorraine Michael

LORRAINE MICHAEL WAS born in St. John's in 1943 to a prominent family of Lebanese heritage. She was educated at Memorial University and the University of Toronto, and was a former nun, as well as a teacher and principal in various communities around the province.

She resigned as a nun after disputes with the Church over their handling of sexual assault accusations.

Moving on from teaching, she became very well-known in Canada and internationally for her activism in achieving political, economic, personal, and social rights for women, including equal opportunities for females in education and employment. She was noted for her work on social and economic justice generally, having involved herself in a number of organizations with that aim. In the late 1990s, for example, the Innu Nation in Labrador designated her as their nominee on the Voisey's Bay environmental assessment panel.

In the spring of 2006, after Jack Harris had resigned as leader of the provincial New Democratic Party, she declared her candidacy for the leadership. At the convention, a couple of months later, the delegates overwhelmingly elected her to the top job.

Then Danny Williams announced a by-election for November 1, 2006, in Signal Hill–Quidi Vidi, the district Jack Harris had vacated. Not only was Williams himself extremely popular in the polls, but the PCs nominated a star candidate, Jerome Kennedy, to run there. Kennedy was a well-known defence lawyer, frequently in the news for his forthright style; to many onlookers, when Michael ran as the NDP candidate against him, she seemed embarked on a political suicide mission.

The thing became a bit of a battle royal, with Williams campaigning actively with Kennedy, going door to door extensively, and national leader Jack Layton coming down to campaign with Michael.

On election day, a surprising number of regular Tory voters stayed home, and for a by-election, the NDP supporters stayed remarkably solid and came out to vote. It was as if the entire district—voters of all stripes—conspired to put her in. The Tories wouldn't vote against their own party, so a lot of them just didn't vote. And the Liberals didn't even nominate a candidate for the by-election. Michael won with just over 55% of the votes, and Kennedy got just less than 45%.

In March 2007, her sole colleague in the House, New Democrat MHA Randy Collins, was implicated in the constituency allowance scandal and resigned as the Member for Labrador West. This alone hurt the party's chances in the general election of that year. Then the popular candidate she thought she had recruited for Labrador West decided to run for the Liberals, and the president of an important union local backed the Labrador Party rather than the NDP. On election day, the PC candidate won the former NDP seat.

The party had been able to muster 36 candidates for the 48 districts in that general election of 2007. Michael herself was re-elected handily in her own district, but none of the other NDP contestants won. She had to go back to the House by herself, as a party of one.

She seemed to be a presence of far more than just one in the legislature, though, and often bode fair to eclipse the Liberals as the main opposition to the government. Solo, she ranged wide over the political agenda, from air ambulances, to increased funding for gambling addicts and the elimination of video lottery terminals, to a ban on bottled water in public offices, often getting news coverage for the thoughtfulness of her topics.

Leading up to the general election of 2011, the polls showed the NDP gaining in popular support well beyond their traditional single-digit percentages. Their campaign slogan was "It's Time." A substantial portion of the electorate seemed to agree.

On election day itself, the PCs under Dunderdale lost half a dozen seats but won yet another big majority government with 56% of the vote. The Liberals won a couple of seats more than they had at dissolution, but their popular vote dropped marginally to 19%. The big story was the NDP surge.

Their popular vote had increased to over 24%, in effect shaming the Liberals. But, because of the way the votes were unluckily distributed, the New Democrats won only 5 seats to the Liberals' 6. The NDP stayed as the third party in the House while the Liberals kept their status as the official Opposition. Michael easily won her own seat.

IN OCTOBER OF 2013, while Michael was away on vacation, her four colleagues in the NDP caucus drafted a letter to her demanding a party leadership convention in 2014. The four of them, evidently forgetting they'd been towed into the House two years before, largely on Lorraine Michael's popularity, wanted a renewal in the party to attract good candidates and popular backing in the next election.

The letter was leaked, and Michael was naturally shaken by its publicly revealed contents. She told the media she was going to have a sit-down with these comrades who had betrayed her and make a decision on what she should do.

A big public scrap in the NDP caucus and executive now ensued, with plenty of conflicting commentary thereon from pundits and citizenry.

Then, MHAs Gerry Rogers and George Murphy suffered conspirators' repentance. They withdrew what they'd written and got back behind Michael. Chris Mitchelmore and Dale Kirby regretted nothing, though, and reiterated their position. Within days, they walked out of the NDP caucus to sit in the House as Independents. And before long, in the winter of 2014, they were welcomed into the Liberal Party and caucus.

That spring, the NDP held a convention where Michael's leadership underwent a review, including a vote of delegates. Despite the fact that, earlier, some executive members of the party had resigned in solidarity with the disenchanted MHAs, now 75% of the delegates present at the convention supported her leadership.

In November of that year, 2014, the party endured dismal results in by-elections. In Conception Bay South district the party dropped from 24% in the general election three years before, down to about 3% now. In Trinity–Bay de Verde, the vote declined to 5.4% compared to the earlier 14%, and in Humber East it was 7.8% versus 13.28% in the general election.

Not surprisingly, after everything that had happened, these returns were disheartening to Michael. Very early in 2015, the general election year, she announced her retirement as NDP leader as soon as a convention could be held to elect a new one. In March, by an electronic and in-person vote, members of the party elected Earle McCurdy as leader.

In the immense Liberal victory in the provincial general election on November 30, Lorraine Michael, in her district of St. John's East–Quidi Vidi, nevertheless got personally elected. I live in her district, and found that more than a few of her constituents, and not only NDP supporters, were absolutely gleeful at her continued personal election success. One said to me, "Lorraine is great: She's better than the Energizer Bunny—she just keeps going and going."

In December of 2016, she went public with the news that she had earlier been diagnosed with breast cancer and that it had been treated. Her prognosis was excellent, she said, and she wanted to share what she'd been through to give other women hope, because it had been a very hopeful experience for her.

I'd award Lorraine Michael, as a political leader, a ranking of 65%.

Paul Davis

PAUL ALFRED DAVIS was born in 1961. He went to Holland College, a community college in Prince Edward Island, and joined the Royal Newfoundland Constabulary in 1985. He worked in Corner Brook and in the Criminal Investigation Division in St. John's, including major crimes and child abuse units. He became well-known to the public latterly as the RNC media relations officer.

During his police work he earned the Crime Stoppers Police Officer of the Year Award and the Police Exemplary Service Medal. Meanwhile, he got elected as a town councillor and deputy mayor in Conception Bay South.

When Prime Minister Stephen Harper appointed Elizabeth Marshall to the Canadian Senate on January 29, 2010, she resigned as MHA for Topsail district. Davis won the PC nomination for the by-election there. On polling day, he won over 81% of the vote. Shortly after that, Premier Williams appointed him as a legislative assistant in the House of Assembly.

The next year, after winning the PC nomination for the general election called by Premier Kathy Dunderdale for October, Davis announced that he had been diagnosed with non-Hodgkin's lymphoma.

His cancer treatments kept him from campaigning publicly during the election, but he obtained 68% of the votes, and Premier Dunderdale put him in her cabinet.

As minister, Davis had to cope with some controversies. When he became minister of Transportation and Works, he was faced with how to deal with a ferry called MV *Nonia*. Back in 1999, the vessel had been purchased by the Liberal government for $1 million. From the start, the craft was a disaster, with $20 million having to be spent between then and 2013 to keep it from sinking to the bottom.

Davis decided to get rid of it, and the government announced that the vessel would be sold. It came out that $3 million had been spent on patch-ups just months before the sell decision. When the derelict was sold on tender, it fetched a little over $76,000 and was scrapped in St. Mary's Bay. (You can see what I meant when I said Brian Peckford was too greatly tainted by the Sprung greenhouse, as if it was something very exceptional in the history of government misspending fiascos in the province.)

In the spring of 2013, when Davis announced that Shoal Arm would be removed as a stop on a Green Bay ferry route, he was condemned by the Opposition as heartless. The year before, the ferry had recorded an average of three vehicles and five passengers on each run between Shoal Arm and Little Bay Islands.

That fall, after he was made minister of Child, Youth and Family Services, he had to act on a serious disclosure earlier in the year regarding Innu children. The chief of the band council in Natuashish, Labrador, had reported that he'd found children under twelve, in a house without adults, sniffing gasoline. Davis cited problems with recruitment of social workers for the remote community and had to tackle the crisis by flying workers in and out on a two-week basis.

In December, he brought in changes to open up, expand, and generally modernize the province's adoption laws.

Interim premier Tom Marshall, in May of 2014, appointed Davis minister of Health. There were allegations that Marshall had a selfish ulterior motive in doing so. The minister of Health whom Davis replaced, the highly competent and respected Susan Sullivan, was apparently of the decided view that the population to be served by a new Corner Brook hospital could not justify the provision of certain expensive cancer treatments there. Marshall, whose district of Humber East was in Corner Brook, didn't like that. When he became premier, he announced that such cancer therapy and equipment would indeed be included in the hospital.

Two months later, Davis resigned from the problematical portfolio to run for the leadership of the provincial PC Party.

A leadership convention had been called when Kathy Dunderdale resigned as premier and PC leader in January 2014. The contest to replace her did not go smoothly. Indeed, the machinations involved in the convoluted process had, from start to finish, all the elements of a Three Stooges farce.

At the beginning, three candidates had emerged to be nominated for the leadership contest: Frank Coleman, Bill Barry, and Wayne Bennett. The Bennett candidacy ended when he was booted out of the race for comments involving the untrustworthiness of Muslim women and children and for supporting the NDP candidate in a by-election.

Bill Barry attempted to distance himself from the party hierarchy and establishment, but he may have gone a little too far. He launched his campaign by stating that Members of the House of Assembly were brain-dead and wouldn't get it if a bucket of shit were plunked on their heads. His error may have been that he hadn't excluded the Tory MHAs in his graphic portrayal of the lawmakers. At any rate, he seemed to feel hurt, as his campaign progressed, that no PC members were supporting him. By the time he pulled out of the contest in despair in April, he appeared to have had an epiphany that part of his problems may have been self-inflicted.

That left some person by the name of Frank Coleman, widely considered Danny Williams's recruit, as leader-designate by acclamation. Without ever, as far as I know, being elected so much as dog catcher at any point in his career, he was due to become leader on July 5, and then automatically premier. But suddenly and brusquely on June 16, 2014, he declared publicly that a mysterious "significant and challenging family matter" was forcing him to leave politics before he even got into politics.

There was much speculation on why he bailed out. Perhaps his naivety about politics came home to him when he found himself bombarded with questions and criticisms over his position on abortion. His wife and some of his children and grandchildren had attended a Good Friday anti-abortion rally in Corner Brook while he was campaigning for the leadership. What was his own position? He was opposed to abortions, he said, and he had personally participated in that anti-abortion rally in past years. But as premier he would not impose his personal views, of course.

The questions and criticism remained, culminating in a column in the St. John's *Telegram* by Bob Wakeham on April 26 called "Time for Coleman to Come Clean." It was one of the best analyses of women's right to abortion, and to their absolute freedom of choice in the matter, that I've ever read. And it was scathing regarding Coleman's past position and actions. I'd be surprised if the column didn't have an impact on Coleman's decision to get out.

But added to that had been his involvement in a dubious activity just before he'd announced he was running for the leadership of the governing PC Party. Humber Valley Paving Limited, a company Coleman had controlled and managed until February of that year, was compensated for a contract it hadn't finished on the Trans-Labrador Highway, and the government forgave the company millions of dollars in completion bonds. There were allegations of secret communications between company principals and government ministers, and of special treatment for Coleman and the company. Interim premier Tom Marshall was forced to ask the Auditor General to investigate the controversy.

Announcing his withdrawal, Coleman made one of the greatest understatements of all time. This, he said, "has a bad look to it." Following his news conference, the video and photo of his wretched trudge back to his car, all alone, to drive home out of it, were among the most pathetic I've ever seen in public life.

The PC leadership contest was now postponed till September 13, 2014. A number of high-profile Tories were touted as possible candidates, including prominent lawyer Ches Crosbie, Senator Fabian Manning, national commentator Tim Powers, and Minister Susan Sullivan.

Meanwhile, numerous prominent members of the PC Party, as well as many in the rank and file, had been practically begging caretaker premier Tom Marshall, in his late sixties, to run for leader. I haven't ranked him in this book because he didn't lead his party into an election, but he certainly warrants a summary of his career.

Tom was the son of Jack Marshall, the highly popular Tory MP for ten years from Humber–St. George's–St. Barbe riding. And Jack was a man I admired. I had heard from my Uncle Stan Butt, himself a wounded Second World War hero, that Jack had gone ashore as an officer cadet with the Canadian Army right at the beginning of the allied invasion of Normandy. Being Jewish, Jack was no doubt motivated beyond even his strong call of duty.

In 1968, he ran in the federal election and got elected along with five other Newfoundland and Labrador PC candidates. They were dubbed "The Noisy Six" for the way some of them made Prime Minister Pierre Trudeau's life miserable, provoking him to invent a brand new swear word, "fuddle duddle." But the moniker hardly applied to Jack Marshall. He spent his time looking after his riding and helping veterans.

In 1978, Liberal prime minister Pierre Trudeau asked me, as provincial Liberal leader, who I thought should be appointed to a Senate vacancy from the province. I surprised him, but only momentarily, by suggesting Tory Jack Marshall, and I could see that he was thoughtfully chewing it over. I don't know for sure what impact my suggestion had, but I was happy to see during that same year that Trudeau made Jack Marshall a senator. So, such was the political heritage that Tom Marshall was part of.

Tom practised law, prominently and successfully, for thirty years, and then ran in Humber East in 2003 for Danny Williams's PC steamroller. He defeated incumbent Liberal MHA Bob Mercer, taking over 60% of the vote. In the next election under Williams again, in 2007, he collected 84% of the votes cast, and in 2011 under Dunderdale, he won once more with 78%.

From his start in the House of Assembly he became minister of top portfolios—Finance, Justice, Treasury Board, Natural Resources, Intergovernmental Affairs. His budgets as Finance minister were characterized by record surpluses, no matter how spendthrift or extravagant the government was in its expenditures. In his 2011 budget, his first under newly appointed premier Dunderdale, an earlier forecast deficit was transformed into a nearly half-billion-dollar surplus. Returns from the oil fields were higher than expected, was the government's rationale for the off-target prediction.

The Opposition MHAs had a couple of other theories. One was that Marshall had earlier understated projected revenues deliberately so that, when the actual revenues came in, they would make the government's performance look good. The alternative Opposition theory was that it was all bullshit: The PC ministers had no idea what they were doing, and their sole motivation was to say whatever was necessary to paint the Tories as competent and successful leading up to Dunderdale's forthcoming election call.

On January 24, 2014, Tom Marshall was appointed interim premier on Dunderdale's resigning recommendation. He was Newfoundland and Labrador's first Jewish premier, and only the second in Canada's history, following BC's Dave Barrett way back in 1972. But some of the honour of that was diminished by the fact that Marshall hadn't been chosen by a party convention, let alone by a mandate from the electorate. A lot of people thought that, when Danny Williams had resigned in November 2010, Tom should have gone for the PC leadership and then taken the party's candidates into an election, but instead he announced he'd be opting out of running himself to support Dunderdale's candidacy.

One top Tory I talked to at the time commented that being Jewish might be a negative attribute regarding Tom's ability to get elected leader and premier. Judging by the returns Tom had received in his own district, and his father before him in a large federal riding, I replied that the comment was utterly ridiculous on the face of it.

There was a more pertinent criticism of his temporary premiership, however: Premier Marshall, being such a naturally nice guy, and having no stake, as a politician, in the future governing of province, was way too free and easy with government money during his short tenure. He seemed more interested in present popularity than in avoiding the problems that future record-breaking deficits would bring down on his successors. Certainly, the polls showed greater satisfaction with his government than with Dunderdale's, and he even seemed to be creeping up on Liberal leader Dwight Ball and his party.

I've touched on Tom Marshall in some detail because there was widespread feeling that, if he had gone for the leadership upon Dunderdale's resignation, the future of the Tory government might well have been different.

IN THE END, the three candidates for PC leadership were Minister Paul Davis, who had declined to run in the earlier round because of health considerations, Minister Steve Kent, and former minister John Ottenheimer. Davis attracted the support of more current and former MHAs than the other two, although each had a good share of high-powered politicos behind him.

At the beginning of the race, Davis was considered by many to be the front-runner. And by August 8, 2014, just over three weeks before the convention, Abacus Data issued a poll showing Davis ahead, Kent second, and Ottenheimer third.

At the convention itself, though, it turned out that John Ottenheimer had attracted more delegates than the other two. On the first ballot, he received just over 42% of the votes cast compared to 37% for Davis. Kent was third and last, with nearly 21%, and had to drop out.

It was now down to a two-man race, and there was much to-ing and fro-ing as party apparatchiks begged for Kent's support for their candidate. Some stated that he should free his delegates to support whomever they liked. But the main rumour circulating the floor was that Kent had already made a secret deal with Davis. And shortly after the first ballot results were announced, he did come out for Davis, with alacrity. It indicated to disappointed Ottenheimer supporters that a partnership had been cooked up before the convention.

When the second ballot votes were counted, the result was a doozy. One vote separated the contenders. Ottenheimer had 339, and Davis 340.

The party constitution required a winner to obtain "more than 50% of the valid ballots cast." And it would appear to have been clear that Davis had garnered more than 50% of the valid votes cast. But according to the returning officer, John Noseworthy, a former Auditor General for the province, Davis had not reached the required magic number.

There was one spoiled ballot, and I don't know if that was somehow added to the total of "valid" votes cast, giving Davis exactly 50%, and not the necessary "more than 50%. . . ." Or perhaps the "more than 50%" requirement was interpreted as meaning 50% plus one, in which case Davis had fallen short by a fraction of a vote.

Whatever was going through the returning officer's mind, he decided there had to be a third ballot between the two remaining contenders to try to get a clear majority. Ottenheimer and his team were absolutely delighted, but Davis's people were less so. Lawyer and former minister Jerome Kennedy said that the Davis camp had approached the rules committee on the matter. "Hopefully there's enough lawyers around," he said, "to see if that interpretation is correct." And strong arguments, some statesman-like for TV, and some cast in the more normal gutter lingo of political backrooms, were flung around the convention floor with lawless abandon.

John Noseworthy's interpretation may well have been wrong logically, mathematically, and constitutionally, but surely it was right pragmatically and politically. Could a leadership candidate be deemed to have a mandate from the party if he'd won his leadership by some small disputed fraction of a percentage point? The air had to be cleared. (Interestingly, though, the national Conservatives elected a new leader in May 2017 with 50.95% of the vote.)

But the problem by this time was that many delegates, especially those from out of town, had started to drive home. Reasonably, they'd thought that in a two-man race, one combatant was likely to win. Now they were hearing on the car radio that they had to drive back to vote in another ballot.

One MHA was forced to tear himself away from his daughter's wedding to return to the hall and vote. And the dedication of supporters in general was seen from the fact that there were only two fewer votes cast on the third ballot than on the second. Davis, with nearly 52% of the votes this time, compared with Ottenheimer's 48%, won with a small but absolute majority.

Lieutenant-Governor Frank Fagan swore Paul Davis in as premier on September 26, 2014, and both Kent and Ottenheimer obtained appointments from the new boss. Kent got the position of deputy premier, and Ottenheimer became head of the Newfoundland and Labrador Housing Corporation.

An interesting side note: Davis was likely the first police officer in Canada to have become a premier. But not everyone was captivated by his background. Some among the Liberals and the media could be heard to mutter, sneeringly, that the man never rose above police constable.

Others were dismayed by what appeared to be his "police-think." On becoming premier, he immediately stated that he would be setting up as a priority an advisory committee on crime. He had earlier linked the move to the stabbing of an eleven-year-old soccer player on a field by an older boy in an incident that was clearly a serious, individual, mental health issue, rather than a matter of regular, everyday criminality.

A few days later, when his cabinet ministers were sworn in, he announced that the name of the Department of Justice would be changed to the Department of Public Safety. This action amazed many; the political tin ear at the head of the Tories would just not seem to go away.

Of all the words associated with government, the term "justice" was one of the few which still carried positive connotations. Others thought a government department named "Public Safety" belonged in a book by George Orwell, along with "goodthink," "thoughtcrime," and "unperson." Following a meeting with the appalled provincial branch of the Canadian Bar Association a week later, Davis announced a compromise; the department would henceforth be dubbed Justice *and* Public Safety.

Davis also hired the former Royal Newfoundland Constabulary

chief of police, Joe Browne, as his chief of staff in the premier's office. And, in a tragically eerie development, an RNC member of the premier's security detail, Joe Smyth, apparently checking out an impolite tweet from Donald Dunphy, visited the man alone in Mount Carmel on Easter Sunday, April 5, 2015, and ended up shooting him to death in his own home.

AS MINISTER OF the new Department of Justice and Public Safety, Davis announced the appointment of an unelected lawyer, Judy Manning. The fact that she didn't having a seat in the House of Assembly from which to answer for her department caused immediate criticism, even though the appointment was a perfectly acceptable practice as long as it was clear that she would seek a seat at an early opportunity. But the criticism intensified when, instead, she made it clear that she would not contest any of some three upcoming by-elections; she was going to wait and run in the next general election in her home district of Placentia–St. Mary's.

Davis later pulled the rug out from under her concerning her negotiations with the City of St. John's about responsibility for the 911 service on the Avalon Peninsula. When she had reported publicly that the talks had reached a deadlock, Premier Davis stepped around her and negotiated an agreement with Mayor Dennis O'Keefe that was contrary to the minister's position on the matter.

The next month, in March of 2015, Davis dismissed her and two other ministers from his cabinet. He stated as his rationale for jettisoning Manning that he had intended to call an election that spring, but his plan to reduce the number of seats in the House had postponed the election till that fall; hence, he could not allow her to serve as unelected minister for an entire year. There was also some chit-chat that MHA Felix Collins had gone back on a plan to retire earlier from the House, and such retirement would have allowed Manning a chance to run in a by-election in the home district she had her heart set on.

Say whatever he might, though, it was difficult to avoid the conclusion that Judy Manning was enticed into an untenable situation by Davis. She was set up for a fall by experienced politicos who should have known better, and she was ultimately flushed down the drain when her presence became too tiresome to tolerate any longer. From start to finish, she was treated shabbily.

AT THE BEGINNING of 2015, Davis opened the House of Assembly to begin the process of legislating a reduction in the number of electoral districts. He wanted to cut 10 seats, bringing the total down from 48 to 38, in time for the fall election. The reduction, he said, would save the government $10 million over the following four years.

But not everyone thought the decrease was a good idea. Some thoughtful persons believed that, for the good of democracy, there should be more, not fewer, seats in the House: Political power should be more widely shared, with more MHAs to control ministers, and also provide a more effective committee system. Neither the Liberals nor the NDP opposed the reduction, although there was some quibbling over the process. In the end, the number of seats was only dropped to 40.

Davis also said he wanted to review the MHA gold-plated pension plan, but the unholy fuss that ensued over that from both sides of the House at the time indicated just how reluctant members were to relinquish their self-endowed perks of office.

DURING HIS SHORT tenure as premier, the government announced some policies in education, health, and housing, but none of it seemed to resonate in the public consciousness. In education, for example, the Speech from the Throne mentioned the creation of a twenty-first-century curriculum for schools and touched on some other plans for education. But much of that was drowned out by the public reaction to the Education minister's announcement less than a week later that teaching positions would be cut for 2015–2016 and class sizes were to go up slightly.

AFTER YEARS OF living high on the hog from oil revenues, Finance Minister Ross Wiseman had to bring in a budget in April of 2015 that killed the Tories' chances in that election year. Oil prices had plummeted since the provincial budget a year ago, and as a result, Davis and his Finance minister brought down one of the harshest budgets ever imposed on the beleaguered province.

Jobs were cut, taxes and fees and borrowing went up, spending decreased, and projects were delayed. And still a deficit of $1.1 billion was projected. The already horrendous provincial debt was slated to go up accordingly.

Public-opinion polls had shown the popularity of the PC government steadily decreasing over the past two or three years. Not long before Davis was elected leader of the PC Party, a Corporate Research Associates survey placed the Liberal Party over 30 percentage points ahead. And there was no significant, consistent improvement in Tory fortunes afterwards.

Nothing seemed to go right for them. The federal Liberals under Justin Trudeau won a majority government in the October 2015 election, and support for the provincial Liberal Party jumped, too. Polls taken in the days before the call for a November election here pegged the Liberals at about 65%, the PC Party around 20%, and the NDP 15%.

In the election, the Liberals won 31 seats, the PCs 7, and the NDP under Earle McCurdy kept 2. The Liberals received 57% of the popular vote, the PCs 30%, and the NDP 12%.

According to polls, Davis had actually raised the popularity of the PC Party during the campaign. Some observers I talked to mentioned that he was an excellent campaigner and that he was impressive to meet and chat with in person. But with this election, he achieved an unfortunate national distinction: The defeat of the Progressive Conservative Party in Newfoundland and Labrador under his leadership meant that there was now not one government in Canada, federal or provincial, containing the name "Conservative" in its name. That hadn't happened in the country since the Second World War.

Less than a year after the election, Davis announced that he was going to step down as PC leader when a successor was chosen at a leadership convention. But as of this writing, he's still there and perhaps may even end up running.

As a political leader, to date, Paul Davis is accorded a ranking of 50%.

Earle McCurdy

EARLE MCCURDY WAS born in Halifax in 1950. He grew up in St. John's, Newfoundland, where he went to school, and graduated from Memorial with a B.A. in the early 1970s. Thereafter, he was a prominent reporter with the *Evening Telegram* for a few years before becoming involved with the Fish, Food and Allied Workers Union in 1980. Many of us involved in politics at the time missed his incisive, if frequently unflattering, journalism.

He was the secretary treasurer of the FFAW Union until Richard Cashin resigned as president in 1993. Then he took over and stayed as elected president for a couple of decades until he retired in 2014.

Retirement didn't seem to agree with Earle. Upon Lorraine Michael's resignation as leader of the NDP the next year, he easily allowed himself to be persuaded, endorsed by then NDP MP Ryan Cleary and MHA Gerry Rogers, to run for the post. He won the leadership over two other contenders with nearly 70% of the votes. Half a year later, he was in the middle of the November 2015 provincial general election.

He ran in the district of St. John's West against former Liberal MP Siobhan Coady and PC cabinet minister and incumbent MHA Dan

Crummell. Coady won with 46% of the vote. McCurdy came second with 27%, just edging out Crummell.

In the previous election of 2011, the NDP candidate in that district, Chris Pickard, had received over 37% of the votes, but this time there seemed to be a sentiment among the voters in favour of dumping the Tories and putting in the Liberals. Not for the first time, the NDP was caught in the squeeze between the two "naturally governing" parties.

The NDP as a whole in the 2015 election got 12% of the popular vote throughout the province. That was less than half the percentage obtained in the 2011 election under Lorraine Michael. But still, the percentage received under McCurdy was the second-highest popular vote in the party's history.

Two New Democrat MHAs were elected to sit in the House, but leader McCurdy had to content himself with looking down mutely on proceedings from the gallery. That didn't stop him from demanding outside the House, the year after Dwight Ball's election as premier, that he resign.

There appeared to be no clamour inside the party for the highly regarded McCurdy to step down as leader.

I'd be surprised if he doesn't add to this grade in the future, but, as a political leader, to date, Earle McCurdy merits 40%.

Dwight Ball

BALL WAS BORN in Deer Lake in 1957. He went to Memorial University, became a pharmacist, operated a drugstore in Deer Lake, and later bought another one in Springdale. Both those towns have named him Employer of the Year. He was also awarded the Bowl of Hygeia, considered the highest award for community pharmacists.

A Canadian pharmacist told me, however, that some of the shine may have been taken off the honour by the action of some loony southern Americans. He googled for me a Bowl of Hygeia award that had caused a lot of controversy. In 2015, the American Pharmacists Association Foundation sponsored the award to be given to a druggist in Louisiana who had refused to fill prescriptions for birth control pills on the grounds that the estrogen in them was increasing the number of homosexual men being born. Moreover, the awardee claimed, since the pills had been tested in Haiti, a high percentage of the population there were turned into homosexuals. Plus Haiti had brought the AIDS virus to the Western Hemisphere by some sort of population transfer from Zaire, where it had been created by "errant vaccine experiments."

My pharmacist friend told me that many professionals have dearly hoped, for the good of the Bowl of Hygeia, that the Louisiana guy would turn out to be an aberration among the awardees. The American foundation has apparently stood by its decision.

Highly successful in his profession and in business, Ball branched out into care homes for seniors, real estate, and venture capital investments. He also became president of the Canadian Pharmacists Association.

Despite the esteem in which he was held as an employer by the Town of Deer Lake, Ball had his ups and downs trying to get himself elected in the district of Humber Valley, where that municipality is located. When he ran for the Liberals in the 2003 provincial election, PC Kathy Goudie defeated him for the Tories as part of Danny Williams's first victory. At the beginning of 2007, after the Auditor General named her among many other MHAs for double-billing her expenses, she claimed clerical errors, and paid it all back, and was not criminally accused but resigned from the House.

Ball ran in the ensuing by-election against PC candidate Darryl Kelly and won by 7 votes. In the general election in October of that year, Kelly took him on again and beat him by 254 votes. A rematch four years later, in the 2011 general election, saw Ball edging out Kelly by 68 votes and just over 48% of the popular vote.

Within weeks, owing to Liberal leader Kevin Aylward's failure to win a seat in the House, the Party made Ball interim leader, and he replaced Yvonne Jones as leader of the official Opposition. As he took the temporary leadership, Ball made public that he intended to vie for the permanent position at the party's next convention, later announced for November of 2013.

Some other party stalwarts jumped into the race, and some heavyweights stayed out. In addition to those who did run, many party faithful hoped that MP Gerry Byrne, former MP Siobhan Cody, businessman Dean MacDonald, MHA Andrew Parsons, and MP Scott Simms, among others, would throw their hats in.

Top St. John's businessman Paul Antle did take on the challenge. Antle's resumé was impressive, with many entrepreneurial awards and recognitions. His supporters for the leadership included former leader Kevin Aylward, MPs Scott Andrews and Scott Simms, and senators George Baker and George Furey. Antle had run unsuccessfully in the 2006 federal election.

Cathy Bennett, another prominent Newfoundland entrepreneur with a similarly impressive number of awards and positions, including president of the St. John's Board of Trade, also ran. She was supported by former interim premier Beaton Tulk, former MHA and minister Tom Lush, former MP Siobhan Coady, international singing superstar Alan Doyle, and business luminary Dean MacDonald.

Danny Dumaresque took a shot at it, too. He was a former MHA for Eagle River from 1989, until defeated by Yvonne Jones as an Independent candidate in 1996. Danny was president of the Liberal Party in the 2000s, and he was supported in this leadership race by former MHA and MP and provincial and federal cabinet minister John Efford. Dumaresque had been Efford's top organizer in Efford's close-run leadership contest against Roger Grimes.

Jim Bennett threw his hat in. He was a lawyer, and possessed a considerable background of legal education and practice both in Ontario and back home on the Great Northern Peninsula. He had been leader briefly in 2006 and was elected in St. Barbe district in 2011. His greatest supporter, who eclipsed all others, was his wife, the impressive former Ontario cabinet minister Sandra Pupatello.

Dwight Ball had the greatest number of political notables behind him. They included MHAs Lisa Dempster, Randy Edmunds, Eddie Joyce, Tom Osborne, and Andrew Parsons; former MHA and Liberal leader Gerry Reid; and federal MPs Gerry Byrne, Judy Foote, and Yvonne Jones.

The Liberals had changed their system of voting for this leadership convention. Instead of the traditional balloting by ex officio and elected delegates in person at the convention itself, this time the system used was the preferential one-person, one-vote method, weighted by provincial district. Only registered members of the party could vote, and balloting was opened up to include modes of electronic voting.

Ball's campaign was strenuous and tireless but low-key. He was not a demonstrative or loudmouth politician, and I practically had to put out a missing-in-action appeal to him on the air to get him to phone *Open Line* occasionally and tell us how he was doing. But meanwhile, he was beating about the province non-stop, cajoling supporters to register and vote for him.

The actual voting for leader put Ball ahead from the start. But it still took three ballots. In the first ballot, Jim Bennett got 2.67% of the votes, Danny Dumaresque 2.74%, Cathy Bennett 22.69%, Paul Antle 27.52%, and Dwight Ball 44.38%. Because Jim Bennett and Dumaresque got less than the required 5%, they had to drop off the ballot, and their second choices went to those remaining.

In the final ballot, Paul Antle got nearly 41% and Dwight Ball got 59%, to be declared the winner of the Liberal leadership.

For the next two years in Newfoundland and Labrador, the old political adage "oppositions don't win, governments lose" applied with a vengeance. Seemingly, the PC government could do no right, and the Liberals could do no wrong; in fact, the Grits didn't have to do a darn thing.

The Liberals approached the November general election with the great political momentum of a party filling a vacuum. They'd won half a dozen by-elections, and a couple of Tory MHAs had bailed out of their caucus to join the Liberals. In addition, the NDP, who'd been riding high since the last election, imploded with a caucus revolt, with two of its MHAs also hooking up with the Grits.

Then a murder near midnight on October 3 in the bar of a hotel called the Captain's Quarters on King's Bridge Road, in St. John's, had an ominous connection with Dwight Ball's family. It threatened, in some minds, to derail his campaign.

A sixty-three-year-old man, Larry Wellman, attempted to prevent an armed robbery in the hotel and was shot by the perpetrator. A police manhunt went on for a week before twenty-seven-year-old Brandon Phillips was arrested as a suspect and charged with armed robbery and first-degree murder.

Before his arrest, he'd been holed up at a house on Quidi Vidi Road, in the company of his mother and his girlfriend, Jade Ball. She turned out to be the daughter of Dwight Ball, the leader of the Liberal Party heading into an election. The police questioned her, but no charges were laid.

Dwight Ball offered his condolences to the family of the victim but would comment no further because of the ongoing RNC investigation. During a conference call with his election candidates, Ball said it was a family matter having nothing to do with him as a public person and that it would work its way through the courts like any other case.

The connection to Ball didn't seem to bother the electorate very much. In the general election of November 2015, his Liberals won 31 out of 40 seats for a solid majority government, the first for the party in twelve years. Ball himself, far now from the razor-edge wins and losses he'd incurred in the past, won his own district of Humber–Gros Morne with 76% of the vote. He was eclipsed, though, by one of his own MHAs: Andrew Parsons attracted 96.5% of the votes in Burgeo–La Poile against two other candidates. If that wasn't an all-time record for a contested district election, someone please show me the actual historical champ.

However, the low level of excitement generated by the election as a whole may be seen from the voter turnout. Only 55.2% of the electorate bothered to cast a ballot—the smallest number since we became a province.

Ball was sworn in as premier, plus minister of Labrador and Aboriginal Affairs, in December 2015. Some criticized him for taking on that extra portfolio, because he was neither Labradorian nor aboriginal—whatever relevance that might have. Many thinking people believed that the premier becoming minister of those important concerns indicated the priority his government was giving them. Former Labrador MP Todd Russell, president of NunatuKavut, agreed with Ball's decision.

One of the items Ball dealt with was the announcing of yet another study of a fixed link between Newfoundland and Labrador. That possible project, for past decades, had been both advocated for convenience and economic development, and derided on grounds of cost, technology, remote geography, and miniscule population.

Meanwhile, the government announced that three major public inquiries would be taking place concerning untoward events under the previous Progressive Conservative government's watch.

The first would look into the violent shooting death of Don Dunphy by an RNC member of Premier Davis's security detail. As of this writing, the inquiry has taken place under Supreme Court Justice Leo Barry, and his final report has been submitted.

The second inquiry would investigate the tragic death by hypothermia of lost teenager Burton Winters.

And the third would inquire into events that were in the nature of a political and financial boondoggle: The company called Humber Valley Paving, which had been associated with erstwhile premier-designate Frank Coleman, was released by the PC government, under questionable circumstances, from an unprofitable contract to pave the Trans-Labrador Highway.

THE FIRST BUDGET of the Ball administration, tabled in April 2016, drove his approval ratings drastically down from the 55–60% he'd been enjoying. Tax increases, spending cuts, and a huge deficit were projected. A poll at the time showed the Liberals, PCs, and NDP just about tied in popular support, a catastrophic drop for Ball in less than half a year.

Cathy Bennett, the minister of Finance, said that the province could not expect to have a surplus for at least six years. Since that would be based largely on the international price of oil, a figure impossible to predict with any accuracy, many commentators found it hard to see what her "optimism" was based on.

Bitter protests took place against the austerity, based at least partly on the vast difference between Liberal promises before and during the election campaign, and the reality they were forced to present to the people immediately afterwards. Ball was also being blamed for incompetence or duplicity regarding the circumstances surrounding the departure of Nalcor CEO Ed Martin, from the corporation responsible for building the wildly out-of-control Muskrat Falls project. Did Martin quit or was he fired?

The controversy was referred to the province's Auditor General, Terry Paddon; he found that Martin had been essentially terminated without cause—constructive dismissal—and was therefore entitled to his multimillion-dollar severance package and lump-sum pension.

Ball could blame the governments of Danny Williams and Kathy Dunderdale all he liked for the Muskrat Falls costs—double what were stated at the start—but the fact was that the budget, the perceived broken promises, the outrage surrounding Ed Martin's golden parachute, and the perception that the government was out of its depth had all combined to make him beat even Premier Kathleen Wynne of Ontario as the most unpopular premier in Canada. She had an approval rating of 24%. Ball's was at 17%.

It must have been the shortest honeymoon for a newly elected premier on record. There have been public calls and petitions demanding his resignation. But Ball has made it clear that he was staying put, and he tried to reassure the populace that the province of Newfoundland and Labrador was not facing bankruptcy. A diminishing number of citizens appeared to have faith in his assurances.

During the first year of his tenure, there were rumblings of discontent from party members and even a petition or two from districts calling upon their MHA to abandon the Liberal caucus. Paul Lane, who'd earlier crossed the floor of the House from the PCs to join the Liberals, criticized the budget publicly and got suspended from the Liberal caucus. Thereupon, he was forced to sit as an Independent MHA.

Even former premier Roger Grimes chided Ball for being too soft in letting himself take it on the chin from his critics, including the Nalcor board that had resigned in the wake of the Ed Martin debacle.

NEWS BROKE IN June 2016 that a man charged with possession of oxycodone for the purposes of trafficking had won a legal decision of $4,820 against Premier Ball and his daughter, Jade, over a landlord-tenant dispute. Dwight and Jade were ordered to pay the money to two former tenants, male and female, for their belongings that went missing after Jade Ball had kicked them out, and for the return of their security deposit.

According to reports, Jade Ball had evicted them, reasonably enough, when she discovered the drug charges. According to the accused drug trafficker, when he went to get his stuff from the flat—couch, dresser, kitchen table—everything was gone. After the award, he reported, rather superfluously, that he and his co-tenant were happy to receive the compensation.

To add insult to injury, the premier and his daughter were also ordered to pay for the hearing expenses to the tune of $20. Ball must have wondered where the hell Judge Judy was when you needed her.

Meanwhile, Premier Ball said he didn't know anything about the matter. All he did was invest money in the property with his daughter, and, although both he and she were apparently listed as landlords, she ran the show. He wasn't even aware of the hearing. He has now retained a lawyer, perhaps a little belatedly, to look into the thing.

This, on top of allegations of ineptitude and hollowness against him for his handling of Ed Martin's resignation or dismissal, whatever it was, plus the doubling of the gas tax, on top of the breach of his promise not to raise the harmonized sales tax by the 2% which had been proposed by the Tory government, all undermined his credibility as a statesman.

He spurred perhaps the greatest amount of focused, vocal fury by closing down more than half the province's rural libraries, of all things, to save peanuts in costs (an outrage later reversed, at least temporarily), and by extending the provincial sales tax to books, making Newfoundland and Labrador the only province to do so.

His claim that he would deal with the monstrous deficit by increasing revenues to the government by means of economic stimulus and diversification was largely derided by partisan opponents and objective economists alike.

Then came the Bernard Coffey fiasco. In the fall of 2016, Premier Ball appointed Bernard Coffey, Q.C. as the Clerk of the Executive Council. Coffey had solid partisan credentials, having been a Liberal appointment to an electoral boundaries commission and an earlier candidate for the leadership of the party.

He also had solid credentials as a lawyer. For example, he had been an effective co-counsel for the commission of inquiry chaired by Justice Margaret Cameron into whether a health board was blameworthy in reporting wrong and belated test results to patients suffering from breast cancer, and then neglecting to disclose the complete range of the erroneous results.

Thus he would have seemed to be a good fit for a job, if you could tolerate the partisanship side of the appointment, which essentially combined the position of top civil servant in the province with that of secretary to the cabinet and deputy minister to the premier.

But there was a small problem: Unbeknownst to the public, when Coffey took the job, he didn't give up his law practice. Some six months into the position, he even launched an action on behalf of a client against the government's most significant Crown corporation, Nalcor Energy. The situation has been described, to no reasonable dissent, as beyond bizarre.

Called out on it, Premier Ball defended the circumstances of Coffey's blatant conflict of interest. There were explanations about a period of transition as Coffey moved fully from his private practice into his public service and about the existence of a "Chinese wall." This was a fatuous reference to a barrier sometimes established inside a business organization to stop exchanges of information or any communication that might result in conflicts of interest.

But as numerous public and private persons have pointed out, you can have all the Chinese walls you want, but there's simply no way of avoiding egregious conflicts of interest between the Clerk's pervasive and comprehensive public duties and any private practice he may be moonlighting at on the side. Or, as a friend commented to me, "Chinese wall? More like Donald Trump's Mexican wall—talked about ad nauseam, but totally non-existent!"

It would be incredible to think that a premier didn't realize all that.

One can only assume that he must have been kept in the dark at the time of the appointment and that, when he found out, he acted properly and effectively in demanding Coffey's resignation. Too bad, in the minds of many, that he then felt some need to set up a rearguard defence of the appointment.

Ball's Liberal government has been in power for less than two years. No new government in our history has come into office with more seemingly insurmountable challenges facing it, especially the ongoing annual budgetary deficit of hundreds of millions and the Muskrat Falls back-breaking mess.

Each of these intractable financial trials by itself threatens to render the province insolvent. Together, in terms of the province's nightmarish future, they hardly bear thinking about. This is the hand Ball has been dealt, and he has to play it. To say the least, it has been a steep learning curve for him and his novice colleagues in cabinet.

I can't rationally judge him, let alone condemn him, after such a short time in office. His proper grading can only take place after his first full term, or when he gets out, whichever happens first. Meanwhile, considering what confronts him, I'm giving him the benefit of the doubt in his efforts to grapple with the monsters.

I'd grant Dwight Ball, as a political leader, to date, the middle-of-the-road rating of 50%. But stay tuned.

Acknowledgements

My deepest gratitude to Garry Cranford, Margo Cranford, Jerry Cranford, Nick Cranford, Laura Cameron, Peter Hanes, Jennifer Konieczny, Ed Oldford, Gerard Murphy, and Bob Woodworth at Flanker Press for invaluable help and encouragement in creating this book and presenting it to readers. And once more, my heartfelt thanks to Graham Blair for his outstanding graphic design.

Born in Newfoundland, Bill Rowe graduated in English from Memorial University and attended Oxford University as a Rhodes Scholar, obtaining an Honours M.A. in law.

Elected five times to the House of Assembly, Rowe served as a minister in the Government of Newfoundland and Labrador and as leader of the Official Opposition. He practised law in St. John's for many years and has been a long-time public affairs commentator, appearing regularly on national and local television, as well as hosting a daily radio call-in show on VOCM and writing weekly newspaper columns.

Rowe has written eleven books, including *Clapp's Rock*, a bestselling novel published by McClelland & Stewart and serialized on CBC national radio; *The Temptation of Victor Galanti*, a second novel published by McClelland & Stewart; the critically acclaimed political memoir *Danny Williams: The War With Ottawa*, which appeared on the *Globe and Mail*'s bestsellers list; *Rosie O'Dell*, a critically acclaimed crime novel; *The Premiers Joey and Frank*, a *Globe and Mail* bestseller and selected by the *Hill Times* as one of the best books in politics, public policy, and history in 2013; *The Monster of Twenty Mile Pond*, the much-loved novel of a legendary monster who engulfed the lives of two teenaged girls; *The True Confessions of a Badly Misunderstood Dog*, a fictionalized account of the frantic years when a Labrador retriever and two cats lived with the author's family; *No Punches Pulled: The Premiers Peckford, Wells, and Tobin*, a political memoir which also appeared on the best books list of the *Hill Times* in Ottawa, and now *The Worst and the Best of the Premiers and Some We Never Had.*

Rowe is a member of the Writers' Union of Canada and has served on the executive of the Writers' Alliance of Newfoundland and Labrador. He is married to Penelope Ayre Rowe CM of St. John's. They have a son, Dorian, a daughter, Toby, and three grandchildren, Rowan, Elizabeth, and Phoebe.

Index